The Special Economic Zones of China and Their Impact on Its Economic Development

The Special Economic Zones of China and Their Impact on Its Economic Development

Jung-Dong Park

Westport, Connecticut
London

Library of Congress Cataloging-in-Publication Data

Pak, Chŏng-dong.
    The special economic zones of China and their impact on its
economic development / Jung-Dong Park.
        p.   cm.
    Includes bibliographical references and index.
    ISBN 0–275–95613–X (alk. paper)
    1. Economic zoning—China.   2. China—Economic policy—1976–
3. Investments, Foreign—China.   I. Title.
HC430.Z6P35   1997
338.951—dc20   96–26875

British Library Cataloguing in Publication Data is available.

Library of Congress Catalog Card Number: 96–26875
ISBN: 0–275–95613–X

First published in 1997

Praeger Publishers, 88 Post Road West, Westport, CT 06881
An imprint of Greenwood Publishing Group, Inc.

Printed in the United States of America

The paper used in this book complies with the
Permanent Paper Standard issued by the National
Information Standards Organization (Z39.48–1984).

10 9 8 7 6 5 4 3 2 1

To my wife, Hye-Young

Contents

Figures and Tables

Prologue

At the Third Full Meeting of the Central Committee of the Eleventh Term of the China Communist Party in December 1978, the Four Modernizations (agriculture, industry, defense, and science & technology) was added to the Revised Rules and New Constitution of the Communist Party. To achieve these "modernizations," China engaged in economic reform centered on the introduction of an open market economy. The reform covered most areas of the economy, including agriculture, corporate business, price structure, financial structure, trade and direct investment, and distribution structure.

The report on the Third Full Meeting states that "its purpose, which is founded on a philosophy of self-reliance, is to actively seek to develop mutually beneficial economic cooperation with other world countries, to work for the introduction of advanced technology and facilities from foreign countries and to put effort into science and education projects necessary for the realization of modernization." Although this report has the condition "with the philosophy of self-reliance," the active development of economic cooperation is actually emphasized more. It can be said that since the meeting, China has undertaken the promotion of various economic cooperation programs with western capitalist countries.[1]

This policy of reform and openness, which is still in full force, has brought drastic changes in the economy and society of China. Perhaps the biggest change has been the establishment of the special economic zones, signaling the appearance of market economies in a socialist economy, bringing a high economic growth rate, and acting as a production base for Asian manufacturing industries. This policy also has caused great political upheaval, as demonstrated by the Tiananmen Square massacre. However, China is showing relatively stable and steady economic growth compared to the economic chaos of the countries of the former Soviet Union and Eastern Europe. With socialist China undergoing such dramatic change, one cannot help but ask the following questions: Why does China have to change so drastically? What is the essence of this change? Where is China headed? This book aims to uncover the significance of the socialist system under Mao Zedong that is the background of the current policy of reform and openness, the essence of the special economic zones, and the effects of the special economic zones on the economy of China.

Because a study of the special economic zones is meaningless without on-site investigation, this book, unlike other books on China, utilizes internal statistics and the first-hand methodology of on-site investigation. It is extremely difficult for foreigners to enter China to do on-site research, and much of the information in this book has never been disseminated outside China. Most studies of China, especially of the special economic zones, were conducted using formal statistics handed out by Chinese authorities. This study focuses on microeconomics and statistical analysis, not because I deny the importance of macroeconomics, but because I do not think that a macroeconomic perspective is relevant in analyzing the economy of China, especially the special economic zones.

It has been over eight years since I first began to study the economy of modern China at the University of Tokyo. I received much assistance from professors, colleagues, and friends during my stay at the University of Tokyo, both as a student and as a researcher, and as a visiting professor to the University of Peking and Harvard University. I would like to take this opportunity to thank all the people who have helped me with this project, including Kyunghwa Lee and Cyrus Yun of the Korea Development Institute (KDI) for their assistance in editing this book. All theories and statistical data expressed in this book are my sole responsibility. It is my hope that this book will assist the reader in understanding the Chinese economy.

Introduction:
Problems and Methodology

Many studies evaluate the role of special economic zones, the majority produced in China. Since most were conducted by administrative officials, they focus on policies and their contents are usually introductory or educational. Those studies considered major include *Ten Years of Chinese Special Economic Zone: Shenzhen,* edited by Zheng Tianlun and Chen Zhuohua in 1990; *Ten Years of Chinese Special Economic Zone: Zhuhai,* edited by Yang Chanzhu in 1990; *Ten Years of Chinese Special Economic Zone: Shantou,* edited by Fang Lingsheng; and *Ten Years of Chinese Special Economic Zone: Hainan,* edited by Su Yucai. These works are judged the most outstanding studies of the four special economic zones, excluding Xiamen, produced during the past ten years. They deal with a wide range of topics, such as the investment context of the zones, their economic performance, the current status of economic reform, and the economic relations of the zones with internal corporations or with Hong Kong. However, the evaluation standards of these studies are much too simple. They simply compare economic performance before and after establishment of the zones. With some indexes, a simple comparison like this can be useful. However, a more important consideration in evaluating the zones is not performance, but background factors. Previous studies do deal with the introduction of various types of market economies (unthinkable in traditional socialist China) in order to reform the economic system. However, they do not comment on the problems encountered in introducing a market economy to the zones. The zones' economic relationships with domestic firms and Hong Kong are mentioned, but their role in those relationships and in the Chinese economy is almost neglected. Moreover, as a result of overemphasizing macrodevelopment issues, structural problems are hardly mentioned.

Ten Years of the Shenzhen Special Economic Zone, published by the Office of Policies of Shenzhen (Shenzhenshi zhengzhi bangongshi) in 1990, for example, deals inadequately with structural aspects, such as the transfer of foreign capital and technology. This is measured by the import of a few very expensive machines, yet how effectively they have been used is not considered. A thorough evaluation should consider whether laborers have benefited from the transfer, instead of focusing solely on surface factors such as the cost of machinery. In order to appropriately discuss the role of the special economic zones, economic development and changes in economic structure should be analyzed in greater depth, based on research into current conditions.

Naturally, Hong Kong has shown great interest in the zones. The Hong Kong studies, however, tend to overemphasize theories constructed from Hong Kong's point of view, examining the political ramifications of the return of Hong Kong and many of its corporations to China in 1997. Analysis of the zones was made from the perspective of the China–Hong Kong economic relationship. While this is important it is nevertheless insufficient for understanding the effects and future of the zones. Another weakness of the Hong Kong studies is that they concentrate on the advantages or disadvantages for foreign corporations entering the zones, while the benefits to China from attracting foreign corporations to the zones are only skimmed. The leading Hong Kong scholars on the economic zones are Wong Puiwee and Thomas M. H. Chan. Wong, director of the China Special Economic Zones Data and Research Unit at the Center for Contemporary Asian Studies in the Chinese University of Hong Kong, has published many dissertations on the zones. His major works include *China's Special Economic Zones: Towards Industrialization and Internationalization* (1988) and *Economic Relations Between China's Pearl River Delta, Special Economic Zones, and Hong Kong* (1988). These studies analyze the future prospects of the zones and the economic relationship between the zones and Hong Kong, but do not discuss the relationship between the zones and nonzonal (internal) areas. Moreover, although the economic development of the zones is mentioned, the specific nature of the development and the change in economic structure are hardly considered.

Chan analyzes the status of industrialization of the zones in terms of the flow of funds. In "A Critical Review of China's Special Economic Zone Policy: Based Primarily on the Experience of the Shenzhen Special Economic Zone" (1988), he predicts an unclear future for the zones owing to the possible emergence of rivals. He also labels industrialization of the zones as "indebted industrialization." Chan's observations are important considerations in analyzing the zones. However, he rarely analyzes the problem of economic structure and the relationship between zones and nonzones or between zones and Hong Kong, and he overemphasizes the flow of funds. A thorough evaluation requires coverage of all these aspects.

The weaknesses of previous studies on the special economic zones are: (1) they did not cover in detail how economic progress in the zones was accomplished because they were based on a simplistic before-and-after comparison, (2) corporate structure in the zones was inadequately analyzed, and (3) an objective judgment on the effects of the zones was not made. This book focuses on economic effects (economic progress and corporate structure) of the zones, evaluation of the zones (taking these aspects into consideration), and the role of the zones in modern China.

Research for this book was conducted on three occasions. The first phase took place from July 30 to August 22, 1989 with a scientific scholarship from the University of Tokyo on the occasion of its 100th anniversary. The main objective of this research was to observe and collect data on the overall conditions of the Chinese economy and the special economic zones. The second phase took place from January 4 to February 27, 1991. I visited Hong Kong, Macao, and the five special economic zones. Research centered on foreign corporate management styles and data collection. The final phase was conducted from April 16 to May 15, 1992 and focused on observing Chinese corporations' management styles and collecting additional data on foreign corporations.

To gather data, I traveled to Hong Kong, Macao, China, and Korea, where I visited corporations from Hong Kong, Japan, Korea, Taiwan, and the United States. This book has already been published in Mandarin, Japanese, and Korean and is now being released for the first time in English because of its relevance to anglophone countries trading in Asia. Research categories were reformulated according to each area's conditions with reference to T. Abo, *Japanese Manufacturing in America: Automobiles and Electronics: The Application and the Adaptation of Japanese Management* (1988).

Part I first reviews the background of the establishment of the special economic zones, which are a symbol of China's reform and open policy, along with their characteristics and purpose. Previous Chinese economic development strategy is then explained, which leads to a discussion of the background and necessity of forming such a policy. This is necessary to understand the role of the special economic zones in the Chinese economy, the establishment of which was the first step toward the reform and open policy

Part II examines the consequences of special zone development. Chapter 5 examines the development process of the zones. Chapters 6 and 7 analyze the effects of foreign capital on the zones, using factor analysis. Factors include labor absorption effects, wage gain effects, industrial structure improvement effects, improvement of international balance of payments through trade, and industry-related effects. Chapter 8 analyzes economic progress through investments by central, provincial, and municipal governments, as well as by internal corporations (corporations outside the special economic zones). It also takes into account geographical advantages, and advantages gained from being a trade transit area.

Part III reviews the corporate structure and transfer of technology and managerial techniques in terms of countries, investment types, and industry types in China. The current status of employment is reviewed in Chapter 9, fostering of manpower in Chapter 10, production management in Chapter 11, forward and reverse interindustrial effects in Chapter 12, and actual conditions of business management in Chapter 13. This analysis is based on research conducted over six months in the special economic zones. Thirty corportions were used as subjects, including Chinese state-run companies and local and foreign corporations.

Part IV reveals the significance of the special economic zones in the Chinese economy. The significance of the zones in economic relations with Hong Kong, Macao, and Taiwan is discussed in Chapter 14, and with internal companies located outside the zones in Chapter 15. Chapter 16 discusses the significance of the zones from the perspective of the multipolar economic block.

Finally, the Summary and Conclusion deals with the research findings and the problems found in the zones. This part focuses on the formation of the Southern Chinese Economic Block and its relationship with China's special economic zones.

PART I

Formation of Special Economic Zones

1

Reasons for Formation

THE ESTABLISHMENT OF SPECIAL ECONOMIC ZONES

In December 1978, the Department of State submitted plans for constructing Baoan Xian (renamed Shenzhen City in March 1979) in the Guangdong Province, China's product manufacturing area, and for simultaneously developing the area into a new type of city to absorb tourists from Hong Kong and Macao. In January 1979, the Party's Central Department of State decided to establish a public corporation at Shakou in Shenzhen City. In April of the same year, during the Central Maneuvering Meeting, when the secretary of the Guangdong Province Council, Xi Zhongxun, discussed the advantages of Guangdong Province, Deng Xiaoping reportedly said, "It is fine to call a certain area a 'special zone.' Wasn't Shan Gan Ning [the free zone established during the Sino-Japanese War, comprising the provinces of Shaanxi, Ganxu and Ningxia] a 'special zone'? The central government does not have enough funds; you yourselves have to seek your own ways."[1] Later, in May, the Guangdong People's Government submitted The Initial Plan For Conducting Pilot Zones For Exports in Shenzhen, Zhuhai, and Shantou, and in July, the Party's Central Department of State formulated a special policy in Guangdong and Fujian Provinces.

There are three reasons why China established the special economic zones in Guangdong Province and Fujian Province, located near Hong Kong, Macao, and Taiwan. First, China promises one state–two systems to Hong Kong, Macao, and Taiwan, which would allow capitalist and socialist areas to co-exist in one state. The special economic zones can be seen as a trial area for the construction of socialism based on this one state–two systems, idea which is unique to China. Accordingly, it can be assumed that China selected the zones because they are close to Hong Kong, Macao, and Taiwan, target areas for one state-two systems. In addition, the opening of southern China to foreign countries and the strengthening of its economic power were necessary to solve the political problem of sovereignty in Hong Kong and Macao and for the political settlement with Taiwan. The construction of the Shenzhen Special Economic Zone is of particular significance in the China-England negotiations for the future return of Hong Kong. This is why China concentrated its efforts in Shenzhen rather than other zones.

Second, potential use of economic power of overseas Chinese: The nearby presence of the strong economic power of Hong Kong, Macao, and Taiwanese businessmen was an important consideration in establishing the special economic zones of Shenzhen, Zhuhai, Shantou, and Hainan in the Guangdong area and Xiamen in the Fujian area.

Third, the multiple layers of China's unique economic structure necessitates a development strategy satisfying the features of each area instead of implementing a nationally uniform strategy. In other words, China can achieve advancement of the entire state economy only through the improvement of each economic area.

Major points of the special policy in Guangdong and Fujian Provinces are:

1. Guangdong and Fujian Provinces are to be granted some autonomy in financial and foreign currency management;

2. commodities are to be regulated by the mayor under the guidance of the state plan;

3. the power of the local government is to be expanded in the areas of planning, pricing, labor, wages, and economic activities with other areas; and

4. Shenzhen and Zhuhai are to become special economic zones first, and, based on their results, Shantou and Xiamen are to be considered.[2]

The decision to begin construction of the Shakou Industrial Zone in the Shenzhen Special Economic Zone was made immediately this special policy was adopted. Officials from the central government and scholars continued to inspect the fields, and in December of the same year at the Second Meeting of Guangdong Province's Fifth Representatives' Convention, the Regulations on the Guangdong Province Special Economic Zones were examined. They were subsequently modified at the Third Meeting of the Counselors of the People's Party of Guangdong Province in April 1980 and were finally determined at the Fifteenth Meeting of Counselors of the Party of the Fifth National People's Representatives' Meeting on August 26, 1980. At the same time, special economic zones were established in Shenzhen, Zhuhai, and Shantou, and on October 7 of the same year the Xiamen Special Economic Zone in Fujian Province was established by the Department of State.

These zones were first called special export zones, but the name was changed at the Guangdong and Fujian Provinces' Meeting presided over by the Vice Prime Minister of the Department of State, Yu Mu, in March 1980. The official name, special economic zone, was first used in a document of the Department of State on May 16 of the same year.

During the initial stages, special economic zones were divided into two types: (1) overall special economic zones and (2) export processing zones. The Maneuvering Meeting for Special Economic Zones presided over by the Department of State in May 1981, classified Shenzhen and Zhuhai as overall special economic zones, while Shantou and Xiamen were classified as export processing zones. However, by 1984, Shantou and Xiamen had dramatically expanded their business scope beyond export processing. Therefore, the two zone classifications were unified as overall special economic zones.

PROS AND CONS OF SPECIAL ECONOMIC ZONES

The establishment of the special economic zones did not progress smoothly. There was much disagreement among leaders in the central government on the progress of the zones and on the open policy. When Prime Minister Zhao Ziyang addressed the Fourth Meeting of the Fifth National People's Representative Meeting at the end of November 1980, he claimed, "It is necessary to carry out an audacious policy in adopting technology and managerial techniques from advanced foreign countries and in using foreign capital."[3] Dissenting conservative scholar Chen Yun pointed out the potential negative aspects of special economic zones. At a discussion meeting of the First Secretaries of Provinces, Cities, and Independent Counties on December 22, 1981, he warned, "We should learn from the combined experiences of Guangdong and Fujian Provinces. A special economic zone should not be established in Jiangsu province. It is necessary to fully consider not only the advantages of the zones, but also the negative effects the zones will bring about." Chen Yun continued to fight against the establishment of special zones at a discussion meeting with members of the National Planning Council on January 1982. He claimed that "all provinces are attempting to achieve breakthroughs by establishing special zones. However, if this is realized, foreign investors and domestic speculators will start speculating on a grand scale."[4]

Despite the prevalence of similarly critical attitudes, in February 1983, Hu Yaobang, secretary of the Party, inspecting Shenzhen, expressed keen approval: "You have already opened a new frontier. This is how I evaluate your efforts: you have wonderfully accomplished the duties given to you by the Party." He added, "The Special Economic Zones need to make things new and special."[5] On April 1, 1984, Deng Xiaoping, chairman and major influence in the Party, visited Shenzhen, Zhuhai, and Xiamen, accompanied by Wang Zhen (vice prime minister of the Department of State) and Yang Shangkon (vice chairman of the Standing Committee of the National People's Representative Convention). Chairman Deng, approving special zone policy, argued for accelerated development:

When I inspected Shenzhen this time, I was deeply impressed by its development. The construction of Shenzhen has been very rapid, especially in Shakou. This is because Shakou was given control over its own development. Shakou's slogan was "time is money, and efficiency is life." Our guiding philosophy was to be clear in establishing special zones and conducting the open policy. That is to unbind, not to bind.[6]

The Central Secretariat Office and the Department of State held a meeting from March 16 to April 6, 1984, during which the opening of fourteen additional coastal cities was suggested. After a meeting at the Party Secretariat Office, a decision to open these cities was reached at the Meeting of the Central Politics Bureau on April 19, 1984 and was officially adopted at the Second Meeting of the Sixth National People's

Representative Convention in May 1984. This marked the second stage of open policy in China, in which development points were extended into lines. Special economic zones, especially Shenzhen, developed rapidly at this time.[7] However, there were many problems in the zones. When Prime Minister Zhao Ziyang visited Shenzhen and Zhuhai in November 1984, he pointed out the problem of balancing foreign capital. Machine accessories and raw materials were being imported and processed, but only a part of the final product was being exported. Thus, the objective of gaining foreign currency was not being achieved.[8]

What was actually happening in the zones? Among the biggest problems were economic crimes, such as black marketeering of foreign currency and smuggling. Using their import and export privileges, businessmen and corporations in the zones imported consumer goods, such as cars, radios, tape recorders, and color TVs with foreign currencies they bought on the black market at the high exchange rate of 60,000–70,000 yuan to one U.S. dollar (2 to 2.5 times the official rate). They resold these goods at high prices to customers from the interior of the country. In this way, special zone autonomy was abused.

While these activities continued, academics debated the future direction of the special zones. The leading disputants were Ru Guoguang (vice director of the Chinese Institute of Society and Science, for the zones) and Wang Zhou (member of the Office for Guangdong Province's System Reform, against the zones). Ru stressed that economic development in special zones should move in "the external (export based) direction," while Wang argued for "the two pivot pins on a fan" policy, meaning that the special economic zones should move like the two pivot pins on a fan and produce not only for export, but also for domestic markets. Wang believed that both product processing and exporting should be permitted in the special zones, and that the import and assembly of parts from foreign countries in the special zones and their sale in domestic markets should be permitted.[9]

This controversy was resolved when the opposing arguments merged at the Maneuvering Meeting for the Nation's Special Economic Zones held in Shenzhen from December 25, 1985 to January 5, 1986. In the meeting, the slogan advocated by Ru Guoguang, "fight for the establishment of an external-directed economy," was adopted simultaneously with the claim that "the special zones must act to the best of their role as the two pivotal pins of a fan, for the mutual benefit of the internal and external economy."[10]

The special zones began as export processing areas, but were gradually transformed into special economic zones. Although there has been no precise reason given it is likely that this step was made to overcome the limitations of export processing areas. If special zones were to function only as export processing areas for Taiwan or Korea, foreign corporations entering the areas would find no advantages other than cheap labor. The benefits for China would also be minimal with limited numbers and types of corporations entering producing only small gains in foreign currency. Most entrants would be either assembling or processing companies, which would not bring the desired transfer of advanced technology. Through these changes, the zones could also be used as a testing ground for reform of the whole economic system.

The zones' special economic activities began prior to the establishment of related regulations and systems. For example, Guangdong Province started signing contracts with foreign corporations before the zone ordinance was officially announced on August 26, 1980. Other regulations, such as Regulations on Entry and Exit to the Guangdong Province Special Economic Zone, Regulations on Wages for Corporations in the Guangdong Province Special Economic Zone, and Regulations on Registration for Corporations in the Guangdong Province Special Economic Zone, were not passed by the Council of the Guangdong People's Representative Convention until November 7, 1981. Official approval by the Council of the All People's Convention was not forthcoming until January 1, 1982.

The gap between the implementation of special economic activities in the zones and their legal codification was probably due to bureaucratic conflicts. There were many disagreements among leaders regarding the special zones, and policy could be established only after these conflicts were settled. Meanwhile, the zones quietly pursued economic activities on their own. It must be noted that the disagreements were about the future direction of the special zones, not about their existence.

2

Objective and Configurational Characteristics

OBJECTIVES OF SPECIAL ECONOMIC ZONES

The objectives of the special economic zones have not been constant. Focus has gradually changed over time. During this first stage, before 1983, primary objectives were transfer of technology, gain of foreign currency, and creation of employment opportunities. This is because the zones were originally intended to serve as export processing areas. In 1984, the objectives of the zones began to change. For example, Gu Liji, noting the need to look at the meaning of the zones from a macroeconomic and long-term perspective, argued that, because the scale of employment or foreign currency generated by the zones would be very small relative to the entire country, foreign exchange and employment opportunities should not be the only objectives of the zones.[11]

During a discussion with leaders of the Central Government in February 1984, Deng Xiaoping defined the zones as "windows to technology, management, knowledge, and foreign policy." Deng's "window" idea stressed absorption of advanced technology and advanced management more than expansion of employment or gain of foreign currency, which were the original objectives of the zones. The phrases "window to foreign policy" and "the window to management" also indicate Deng's belief that the zones must play a role in recovering China's sovereignty over Hong Kong, Macao, and Taiwan, and that the zones' management system should take a leading role in the reform of the national economy.

From these observations, it can be concluded that China wants to reform its domestic economic system centering on the zones. Furthermore, it wants to integrate itself with the international economy, expand employment, gain foreign currency, and obtain technology in the course of internationalization. Finally, through the zones, China wants to solve its political problems with Hong Kong, Macao, and Taiwan (see Figure 2-1).

Figure 2-1
Connection between China's Internal Areas, Special Economic Zones, and Foreign
Countries

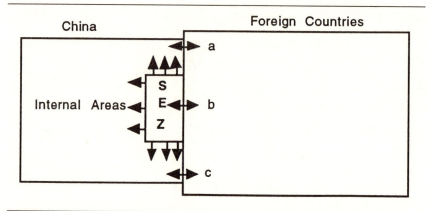

Note: a is the route China and foreign countries can approach most easily; *b* is the route that can be
approached less easily than special economic zones.

TYPES OF SPECIAL ZONES

China's special economic zones can be seen as special areas open to foreign business, finance, and trade. There are, however, other economic areas that can help establish external markets. These include transit zones, free ports, and export processing areas. What is the difference between these economic areas and China's special economic zones? The characteristics of each type are discussed in the following section.

Transit Zone

A transit zone,[12] also called a free zone or a free transit zone, is a port with a bonded warehouse that serves as a trade transit area. This type of zone seeks to extend business advantages to landlocked countries. Goods brought to the bonded warehouse are not regarded as imported, and customs duties are not imposed on them as long as they do not enter the domestic market. The transit zone has a narrower scope of economic activity than a free port or an export processing area.

Free Port

A free port refers to all or part of a trade port designated by the state, at which imported foreign goods are not subject to customs and are permitted to enter freely. It exempts foreign commodities from customs and provides a certain degree of freedom to foreign ships using this port, unlike other ports where customs duties are levied and various inspections and supervisory controls are imposed. At a free port, it is possible to re-export, repack, blend, process, manufacture, and exhibit commodities, as well as establish a sample market. In addition, it is also possible to construct or rent warehouses in which finished products may be stored.

Export Processing Zone

An export processing zone is a designated area near a port which is required to export all or some of the products it manufactures. In the 1960s, Taiwan, Hong Kong, Korea, Singapore, and Mexico established such areas. This indicated that they had changed their economic development strategy from import substitution to export promotion. An export processing area can therefore be characterized as the core of an export promotion industrialization strategy.

Generally, corporations in export processing zones receive special treatment. For example, they are exempt from customs duty on the import of raw materials, finished products, semifinished products, processing facilities, and parts, or on the export of products. Taxes levied on these corporations are low, and tax exemptions are granted for a certain period of time after the corporations' inauguration. Foreign corporations in the processing area can freely transfer their profits elsewhere and are not subject to any restrictions on foreign currency management. The government also provides them with facilities, such as water, electricity, ports, warehouses, factories, and boarding houses and services such as communications (telephone and postal service), transportation, banking, and foreign currency exchange.

In sum, an export processing zone is a special economic area established to facilitate export and trade of wholly domestic products via looser regulations on taxation and foreign currency management.

Special Economic Zones

Since many factors overlap in China's special economic zones, it is not easy to classify them. Special zones do not enjoy a no-tax privilege. There is a 15% corporate income tax, and a personal income tax is levied on monthly incomes exceeding 800 yuan. Materials used for production or consumption are exempted from duties, but materials used for other purposes are taxed. The special economic zones differ from free ports in that not only imported but also domestic raw materials are used in large quantities. They also differ from export processing areas in terms of the variety of industries present, which include commerce, housing and tourism, and public works such as roads or electricity.

In sum, a special economic zone is an area in which a comparatively freer management system and other conditions are set up for the achievement of economic objectives. It enjoys economic cooperation with foreign corporations in various relationships, ranging from mergers to independent management, and is an overall economic development area in which disparate businesses, such as manufacturing, agriculture, livestock, fishing, commerce, housing, tourism, banking, and insurance, are conducted.

3

Characteristics of Special Economic Zones

What essential characteristics of special zones distinguish them from other parts of the country? There are the new managerial systems and administrative measures set up by the central government, but more important is the underlying ideology. There have been many different interpretations of how socialist or Marxist-Leninist ideology and the special policy have been combined in the zones. The three major theories are (1) the special economic zones have socialist characteristics, (2) the special economic zones represent capitalism in a socialist state, and (3) the special economic zones have the characteristics of state capitalism.[13]

These theories differ in the aspect each theorist desires to emphasize. In the author's opinion, the most important distinction is between ownership and the economic management system. Considered from the perspective of ownership, wholly foreign companies in the special zones reflect a capitalist nature. From the perspective of the economic management system, these companies are indirectly controlled by the Chinese planned economic system. Accordingly, the zones display characteristics of both socialism and state capitalism. However, there are many factors that cannot be characterized as either socialism or state capitalism. For example, prices of commodities are mostly determined by market conditions. The market mechanism is also applied to the circulation of fixed capital, such as real estate and land. In addition, there is a considerable amount of production that takes place without the direction of state planning. In these respects, the central government has been gradually loosening control over the special zones. It is clear that neither viewpoint adequately reflects the situation. In the following section, the characteristics of special zones, as stated above, will be reexamined based on research on Shenzhen Special Economic Zone, selected because it is has the longest history and the largest scale of economic activity.

ANALYSIS OF OWNERSHIP IN THE SPECIAL ECONOMIC ZONES

Ownership of Residential Property

In November 1981, Shenzhen Special Economic Zone formulated the Regulations on Land Management in the Shenzhen Special Economic Zone. According to these regulations, any individual may freely sell or buy a factory, warehouse, building, or house. As a result, real estate transactions accounted for 43% and 31% of social gross production and state income, respectively.[14] Most of the transactions were by individuals. For example, 74% of buildings built by the Financial Development Corporation in 1987 were sold to individuals, and only 26% to groups. Of the buildings sold and bought by the Special Zone Real Estate Corporation, 75–80% were sold to individuals.[15]

Selling and Buying According to the Market Price

As of January 1991, a three-bedroom apartment in Shenzhen Special Economic Zone, sold for approximately 200,000–300,000 yuan. Buyers included the following:

1. Anyone with a household register in Shenzhen Special Economic Zone may purchase an apartment at a very low price. People with sufficient money buy several and rent them.
2. Chinese corporations based in Hong Kong entering Shenzhen Special Economic Zone from Hong Kong as well as domestic Chinese corporations may purchase apartments at market prices.
3. Foreign corporations entering Shenzhen Special Economic Zone may purchase apartments at market prices.
4. Foreigners (mostly Hong Kong residents and Taiwanese) purchase apartments mainly for speculation or for relatives.

Many people rent rather than buy apartments. As of January 1991, a three-bedroom apartment in Shenzhen Special Economic Zone carried a monthly rent of 1,500–3,000 yuan. People who rented homes included (1) people from outside areas without a household register in Shenzhen Special Economic Zone who must rent apartments (if they have enough money, they can purchase apartments), and (2) foreign corporations' workers. The Chinese (mainly officials) working for foreign corporations (large-scale companies such as banks and stock companies) and having no household register, as well as foreigners, live either in the corporations' apartments or in rented apartments because they do not receive housing from the local government.

Selling and Buying by State-Owned Corporations

State-owned corporations can supply a three-bedroom apartment at one-fifth to one-seventh of the market price, or about 40,000 yuan. This differs from sales based on market prices in that it is a kind of long-term lease (fifty years on the average). It applies only to the use of the building, and the corporation retains the right to use the land.

If a worker at a state-owned corporation moves to another corporation after purchasing an apartment, the problem can be solved in two ways: (1) The worker's new corporation pays the balance (margin between the current market price and the price at which the old corporation purchased the apartment) to the worker's former corporation, and (2) The worker returns the apartment to the old corporation. The worker pays the original price of the apartment plus interest on the original price.

Generally only married male employees may buy an apartment from a state-owned corporation. However, this is limited by management conditions. For example, Mr. A (thirty-two years old, married, and a college graduate) works in the state trading company and has a record of good performance in the company, but does not have his own apartment yet. This is because his company has poor management conditions and cannot provide housing for all of its employees. He currently shares a four-bedroom apartment with another household.

Sale of Housing by the City Government

City-owned apartments are much cheaper than state-owned corporation apartments. A three-bedroom city-owned apartment is 10,000–20,000 yuan. However, if an employee transfers to another location, he must return the apartment to the city government. For example, Shenzhen University built apartments in the downtown area of the city and supplied them to faculty members who have been with the university since before January 1986. Their right to use these apartments is valid for fifty years and extends beyond retirement.

Ownership of Land

Land is the most important production material. It is the basis of socialist collectivism. In the special economic zones, land (except land in the collective ownership system) belongs to the state and cannot be sold. However, sale of the right to use land is permitted with tax levied on use. Because of this policy, the land market in Shenzhen Special Economic Zone has developed dramatically. There were 184 sales of the right to use land in Shenzhen City from 1988, when it was legalized, to the end of 1989. The total size of the land sold was $427m^2$, totaling about 330 million yuan. Among these sales, 13 (total size: $14.7m^2$) were sold through auction, amounting to 140 million yuan.[16]

Agricultural land use rights could be sold in two ways.

When a collective group has ownership and an individual has right of use:

Mr. A from Shenzhen works for a Japanese corporation in Nan Touqu in Shenzhen Special Economic Zone. With the de-organizing of the *Renmin Gongshe* (People's Communes), Mr. A gained the right to use a plot of the communal land. He rented the right for one year to a farmer who came to Shenzen with his family of four (himself included) from the interior. In 1987, Mr. A charged 150 yuan per mu (6. 67 acres) for one year. In 1990, he increased the rent to 400 yuan, a 230% increase over a three-year period. The farmer cultivated vegetables in an area of 2 mus to sell in the markets. His annual income was around 7,000 yuan.

When the state has both ownership and right of use:

Mr. B, who grows bananas in Nan Touqu, came to Shenzhen with his family of four (himself included) in 1983. He obtained a one-year contract for the right to use 10 mus of land from the Agricultural Center of Shenzhen City. The rent was 100 yuan per mu per year in 1983, which increased to 400 yuan in 1991. His annual income after subtracting overall expenses (including fertilizers) was 8,000–10,000 yuan.

Exact figures regarding the lease of farmland are not available, but a Shenzhen city government official estimates that more than 95% of the right to use farmland in Shenzhen Special Economic Zone is leased out to farmers as in these examples.

Ownership of Other Production Factors

After the establishment of the special economic zones, China granted privileges, such as tax reduction, to foreign corporations in order to obtain their advanced technology and superior managerial techniques. Thus, many foreign corporations, including those from Hong Kong, entered the special economic zones. These corporations were under various types of ownership, such as state-owned companies, collective ownership companies, private companies, joint-venture companies between China and other countries, merged companies and wholly foreign-capital companies. The last three types are considered foreign companies because they are financed partially or wholly with foreign capital. A joint venture is similar to a merger in that both the Chinese company and the foreign capital company invest in kind, but generally not to evaluate the value of the in-kind contributions. In addition, the share of management risk and distribution of profits is predetermined by contract. Liquidation of the company is enacted in the same way by contract, but the company capital is often handed over to the Chinese partner. In a merger, the Chinese partner and the foreign-capital company jointly invest with money (foreign currency and yuan), buildings, machine facilities, rights to use land and patent rights and split profits according to the investment ratio. In addition, the company is liquidated by splitting the remaining capital according to the investment ratio. Because the merged company is a stock ownership type, it must be established as a limited liability company with a corporate position according to the investment ratio. In a wholly foreign-capital company, all fixed capital and funds are personally possessed by the investor and protected by the laws of the special zone. During the contract period, renewal and transfer of facilities and funds are possible, and the investor is fully responsible for production, sales, cost accounting, profits, and losses. When the company leases a factory or land to construct a factory, it pays rental charges for use of the land or factory by negotiation.

By the end of 1988, industrial production in Shenzhen was worth a total of 7,730.97 yuan (at 1980 prices). Of that, state-owned companies made up 2,147.28

yuan, collective ownership companies, 467.27 yuan, and foreign corporations, including wholly foreign companies, 5,100.09 yuan. About 30% of total production was by socialist public corporations.[17] However, much of the production by the socialist public corporations was actually by *Sanlaiyibao* (processing on consignment). There are four types of Sanlaiyibao:

1. *Lailiao jiagong* (processing on commission): The company imports raw materials, accessories, and/or packing materials from the foreign customer and gives the processed products to the customer. The Chinese company is paid for the processing.

2. *Laiyang jiagong* (manufacture on the basis of sample): The company processes products according to samples or instructions from the foreign customer and hands them over to the customer. Chinese raw materials are used for manufacturing.

3. *Laijian zhuangpei* (knockdown export): The foreign customer supplies accessories and the Chinese company assembles products. The customer receives the finished products.

4. Compensation trade: The foreign company supplies raw materials and/or machine facilities and is repaid with products. This is the so-called "distribution method." In other words, in terms of production, socialist public corporations in Shenzhen Special Economic Zone accounted for no more than 27% of the total.

ANALYSIS OF THE ECONOMIC MANAGEMENT SYSTEM

The central government's policy on the operation of special economic zones centers on the market mechanism rather than on government planning, that is, the state is involved in the drawing up of mid- or long-term plans and the introduction of important projects/permission for construction. Materials and energy sources that need state support are included in the plans. Other factors are left to distribution by the market or suggestion by the state.

The classification of ownership of commercial corporations in Shenzhen Special Economic Zone as of the end of 1989 is shown in Table 3-1. As Table 3-1 shows, state-owned, collective, and internal corporations make up no more than 30.1% of the commercial area of Shenzhen Special Economic Zone. In terms of ownership, these corporations are state-owned or collective types, however, in terms of production activities, most are not covered by the state plan system. This is clearly shown by the fact that the market mechanism determines the price of consumer goods produced by these corporations.

Market for Consumer Commodities

Since the special zones were established, the government has been putting its efforts into the formation of a market for consumer goods to increase people's living standards and income. These efforts include activation of the distribution network and price reform. Outside the special economic zones, state-determined fixed prices prevail based on principles centering on the planned economy. Liquid prices that can be moved up or down by both the municipal governments' Bureau of Prices or by the free market take only an auxiliary role. However, the situation is completely different

Table 3-1
Ownership of Commercial Corporations in Shenzhen Special Economic Zone

		1988	1989	Increase from the previous year (%)
	Domestic corporations	6,530	8,069	23.6
Types	State-owned corporations	1,642	1,751	6.6
	Collective corportaions	529	671	26.8
	Internal corporations	28	38	35.7
	Private corporations	4,331	5,609	29.5
	Sectors — Commerce	2,770	3,122	12.7
	Restaurants	476	638	34.0
	Services	1,085	1,849	70.4
	Foreign corporations	113	103	-9.0
Total		6,643	8,172	23.0

Source: From an interview with the staff of the Statistical Bureau of Shenzhen, January 4–May 15, 1991.

in the special economic zones. In Shenzhen Special Economic Zone, price reform has progressed through three stages.[18]

First Stage: From May 1982 to October 1984

Major reforms during this stage include the transfer of management power to lower agencies, the gradual reduction of the scope of state-determined fixed prices, and the expansion of the scope of free market prices. As a result of these reforms, prices of only a few commodities remain under the control of the Shenzhen City municipal government's Bureau of Prices, while the rest are determined independently by corporations. Prices are in principle regulated by supply and demand. After taking into consideration the effects of certain goods on the state economy and on people's living standards, the following price management system was adopted in Shenzhen.

Fixed Prices. The provincial government determines fixed prices for a few important goods (food, oil, fuel, and drugs) and public services (rent, electricity, water, school tuition, and transportation) that are supplied or distributed through state planning.

Liquid Prices. Corporations are allowed to increase or decrease prices for some commodities within a range determined by the municipal government's Bureau of Prices. For example, a liquid price variation of 10–30% can be applied to marine products, and price variation according to quality is allowed. For industrial products, especially domestic electric appliances produced in the area, only a maximum price is set, with no minimum. As for vegetables, the municipal government's Bureau of Prices previously controlled seventy-two items. In March 1982, however, restrictions on fifty-four items were lifted and the Vegetable Corporation was allowed to fix prices within certain limits according to supply and demand. At the end of 1983, restrictions on fourteen more items were lifted, leaving only four vegetable items under the control of the Bureau of Prices.

Market Prices. The ratio of market prices to government-regulated prices in Shenzhen City's price system is gradually increasing. The proportion of market prices in the commodities area increased from 15% in 1979 to about 80% in 1984.

Second Stage: From November 1, 1984 to the End of 1987

Entering the second stage, the Bureau of Prices loosened price controls in the following manner:

1. Price decisions regarding production materials and means, such as wood, electricity installation services, and glass, were transferred to the price-related city department.
2. Price decisions regarding vegetables were given to the mayor to be decided according to supply and demand.
3. Price decisions regarding daily necessities, such as food, cooking oil, and gas, were changed from the fixed price system to the liquid price system. The Bureau of Prices induced a decline in prices by setting a maximal limit. At the same time, price subsidies for four items were lifted. Increased expenditures by city residents were offset by increases in their wages.

With these measures, prices for most agricultural and industrial products were left, within limits, to the market-controlled relationship between supply and demand, outside the control of central or provincial government.

Third Stage: After January 1988

By this stage, prices for most consumer goods were determined by the market. For commodities, market prices prevailed for 91.5%, liquid prices for 6.8%, and state-determined fixed prices for 1.7% of all production. The price system in special economic zone was changed from "one product, multiple prices" (in which state-determined prices and market prices coexisted) to "one product, one price."[19] In addition, the role of the city planning office changed from control of distribution to supervision and management of prices, reflecting the marketization of the economy.[20] Thus, although the ownership of state-run and collective corporations remained with the state or group, most business activities, including price decisions, moved out of the state planning system.

Market for Producer Goods

Under the planned economy, China did not consider producer goods as products. Accordingly, they were objects of controlled distribution, from central to local authorities. However, the management of these authorities was complex and stiff, preventing the smooth circulation of producer goods. Furthermore, economic development and large-scale investment in facilities in the special economic zones greatly increased demand for producer goods. Since this demand could not be fulfilled solely by the central government's controlled distribution, materials had to be bought from domestic or foreign markets. The coexistence of different distribution channels, such as state-controlled distribution and imports from outside markets and foreign countries, made for considerable price differences, and the producer goods market was thrown into chaos. Accordingly, special economic zones applied the market mechanism to the circulation and pricing of producer goods in the hope of promoting their circulation and ensuring secure supply and demand.

Recently, not only large state-run corporations, such as the Shenzhen Production Materials Corporation, the Special Zone Development Corporation, and the Industrial Group of Construction Materials, but also foreign corporations (including wholly foreign companies) have taken charge in the supply of producer goods. In 1987, there were about 700 companies dealing with producer goods in Shenzhen City. Major items included electronic accessories, electrical instrument installation, construction materials (60 companies for steel, 130 companies for cement, and 30 companies for wood), metal materials, and producer goods for agriculture. With the formation of a market for producer goods, pricing shifted from the former monopoly model to a more competitive situation, and market prices prevailed in Shenzhen Special Economic Zone.[21]

Among the producer goods currently being circulated, steel, cement, and wood (which have relatively large effects on investment in facilities and public projects) are under the control of the state. At the end of 1987, 1.2% of steel, 4.2% of cement, and 35% of coal were distributed by the state.[22] However, "the liquid price" system was applied to even these three producer goods on the condition that they did not affect production circulation and the profits of owners. Generally, the selling corporation can freely decide price within 120% of the base price. When the sale price exceeds the base price by 20–30%, the main office of the corporation may determine the price. When it exceeds the base price by 130%, however, the corporation must obtain permission from the Bureau of Prices.

Capital Market

Profits and taxes of state-run commerce and industry were previously concentrated on central and local finance. As a result, government financial agencies had much more power than banks. However, in the special economic zones, government financial agencies have a weaker role than banks and other financial companies. For example, a total of 13.8 billion yuan was invested in basic construction projects in Shenzhen from 1979 to 1988. This is an increase of 27,700% from the 49.66 million yuan invested in 1979. Of this total investment, the combined expenditures of the central and Shenzhen City government made up no more than 16%.[23]

The capital market consists of the following financial agencies: (1) state banks—the Chinese People's Bank (Central Bank), the Chinese Bank (Foreign Currency Exchange Bank), the Chinese Bank of Industry and Commerce, the Chinese Construction Bank, and the Chinese Agriculture Bank and (2) private banks—the Shakou Commerce Bank, the Shenzhen Development Bank, and foreign banks (currently, there are six

Hong Kong banks, four Japanese banks, three French banks, and one English bank in Shenzhen).

Besides banks, there are fifteen other financial agencies in Shenzhen, including trust investment companies, finance companies, lease companies, stock companies, and insurance companies. As Figure 3-1 shows, various agencies exist in the financial market.

Money Market

The money market is made up of debt and credit between banks and corporations, exchange of short-term funds between banks, and debt and credit between financial agencies and corporations.

Debt and Credit between a Bank and a Corporation. The conditions for debt and credit are determined by the market environment. The 1988 savings and loans of each type of financial agency in Shenzhen are shown in Table 3-2. Banks have two types of loans for corporations: the bank group loan and the asset collateral loan. An example of a bank group loan is the Shajiao thermal power plant. There were forty-six banks participating in the group loan for this power plant (worth 3.33 billion Hong Kong dollars), including the Hong Kong branch of the Chinese Bank and the Shenzhen branch of the Hong Kong Shanghai Bank.[24]

Exchange of Short-Term Loans between Banks. Every bank in Shenzhen started a call not only with banks in the Shenzhen zone, but also with internal banks, beginning in 1984. The call money market in Shenzhen City from 1984 to 1988 totaled 16.04 billion yuan.[25] The scope of changes in the rate of interest is determined by the Chinese People's Bank after which it is regulated by the market.

Figure 3-1
Financial System in Shenzhen

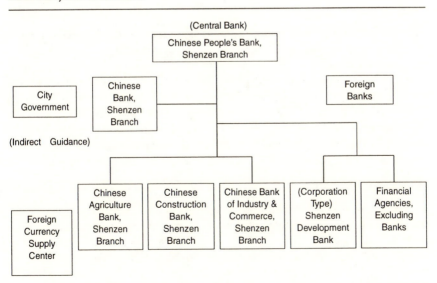

Table 3-2

Savings and Loans of Each Financial Agency in Shenzhen City, 1988

Financial agencies	Balance in Chinese savings (100 million yuan)*	Balance in Chinese loans (100 million yuan)*	Balance in foreign savings (U.S.$100 million)**	Balance in foreign loans (U.S.$100 million)**
State banks	80.3	94.6	—	—
Private banks	7.3	7.2	14.53	18.21
Nonbank agencies	8.2	11.6	—	—
Foreign banks	—	—	3.22	8.06
Total of 1988	95.8	113.4	17.56	26.27
Total of 1979	93.0	169.0	11.7	—

Sources: For *, Liu Zhigang, 1989, p. 833; for **, Statistical Bureau of Zhenzhen, 1989, p. 42.

Debt and Credit between Financial Agencies (Excluding Banks) and Corporations. Financial agencies (excluding banks) currently located in Shenzhen conduct businesses such as consignment loans, investments, and leasing. In addition, they also perform services, such as guarantees of domestic and foreign investment, real estate, stocks, and management advice. As of the end of 1987, there were fifteen financial agencies with capital worth 1.69 billion yuan, occupying 24.1% of the total capital of financial agencies in Shenzhen.[26] As shown in Table 3-2, savings of financial agencies in 1988 totaled 0.82 billion yuan, 8.6% of total savings. Loans made up 1.16 billion yuan, or 10.2%, of total loans.

Stock Market

One of the biggest problems that the Shenzhen financial market faces is the transformation of a considerable amount of unused funds, such as small funds and an agriculture-promoting fund, into an investment fund. In 1983, a stock market was created in Shenzhen with the issuance of stocks by the Shanwa Limited Corporation, Yinghu Travel Agency, and the Lianhe Investment Corporation in Baoanxian. After the Shenzhen municipal government announced "temporary regulations on issuing company bonds in Shenzhen Special Economic Zone" in 1984, stock and company bond markets developed gradually under government control.[27] Currently, company bonds amount to 4.4 million yuan; state bonds, 2.68 million yuan; and valuable securities 10 billion yuan.[28]

Foreign Currency Market

Corporations in the Shenzhen zone enjoy special treatment in foreign currency management. They are granted 100% reservation of income from foreign currency earned through exports. However, under the previous rigid system of foreign currency management, there was no way to smoothly exchange foreign currency and yuan.

Thus, a considerable amount of foreign currency and yuan was exchanged on the black market, resulting in serious problems in the national foreign currency system.

To alleviate this problem, the central government established the Foreign Currency Supply Center in Shenzhen in November 1985. However, this has not eliminated black market activities. At its establishment, deals were very small because a ceiling was set on the supply price and customers could not directly deal, nor could foreign corporations participate. The Foreign Currency Supply Center had deals worth $58.52 million from November 1985 to December 1986. During this same period, black market deals worth $22.28 million were intercepted. Despite the establishment of the Foreign Currency Supply Center, black market activities increased by 150% in 1985. If hidden black market transactions are taken into consideration, the total amount of black market transactions is estimated to be much greater.[29]

In order to strengthen the function of the Foreign Currency Supply Center, the government lifted restrictions in 1987. Prices were to be dictated by the market, and individuals or corporations allowed to freely participate in the trading. As a result of these measures, transactions in the Foreign Currency Supply Center totaled $0.5 billion in the first part of 1988, an 800% increase over the $58.52 million transacted between November 1985 and December 1986.[30] The Foreign Currency Supply Center was able to better satisfy the needs of both suppliers and demanders of foreign currency. For example, in October 1987, Corporation A for Exports/Imports of Spun Products of the Shenzhen foreign trade group had a bank balance of 6 million dollars. However, it still suffered from a lack of funds due to a previous bank loan of 30 million Chinese yuan. This is because the official exchange rate of yuan to dollar was higher than the actual rate for a long time. As a result, the more one engaged in dollar-earning exports, the more one suffered losses. After a free price system was available in the Foreign Currency Supply Center, however, Corporation A could exchange its foreign currency with yuan at a much higher rate than the official rate.[31]

Labor Market

A free labor market now exists in the special economic zone. Before this, the government controlled distribution and management of labor and dictated plans to lower offices; workers were assigned to a corporation by the government and could not be moved thereafter. However, with the establishment of the special zones and the consequent emergence of multiownership corporations not under direct government control, labor can transfer from one workplace to another.

Other labor problems, such as coordination of wages, welfare, social security, and labor shortages (especially of skilled labor), accompanied the economic development of the special zone. These problems could not be solved effectively through government coordination and planning. Therefore, the government granted labor planning autonomy to Shenzhen City, which manages labor according to its social and economic development objectives. The labor mechanism is as follows.

People with Official Household Register

The household register is managed jointly by the city's Department of Labor and the Bureau of Public Welfare. The Department of Labor annually determines and mandates a quantity index for the size of the population (people with official household registers) in the special zone. People with official household registers are mostly permanent laborers with government jobs. Since the Regulations on Business Management in the Guangdong Province Special Economic Zones was announced, most companies in the Shenzhen Special Zone have adopted the contract system for hiring laborers. However, cultural, education, and medical agencies still follow the fixed labor system.

People without Official Household Register

There are many external laborers (people with either long- or short-term temporary registers instead of official registers) in Shenzhen. A person who holds a long-term temporary household register is one who does not need to obtain a permanent household register for moving into the zone although the period of residence in the zone is relatively long (over one year). Typical owners of this register are managers, unskilled laborers, and skilled laborers who come from outside to work temporarily at a Chinese company or with foreign-capital companies. These people usually return to the internal areas after three to five years. Short-term temporary registers are issued to those whose residence period is relatively short, less than half a year. These people obtain a certificate to enter Shenzhen from an armed police side unit located at the border of the special zone and do not need to process a temporary household register. They are recruited, coordinated, and distributed through the market mechanism by agencies, such as the Shenzhen City Labor Corporation, the Zone Labor Corporation, and the Labor Services Station.

Various labor corporations, fifty-four in all, were established in cities throughout China by 1989. These corporations recruited and distributed 800,000 workers to the special zone at the request of corporations.[32] These workers were employed as contract workers, replacement workers, or temporary workers. The entire Shenzhen Special Economic Zone adopted the contract system for hiring new employees in 1982. An employee takes a company entrance exam and is fired if he shows poor work attitudes or performance. Most contract laborers are young middle and high school graduates who often change workplaces because of dissatisfaction. Companies in Shenzhen allied with internal areas use the shifting labor system. Technicians, managers, and skilled laborers assigned to the allied company are replaced with new personnel from the internal areas when they complete their one to two years assignment in the zone. Temporary laborers usually work in areas such as factory assembly lines, civil engineering and construction sites, quarries, transportation, and various repair works. Other temporary laborers work in hospital wards, warehouses, and as part-time housemaids. It cannot be determined precisely how many workers in Shenzhen do not have an official household register and are coordinated by the market mechanism because complete statistics are not available. According to partial statistics, however, about 80% of the total labor force in corporations and offices in the special zone are known to be contract or temporary workers.[33]

China manages the household registers of rural households and urban households separately to restrict movement from rural to urban areas. This system began at the same time as food controls in 1953 and still exists. Movement from rural to urban areas is confined to college entrance, military service, marriage, and job transfers of government officials. However, the illegal entry of labor from rural area to urban areas is openly conducted as a result of the boom in economic activities in urban areas.

Other Markets

After the inauguration of the special economic zone, the Shenzhen municipal government actively promoted scientific projects and introduced advanced technology from abroad. It greatly encouraged the establishment of private corporations by scientists and technicians and the creation of R&D centers within companies. Consequently, the field of applied sciences became strengthened and a technology market was created. In 1987, there were 201 corporations within Shenzhen involved in technology development, technology services, and technology consulting. In Shenzhen Special Economic Zone, an information market was created along with the technology market. Research activities, publishing companies, and consulting services on marketing were vigorously pursued, and the information they collected was marketed. With the formation of a technology and information market, China not only began to import advanced technology, but also exported its own technology. In 1987, technology exports from Shenzhen Special Economic Zone were worth $160 million, and there were 245 information-related corporations in the zone.[34]

DIFFERENT PERSPECTIVES ON THE CHARACTERISTICS OF THE SPECIAL ECONOMIC ZONE

There are currently three viewpoints regarding the characteristics of the special economic zones. One perspective sees the special economic zone as "a socialistic society." Yu Guangyuan gives three reasons supporting this view:

1. In the People's Republic of China, the special economic zone is no more than an area where some special policies are enacted. The special zone is not special politically or socially, but only in terms of economic policy.
2. Many socialist collective corporations exist in the special economic zone. Although Sanlai-yibao business management is followed, there is no change in the socialist characteristic of the Chinese corporations.
3. Even in foreign corporations, workers, wages, and organizations adhere to the characteristics of Chinese socialism.[35]

Liang Wensen, Director of the Department of Special Economic Zones Studies at Shenzhen University, observes that the special zone lies within the land of the People's Republic of China and the central government has sovereignty. It is a part of socialist China which cannot be detached, and it is subject to political and jurisdictional regulations that are declared by the People's government. In the special zone, there exist features of socialism which are completely discordant with capitalism, such as a state-run economy and a collective economy. Although the individual economy in the special zone is related to and affected by non-socialist economic factors, the zone can only be seen as a necessary supplement to the essentially socialist economy.[36]

I disagree. When the characteristics of special economic zones are being discussed, economic factors, not political or social factors, should be analyzed. Accordingly, it is difficult to conclude that the special economic zone is socialistic simply because it does not possess special, nonsocialist political or social features. While there are many corporations with socialist communal ownership in the Shenzhen zone, they only produce about 37% of total production. Furthermore, many corporations with socialist communal ownership depend on production by Sanlai-yibao. When these are taken into consideration, the actual proportion and significance of corporations with socialist communal ownership goes down. Accordingly, in terms of ownership, it is hard to say that the special economic zone has socialistic characteristics. Undeniably the Chinese participate with and influence foreign corporations in terms of labor, wages, and organization. However, it should be noted that this does not greatly affect actual corporate management style. Special zone companies, especially the foreign-capital companies, have greater autonomy than other companies in China. This is because special zone companies conduct activities independently of national planning. Each company can make decisions concerning purchases, sales, investment, and business management strategies. Both Chinese and U.S. partners desire to minimize wages and maximize profits; not a socialist idea. This tendency is stronger when the major investor is a corporation from Chinese areas outside the special zone. In the case of merged companies, workers may be recruited through newspaper advertisements or acquaintances rather than through the Department of Labor. There are no restrictions from municipal government on recruiting laborers and the company can dismiss its workers at any time. See the example of Company A: Company A is a merged manufacturer of bags with 50% each of capital held by its U.S. and Chinese owners. Its workers are temporary workers from the rural area of Guangdong Province with no relation to the original corporate labor units. It bends and abuses the labor laws to maximize profits. For example, when a company hires a worker, the first three months serve as an internship period. Thereafter, the company must pay an amount equal to 25% of the worker's basic wages as social insurance to the Department of Labor. Company A often attempts to extend the internship period to reduce wage expenses. Sometimes, the company fails to pay required social insurance to the Department of Labor. Furthermore, it does not follow regulations on various worker benefits (e.g., overtime and holiday allowances).

My research reveals that many foreign companies (including merged corporations) have similar attitudes. Corporations enter the special economic zone to seek a cheap production base. Chinese companies that merge with these foreign companies put priority on profits, not worker welfare.

Another perspective sees the special economic zone as capitalism in the socialist state. Fu Dabang, at the Bureau of Advertising in Guangdong Province, supports this viewpoint for the following reasons.

1. Capitalists are allowed to operate factories or various businesses to attain profits.
2. All labor employment systems in the special zone are based on production surplus.
3. Various economic relations in the special zone are centered on control of the market.
4. Wholly foreign corporations are private capitalist companies.
5. Merged or cooperative corporations are examples of state capitalism rooted in capitalism, because in such corporations, the exploiting capitalist class and the exploited labor class coexist.[37]

This view is based on the presumption that there is a capitalist class which seeks the creation of surplus. However, this is not enough to clearly reveal that the special economic zone is capitalistic. It is necessary to look for not only the existence of a capitalist class, but also its proportionate size among all classes in the special economic zone. Nor is the abstract argument that economic management is centered on control of the market persuasive. For this view to prevail, it must clearly demonstrate a dominant market mechanism. As mentioned before, the economic management system in the special economic zone operates in a very close relationship with capitalism. However, it is unreasonable to claim that the special economic zone is completely capitalist while strict government restrictions still exist.

For example, wholly foreign corporations must go through the Department of Labor when they hire workers. Workers must be from Guangdong Province. (Workers from other areas, who enter the zone in small numbers, must have special skills). They must register their workers with the Department of Labor, regardless of how they hire them. They must pay social insurance, on top of wages, to the Department of Labor. Furthermore, workers from outside Guangdong Province cannot freely move their household register. As a result, they face many disadvantages: (1) they are not given a housing allowance, (2) in order to send their children to school, they must pay a tuition five times greater than that paid by people with household registers in Guangdong. Consequently, they generally cannot afford to give their children an education, and (3) they must also seek jobs for themselves without government assistance.

In addition, ownership and economic management systems in the zone have the characteristics of a planned economy. Accordingly, when these factors are considered, it is still too early to claim the special economic zone is capitalist.

Another popular opinion views the special economic zone as state capitalism. The major proponent of this perspective is Xu Dixin. He gives the following reasons:

Although an individually invested corporation owned by a foreign investor is a capitalist company, the environment in which it exists is different from that of a private corporation in a capitalist state. Such a company is under the Chinese government and is controlled by the special zone government. It must abide by Chinese rules and regulations and pay a business tax, a real estate tax for houses and lands, and income tax. The range of business management is also restricted by the Chinese government, and it cannot act as it wants to. Accordingly, even an individually invested corporation owned by foreign investors has some characteristics of state capitalism, as a special capitalist corporation under the power and control of China.[38]

Xu acknowledges the pursuit of profits by foreign corporations is an act of exploitation, but he interprets this as a purchasing policy. That is, just as China obtained cooperation from the Chinese bourgeoisie in the beginning stages of its emancipation, it is currently trying to attain the cooperation of foreign capital or overseas Chinese through its purchasing policy. He believes that China wants to introduce outside capital and advanced technology, develop the special zone, and ultimately achieve the modernization of socialism.

The most distinct feature of this interpretation is that discussion of the nature of the special zone is confined to individual foreign companies. It perceives the individual foreign corporations as capitalist in terms of ownership, but sees the zone as essentially following state capitalism because its business management system is subject to many restrictions. However, it should be kept in mind that discussion should not only be on ownership of individual foreign corporations or business management systems, but also on overall ownership type and business management systems. Another problem with this interpretation is that Xu's definition of state capitalism is unclear. In this regard, Xu says, "As a purchasing policy, foreign capital and technology from the foreign capital are first introduced. This will bring about development of the special zone's economy and at the same time, gain of foreign currency and business management techniques. As these expected objectives are accomplished, the foreign capital will gradually achieve socialistic reforms."[39]

However, this begs the question of just how these reforms will be accomplished. Xu vaguely explains that state capitalism in the special economic zone will be realized over a long period, and that state capitalism in the special economic zone is different from the capitalism adopted by and for the national bourgeoisie after the emancipation.[40] If the special economic zone is to be defined as state capitalism, this claim needs to be made more clearly.

In the light of these views, combined with the evidence regarding the actual situation in Shenzhen Special Economic Zone, I define the special economic zone as a capitalist area under the restrictions of a socialist state. This alternative definition is based on the following observations:

1. In areas outside the special economic zone, socialist collectivism is the basic form of ownership and the planned economy is the basic form of economic management system.

2. In the special economic zone, many types of ownership exist but socialist collectivism is the predominant form.

3. The economic management system in the special economic zone is restricted by the government with respect to the overall development plan and the supply of materials

(including labor and basic goods, such as water and electricity). However, economic operations in other respects are mostly governed by the market mechanism.

Most importantly, state restrictions and economic management based on socialist collectivism are being reduced over time. The special economic zone can be said to possess an economic system in a period of transition from socialism (the planned economy) to capitalism (the market economy). It can be seen as a new experiment never experienced before in the socialist economic system.

4

Background to the Establishment of the Special Economic Zones

The history and purpose of the special economic zones and their effects on the Chinese centrally planned economy have been reviewed. Another issue that must now be discussed is why, in the late 1970s, China made such a radical change as the reform and open policy, represented by the establishment of the special economic zones. This change to a development strategy, of course, involved a change in the thinking of new policy makers. In analyzing this change, it is necessary to consider economic and other factors, instead of simplistically interpreting it as new thinking by new policy makers.

ECONOMIC FACTORS

Rural-Urban Two-Dimensional Economic Development Strategy under Less Developed Socialism

After the Revolution in October 1949, China conducted a socialist planned economy while still an undeveloped country with a population of 540 million and 9.6 million square kilometers of land. Two features were prominent at the start. One was an economy with extremely low productivity. Thus, one of the main objectives of the new regime was to overcome underdevelopment. The other feature was a socialist planned economy chosen as its national economic system. Since the revolution, it has promoted economic development within the boundaries of socialism.

The most frequently used method in analyzing China's economy has been the comparative economic system theory. However, the old comparative economic system theory was based on Soviet and Eastern Block economic experiences, in which the market-based economy or the social division of labor was relatively advanced. The focus of the old theory was on comparing the functions of capitalist and socialist economies (e.g., market distribution versus planned distribution), which was its original task, or on comparing various types of socialist economies (e.g., centralized socialism versus noncentralized socialism). This creates limitations in analyzing the Chinese economy, in which planned distribution is maintained by complex system factors. The underdeveloped market economy, the administration system, and the conventional economy that coexist in China cannot be fully explained with the comparative economic system theory. In order to overcome this limitation, the rural-urban two-dimensional economic development model in a less developed social-ist system is used in this paper as the analysis framework, modified from A. W. Lewis's two-dimensional economic development model. A. W. Lewis's double model of economic development is useful as a framework of economic development analysis for undeveloped countries having problems of overpopulation and rural development. However, its application to China is meaningless because although China is an underdeveloped country, it is basically a socialist state conducting a planned economy. Therefore, a new analysis framework is employed that takes into consideration the major characteristics of a socialist planned economy, such as planned distribution of resources, restriction of labor movement, and a distributed wage.

Assumptions of the Model

This model was made based on the following assumed arguments:

1. The means of production are collectively owned and the economy is centrally planned. Here, the collective possession of the means of production implies both state ownership and ownership by the people. In a centralized planned economy, major economic decisions are made by a central agency and lower agencies are only given the power to execute. Therefore, investments, labor, machinery, and all categories of raw materials and working methods are decided by the upper agency, and corporations are simply required to perform the duties assigned to them.

2. The country consists of a rural sector, the traditional center of farming, and an urban sector, the center of modern manufacturing. Labor is incompletely employed in both rural and urban sectors, although unemployment is not a serious problem.[41]

3. With the labor distribution, the migration of rural workers to the urban area is restricted until overemployed labor is fully absorbed in the urban area. The reason for this policy is that the replacement of capital and labor is easier in the rural sector than in the industrial sector.

4. Wages are not determined by supply and demand, but by the distribution principle of the socialist planned economy. (Labor works according to ability and receives a dividend according to the labor.) Wages in both rural and urban sectors are determined by dividing the balance (the total distributing amount), gained by subtracting the accumulation from the total production by the labor amounts of workers. This is called distributed income in this book.

5. The accumulation is all reinvested, and the proportions (for rural and urban sectors) are determined by the state investment policy: Total Reinvestment (T) = Weighted Rate in Rural Sector $(E1)$ x T + Weighted Rate in Urban Sector $(E2)$ x T, $E1 + E2 = 1$, $0 < E1 < 1$, $0 < E2 < 1$.

6. The technology level is invariable until overemployment of labor disappears, meaning here that the proportion of capital and labor to each worker is invariable if employment is sufficient (wage = marginal labor productivity) during each production period.

Economic Development Strategy for the Rural Sector

Figure 4-1 shows the process of extended reproduction in the rural sector. When total production (Qa^1), is assumed to be produced by the input of labor (OLa), to the given farmland, marginal labor productivity (MPL) is determined at the point where the labor input, La^1, meets with the total production curve, at which the wage (Wa) is also determined.

Economic Development Strategy for the Urban Sector

Generally, in a capitalist economy, employment is theoretically determined at the point where marginal labor productivity equals the wage, thus putting other labor in a state of unemployment. Accordingly, the labor in area $OLa–La^1$ is unemployed, because for that section, marginal labor productivity is lower than the wage. However, socialist China cannot abandon its unemployed workers. All labor must be employed, regardless of its marginal productivity. Accordingly, the overall labor (OLa), works to

Figure 4-1
Process of Extended Reproduction in the Rural Sector

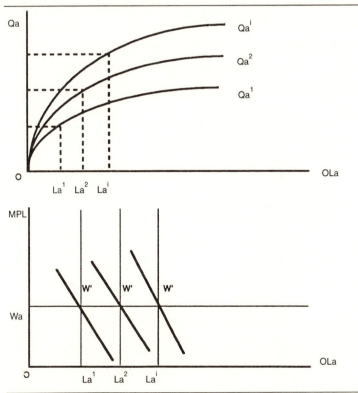

Notes: Optimal labor input during each period in rural sector, La^1, La^2 ... La^i. Production during each period, Qa^1, Qa^2 ... Qa^i. Total labor input, OLa. Production, Qa.

yield the total production (Qa^1). The labor in section $OLa–La^1$ is employed, but it is employed incompletely due to the shortage of capital. That is, it is essentially overemployed labor. To solve this problem, the state increases the accumulation out of the total production as much as possible while reducing the distributed income (Wa) determined by the state as much as possible, uses it for the next production expansion, and thus extends the next total production curve from Qa^1 to Qa^2. This strategy is designed to solve the problem of overemployed labor, and at the same time accomplish economic development by repeating the process of extended reproduction.

In the urban sector the production factors are capital (K) and labor (L). Figure 4-2 shows the loci, Q_b^1, Q_b^2 ... Q_b^i, of the total production curve when the overall labor and captial (OL_b) of each period are combined. The wage (W_b) in the urban

Figure 4-2
Process of Extended Reproduction in the Urban Sector

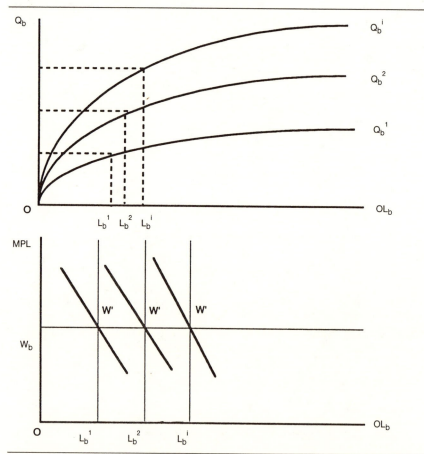

Notes: Optimal labor input during each period in urban sector, L_b^1, L_b^2 ... L_b^i. Production during each period, Q_b^1, Q_b^2 ... Q_b^i. Labor and capital input, OL_b. Production, Q_b.

sector is also determined by distributed income, as in the rural sector. Furthermore, the state tries to extend the accumulation out of total production as much as possible because, as in the rural sector, the urban sector has the problem of overemployed labor. The accumulation is used as a surplus for the expansion of subsequent production, and by this reinvestment the total production curve moves upward from Q_b^1 to Q_b^2.

Policy Suggestions of the Rural-Urban Two-Dimensional Economic Development Model

The model described above suggests the desirability of the following policies, at least from a theoretical point of view.

Population Policy. The population policy should make the population growth rate lower than the economic growth rate. If the population growth rate exceeds the economic growth rate, the total distribution increases as much as the population growth as long as the wage level is kept constant. As a result, reinvestment declines and economic growth rate is restricted.

Capital Accumulation. In the early developmental stage, the state adopts a policy of decreasing consumption as much as possible and increasing savings, because the lack of capital among production factors is most serious. The reason for taking this mode of growth is to attain in the future a distribution exceeding the present average labor production. This is because the future distribution gained by reinvesting part of the present production will definitely be much larger than the present distribution, in which the present production is equally distributed and then completely consumed.

Production Method. Until overemployed labor disappears, production in both rural and urban sectors can depend on sufficient labor. In addition, labor migrates from the rural area to the urban area within the range that the urban sector can absorb. (The range of absorption refers to employment in the urban area and food production in the rural sector both for its remaining population and for the labor that migrated to the urban area.)[42] Furthermore, when both rural and urban sectors reach the point at which overemployed labor disappears, the rural sector must change its production method from production extension based on sufficient labor to labor-saving methods based on modern technology such as fertilizers, pesticides, and farm machinery. When the urban sector reaches this point, it must likewise increase productivity through labor-saving technology rather than sufficient labor, and the production structure must be deepened.

Economic Results Prior to the Reform and Open Policy

The two biggest problems in the Chinese economy prior to the reform and open policy were overemployed labor and paralysis of the accumulation mechanism.

Overemployed Labor

With economic growth, an excess supply of labor occurred as a result of the natural increase in labor and the rise in women's participation in the labor sector, despite the remarkable increase in employment opportunities.

According to the Statistics Yearbook of 1983, the employable population is estimated to be 630,240,000 out of a total population of 1,024,950,000. Of the potentially employable population, 82.7% are actually employed. The unemployed population of 17.3% (190,300,000) is made up of students (18.14%), high school graduates preparing for college entrance exams (1.01%), homemakers (55.18%), retired people—state corporation male workers at 60 and female workers at 55 (7.1%), young people waiting for jobs (2.41%), and others (22.45%). In terms of unemployment among young people, China is no worse than other countries. However, the real unemployment problem in China lies in disguised employment.

The true gravity of China's excess supply of labor is hidden because potentially jobless surplus workers are almost fully employed in the form of overemployed labor. This makes it extremely difficult to determine exactly how many surplus workers exist. Generally, it is estimated that there are about 100–200 million surplus workers in rural areas and 15 million in state-run urban corporations. The figure can rise to 20–30 million if the 15 million workers in the collective corporations are included.[43] The problem of overemployed labor appeared in the late 1970s during which there was a policy of getting young people employed in relatives' or acquaintances' workplaces. These young people were sent to rural areas during the Cultural Revolution and returned to urban areas after the revolution.

Paralysis of the Accumulation Mechanism

Under traditional Chinese economic development, two factors functioned as the major accumulation mechanism: value transfer from the rural sector to the industrial sector by the scissors differential[44]; and the comparatively low wage/high savings of urban laborers. What made this accumulation mechanism possible, of course, was the low price of farm produce.

In value transfer from rural to urban sectors by the scissors differential, if the contribution is estimated in terms of farm tax paid to the state, the rural sector's contribution to state income is very low in proportion to its population density, as shown in Table 4-1. However, the farm tax is not the only contribution the rural sector makes to the state's financial income. In state income, the proportion of the rural sector's contribution is the sum of the farm tax, the margin between the production cost of farm produce and the selling price, and the margin between the original industrial product value and its selling price. It was 44.7–55.9% in 1952, 59.9–72.2% in 1957, and 41.6–55.2% in 1977. For example, when the minimum value (estimation A) of the estimated results of the value difference in 1977 is derived, the total farm contribution was 36.4 billion yuan. This amounts to 85% of the 43.3 billion yuan the state invested in basic construction that same year.

The second factor is the rational low wage system, which refers to low prices of farm produce, low wages, low consumption, and high savings. China also introduced

Table 4-1
Contribution by Rural Sector to State's Financial Income
(goods after construction of value difference*)

	Estimation	1 Farm tax**	2 Financial income**	3 ½%	4 Undergain from selling farm produce**	5 Over-payment when purchasing industrial goods**	6 1 + 4 +5	7 % of 6 in financial income in the year
1952	A	27.0	175.6	15.4	19.0	32.5	78.5	44.7
	B	27.0	175.6	15.4	26.3	44.8	98.1	55.9
1957	A	29.3	310.2	9.4	89.3	66.0	184.6	59.5
	B	29.3	310.2	9.4	112.0	82.6	223.9	72.2
1977	A	29.0	874.5	3.3	213.0	122.0	364.0	41.6
	B	29.0	874.5	3.3	288.2	165.2	482.4	55.2

Source: T. Yamamoto, 1982, p. 169.

Notes: * Difference between the undergain from selling farm produce and the overpayment for the purchase of industrial goods. **100 million yuan.

the system of uniform purchase, uniform income in 1953 to support the rational low wage system. As a result, a market for food, crops, and cotton could not be formed, and prices were put entirely under state control making it possible to fix farm produce at a low price to consumers in the nonrural sector.

This accumulation mechanism, which had been maintained by sacrificing laborers in both rural and urban sectors, should have been able to gradually achieve low wages, expansion of accumulated capital and reinvestment, increase in production, and increase in consumption, in that order, if the mechanism had worked as expected. However, the actual results were that urban wages were pegged or decreased, and farm production did not overcome its stagnation, as shown in Table 4-2. Table 4-3 shows grain production per agricultural laborer. Production levels remained more or less constant from 1952 to 1978. 1978 was a turning point in that for the first time in twenty-one years, grain production surpassed the 1957 level. These statistics starkly illustrate the stagnation of farm production and the impoverishment of farmers and laborers.

The Seventies, a Chinese magazine published in Hong Kong, commented on Chinese living standards: "The people's wages have not increased for several decades, but prices have increased substantially owing to the shortage of commodities. The people's burden for their household economy has increased and the living standard has decreased to a lower level than that in 1957. The people have endured their impoverished living standards for a long time, but their patience has reached the limit."[45] Hu Qiaumu recognized that "the agricultural situation is serious. Food per capita nationwide in 1977 is no more than that in 1955. Food production has

Table 4-2
Average Wages of Laborers and Employees

	Average wage of laborers & employees (yuan)	Index (1952 = 100)		Average wage of laborers & employees in state-owned corporations (yuan)	Index (1952 = 100)		Average wage of laborers & employees in collective ownership corporations (yuan)	Index (1952 = 100)	
		Nominal	Actual		Nominal	Actual		Nominal	Actual
1952	445	100.0	100.0	446	100.0	100.0	348	100.0	100.0
1953	495	111.2	105.8	496	111.2	105.8	415	119.3	113.5
1954	517	116.2	109.0	519	116.4	109.2	464	133.3	125.1
1955	527	118.4	110.8	534	119.7	112.1	453	130.2	121.8
1956	601	135.1	126.5	610	136.8	128.0	547	157.2	147.2
1957	624	140.2	127.9	637	142.8	130.3	571	164.1	149.7
1958	536	120.4	111.0	550	123.3	113.7	470	135.1	124.6
1959	512	115.1	105.8	524	117.5	108.1	430	123.6	113.7
1960	511	114.8	102.9	528	118.4	106.3	409	117.5	105.4
1961	510	114.6	88.5	537	120.4	93.0	380	109.2	84.3
1962	551	123.8	92.1	592	132.7	98.7	405	116.4	86.5
1963	576	129.4	102.2	641	143.7	113.7	371	106.6	84.3
1964	586	131.7	108.1	661	148.2	121.7	358	102.9	84.5
1965	590	132.6	110.1	652	146.2	121.5	398	114.4	95.1

Table 4-2 (continued)

	Average wage of laborers & employees (yuan)	Index (1952 = 100)		Average wage of laborers & employees in state-owned corporations (yuan)	Index (1952 = 100)		Average wage of laborers & employees in collective ownership corporations (yuan)	Index (1952 = 100)	
		Nominal	Actual		Nominal	Actual		Nominal	Actual
1966	583	131.0	110.1	636	142.6	120.0	423	121.6	102.2
1967	587	131.9	111.7	630	141.3	119.5	455	130.7	110.7
1968	577	129.7	109.7	621	139.2	117.7	441	126.7	107.2
1969	575	129.2	108.3	618	138.6	116.1	439	126.1	105.7
1970	561	126.1	105.6	609	136.5	114.3	405	116.4	97.6
1971	560	125.8	105.6	597	133.9	112.3	429	123.3	103.4
1972	588	132.1	110.5	622	139.5	116.8	465	133.6	111.9
1973	587	131.9	110.3	614	137.7	115.2	489	140.5	117.6
1974	584	131.2	109.0	622	139.5	115.9	441	129.7	105.3
1975	580	130.3	107.9	613	137.4	113.9	453	130.2	107.8
1976	575	129.2	106.7	605	135.7	112.1	464	133.3	110.1
1977	576	129.4	104.0	602	135.0	108.5	478	137.4	110.4

Source: State Statistical Bureau of China, 1990, p. 140.

Table 4-3
Grain Production per Rural Laborer (unit: kg)

Year	1952	1957	1962	1965	1970	1975
Production	947	1,010	752	831	863	966

Year	1976	1977	1978	1979	1980	1981
Production	972	963	1,036	1,129	1,061	1,139

Source: State Statistical Bureau of China, 1985, pp. 213–58.

increased just barely enough to meet growing demands of industry and an increased population."[46]

The situation for farmers in areas where agricultural development had lagged was especially miserable. During the Cultural Revolution, Hu Qiaumu noted, the situation was extremely serious: "According to statistics, the yearly food supply for 200 million (out of a total of 800 million) Chinese farmers was 150 kg. per farmer, which meant that they were on the verge of starvation. In the past, farmers in southern Shaanxi Province had food reserves even during times of war. However, they do not have even a single grain now."[47]

In the late 1970s, when China was trying to recover its national economy, it had to drastically increase the procurement price of farm produce and the wages of urban laborers to alleviate the plight of farmers. This explains why the scissors differential and the rational low wage system, which depend on low-price agricultural products, could no longer function as an accumulation mechanism.

Primary Causes of the Stagnation of Economic Operations

Loss of Farmers' Work Initiative Due to the Ownership and Distribution System

Rural Renmin Gongshe's ownership system, after several adjustments, finally took the form of three types of ownership with the production division as a basic accounting unit. Ownership of the basic production means (such as land, livestock, and agricultural tools) generally belongs to the production division (*shengchandai*) and is managed and used by this division. But other production means are owned, managed, and used by the production battalion (*shengchandaidai*) and corporation (*gongshe*). Its distribution system was the partial wage–partial supply system.[48] The biggest problem with this system was that individual efforts did not directly reward individuals since ownership and distribution systems were based on collectivism. How this system discouraged farmers' morale at the time is well described in the following examples.

After people became members of Renmin Gongshe, they became less industrious than before. This is mostly because the result of their efforts was not repaid to them in a tangible form. . . .

Of course, after people became members of Renmin Gongshe, they did not work as hard as before. The evidence is that plenty of crops in the collective farm dried up and died because of shortages of labor, chemical fertilizers, and water. Meanwhile crops in private plots near people's homes were all strong and healthy, which was probably because they were well taken care of. Likewise, chickens in Renmin Gongshe looked like they were going to collapse any moment because of weakness, but the people's own chickens were plump and walking strongly. . . .

This was not the result of a bad crop. There was a great harvest of barley in the areas surrounding our village. However, barley was rotten in the communal field because it was not harvested and taken away to be stored. Vegetables were in the same situation. People were apathetic toward Renmin Gongshe's crops, even though they became rotten and wasted, because people did not think of the crops as being their concern. They did not work carefully because they felt they were helping others and not themselves if they did.[49]

These examples clearly show how much the ownership and distribution system of the Renmin Gongshe discouraged farmers' work initiative. The fact that China had to conduct rural reforms as the first step of the economic reform and open policy after 1978 reflects this situation.

High Population Growth Rate

China before communism had a high birth rate, a high death rate, and a low growth rate. This reversed after Red China was established. China's population policy saw the following results: the birth rate during the first five-year plan (1953–57) was 3%; the death rate decreased from 1.7% in 1952 to 1.08% by 1957. After the 1960s, efforts were made to reduce the birth rate, but the chaos of the Cultural Revolution caused birth control policy to be neglected. As a result, a baby boom took place from the 1960s to the early 1970s.

As the seriousness of population growth became apparent, birth control and late marriage were encouraged in the early 1970s. However, birth control was not achieved as planned because the population explosion theory and the theory of resource depletion were still regarded with skepticism at the time. In January 1979, however, the Director's Meeting of the National Planned Birth Council decided to enact a policy to reduce the population growth rate to 1% by the year 1980. It stressed that "it is desirable for each family to have one child. Each family can have no more than two children, and the birth interval should be more than 3 years."[50] With this, the one-child policy and full-scale birth control began to be strongly promoted.

In terms of economy a human being is not only a producer but also a consumer. These two roles appear as different forms depending on time and place. Recently the negative effects of population growth in China have grown because the increased population apparently functions as consumers, while their production scope is limited due to a shortage of capital. When the consumer function of increased population is bigger than its producer function, unless wages go down, the distributed share increases with population increases, accumulation decreases, and economic growth becomes restricted, that is, the standard of living goes down.

Investment Policy with Emphasis on Heavy Industries

The traditional Chinese investment and distribution policy put priority on the capital material sector. As shown in Table 4-4, heavy industries were already stressed in the first five-year economic development plan (1952–57), and budget allotment to heavy industries was more heavily weighted during the Great Leap (1958–60) and the Cultural Revolution (1966–76). According to budget statistics from 1952, the proportion of the budget for the rural sector was 57%, for heavy industries 15%, and for light industries 28%. However, these proportions changed in 1979, with heavy industries at 41%, light industries at 32%, and the rural sector 27%.

Besides the discriminatory distribution of the budget, a policy emphasizing heavy industries was adopted in terms of pricing. That is, prices of agricultural inputs, such as industrial goods, agricultural machinery, chemical fertilizers, and insecticides, were maintained at a high level, while prices for farm produce were kept at a low level.

The heavy industries policy that continued for about thirty years brought about the so-called heavy industries syndrome. Self-sufficient heavy industrialization came to satisfy only the needs of heavy and related industries. That is, the steel, petroleum chemicals, nonferrous metals, and heavy machinery industries supported only related industries, such as railroads, electric power, and mining, but did very little with farming based on traditional techniques, rural industry, or small- and medium-sized corporations.[51] As a result, the high accumulation rate intended for Chinese socialist economic development and the people's efforts to achieve it, could not make a return to the people because of the investment policy of heavy industries for heavy industries.

Problems in the Corporate Management System

The corporate management system was another important factor in economic stagnation:

1. Corporations are not independent from government administrative agencies. Instead, the two are interlocked in a tight vertical relationship. Corporate management usually follows commands given by upper administrative agencies, which convey these commands through instruction-type input-output indexes.[52]

2. All investment funds are handed over to corporations by the government's Financial Fund Exchange. There are no repayment obligations or interest burdens for these funds. Therefore, corporations try their utmost to secure investment funds from the Financial Fund Exchange in order to ease their management operations, even though their potential financial gains are small or even negative. With these investments, corporations can increase their fixed capital and production, thereby expanding welfare benefits for their employees and enhancing their prestige and power. This arrangement creates an Iron Castle situation in income distribution, wherein corporations are guaranteed survival by the state (through investment funds handed out by the government), regardless of their performance, and employees are guaranteed survival by the corporation (through wages and other benefits).[53]

Table 4-4
Growth and Structure of Chinese Industry (unit: %)

			1953–57	1958–62	1963–65	1966–70	1971–75	1976–80
Overall production in agriculture and industry	Agriculture		4.5	-4.4	11.1	2.9	3.4	3.2
	Industry		38.3	7.7	36.1	23.7	18.2	19.7
		Heavy industries	25.4	6.6	14.9	15.0	10.3	8.2
		Light industries	12.9	1.1	21.2	8.7	7.9	11.5
Distribution of investments	Agriculture		7.1	11.3	17.6	10.7	9.8	10.5
	Industry		42.6	60.4	49.8	55.5	55.4	52.6
		Light industries	6.4	6.4	3.9	4.4	5.8	6.7
		Heavy industries	36.2	54.0	45.9	51.1	49.6	45.9
	Other		50.3	28.3	32.6	33.8	34.8	36.9

			1952	1957	1965	1975	1979	
Structure of overall production in agriculture and industry	Agriculture		56.9	43.3	37.3	28.2	26.6	
	Industry		43.1	56.7	62.7	71.8	73.4	
		Light industries	27.8	31.2	32.3	31.6	32.1	
		Heavy industries	15.3	25.5	30.4	40.2	41.3	

Source: State Statistical Bureau of China, 1990.

3. Local governments and corporations both have a closed, self-contained, and self-sufficient organizational structure. This structure is called big and all, small and all because all organizational bodies (such as schools, health care services, and communist ideological groups) in, for example, a large city, can also be found in much smaller organizations, such as business corporations.

Such corporate management has hindered the development of role specialization and effective division of labor in both corporations and government agencies. Resources have been wasted, products have not been distributed efficiently, and tensions have arisen between supply, production, and sales. In order to solve these inefficiencies, more money was poured in, creating a vicious cycle of greater and greater investments. These problems in the corporate management system have stalled China's economic recovery.

SUMMARY

To this point, the background leading to the reform and open policy has been examined from the perspective of the high accumulation mechanism. First, the ownership and distribution systems weakened the farmers' work initiative and morale, and consequently, agricultural production declined. Second, the high population growth rate resulted in a rise in total consumption, which increased at a rate faster than that of total production levels. Third, accumulation from the people's savings and low consumption levels was invested mainly in heavy industries. Fourth, the problems in the corporate management system propagated economic stagnation. Finally, add the sudden influx of young people, who had been forcibly sent to the countryside during the Cultural Revolution, into the urban areas, which further burdened economic policy became with the difficult task of providing jobs for these youths. Faced with these economic crises, China had to reform the rural economic system, where the accumulation mechanism originated. It also had to search for new sources of accumulation. The latter task was accomplished by introducing foreign capital.

OTHER FACTORS

Economic Gap between China and Newly Industrialized Countries (NICs) in Asia

The first factor in the external background to the policy change is the economic development of NICs in Asia and its effects on China. Facing the return of Hong Kong in 1997 and Macao in 1999 and political problems such as unification with Taiwan, China had to pay attention to the economic development of these and other NICs in Asia. Regarding this matter, Sato Taune Aki believes that the reform and open policy was brought about by pressure to reduce the economic gap with NICs and eventually keep pace with them. He observes:

China has a double personality of a socialist state and a developing country. One of these appears more visibly than the other according to the time and situation. If one considers the fact that China lost almost 20 years after the Great Leap and that the economic gap between China and the NICs is increasing, it is not strange at all that China is using very bold measures in order to recover lost time.[54]

Uehara also explains the external background to the reform and open policy from the perspective of the coexisting competitive relationship with capitalist nations, including the Asian NICs (such as Hong Kong and Taiwan) and other countries that have different economic policies:

When "one state-two systems" becomes a real issue after the return of Hong Kong in 1997, the biggest question will be which system, the socialist state or the capitalist state, is more rational and can provide a better life for people. This issue is also related to the question of how China, as a socialist state, will act in today's world of extremely competitive international society and technology revolution.[55]

Okabe also uses a comparison between China's deeply rooted backwardness (barriers to modernization) with the situations of Asian NICs to explain the features of the reform and open policy. Presenting the examples of Hong Kong, Taiwan, and Singapore to support his theory, he claims that barriers to modernization, such as bureaucracy, lack of modern spirit, and the ideology of self-sufficiency, will be removed when the nation becomes accustomed to market conditions and competition in a stable political order. This is not mere theory. The validity of Okabe's theory is well proven by the remarkable economic development of Hong Kong, Taiwan, and Singapore, whose citizens had a comparable mentality. He comments that people living in these countries, through being immersed in capitalism, lost the mentality that remains in China as a barrier to modernization.[56]

These scholars believe that the economic disparity between China and the NICs must have put great pressure on China to open up and reform its economy—especially since political confrontation between these countries is expected.

National Unification with One State–Two Systems

Another major factor leading to the reform and open policy is China's plan for eventual national unification with Hong Kong, Macao, and Taiwan. Hong Kong will be returned to China from England in 1997, while Macao will be returned from Portugal in 1999. If Hong Kong and Macao maintain their present systems, China will become one state–two systems, in which capitalism and socialism coexist. It is envisioned that socialism will constitute the state's ideology and that the present socialist system will be maintained in most parts of the nation. The Chinese mainland will represent the state, while Hong Kong, Macao, and Taiwan will become local administrative units or individual local governments.

In one state–two systems, special administrative districts have legislative power. Regulations passed by the legislative organ of the special administrative district do not need to agree with those of other districts in China. They are all valid as long as they agree with the basic law and legal procedure of the special administrative district. The Hong Kong special administrative district will continue to maintain the economic and social systems of capitalism even after 1997, and private ownership will be protected by law. The central people's government will uniformly manage diplomatic affairs after the return of Hong Kong and the unification with Taiwan, and only the People's Republic of China will represent China internationally. However, at the same time, the central people's government will provide Hong Kong and Taiwan with diplomatic rights to deal with some foreign affairs. The Hong Kong special administrative district will maintain financial independence in areas such as finance, military, customs, issuance of its own currency, and conduct an independent monetary policy. Taiwan will decide freely its own foreign policy and keep its own army within a scale that does not threaten the mainland. The independent judicial power of the Hong Kong special administrative district will be ensured even after 1997.

The one state–two systems idea can be seen as a proposal for the peaceful unification of China. By this system, China hopes to assure Hong Kong, Macao, and Taiwan of its willingness to guarantee their future security. Since the economic gap between the mainland and other areas must be narrowed for the system to prevail, it had to prove that it recognizes both systems, acknowledges the advantages of capitalism, and is willing to apply the advantages of capitalism for the reform of the economic system. It also had to show that it possessed a policy that could be used immediately to implement economic reform. Finally, China had to prove that these ideas were not mere political propaganda for the people of Hong Kong, Macao, and Taiwan.

The first concrete step of China's movement toward achieving one state–two systems was its reform and open policy, and that the core manifestation of this policy was the establishment of the special economic zones. By creating in advance areas with an economic system differing from other parts of the country, China founded a pilot system that can serve as a model. China has actively supported one state–two systems in selected areas because of their significance not only in political, but in economic terms. This is because these areas act as vital sources of foreign currency and important export markets.

One area with tremendous economic significance for China that will eventually become part of the one state–two systems is Hong Kong. Hong Kong has acted as a window for China's important exports by consistently being its first or second largest trading partner since the 1960s. China's exports to Hong Kong are increasing every year, and China constantly records a trading surplus with Hong Kong (see Table 4-5). China has been making up for its increasing trade deficits with western advanced countries every year with the surplus gained from Hong Kong. In addition, Hong Kong is a very important trade broker, connecting China with Southeast Asia and Europe, and international financial center, the fourth largest after New York, London, and Tokyo. This will bring to China many advantages, such as fund security and an extensive information database, when the Chinese economy is transferred to the international economy in the future. Moreover, Hong Kong is abundant in various resources, accumulated over a long time, such as corporate management skills and skilled labor. Because of these advantages the maintenance of a thriving Hong Kong economy is an essential element in Chinese economic development policy.

The extent to which China values Hong Kong can also be seen by its active interest in Hong Kong investments. China's investments in Hong Kong have increased tremendously over the past several years, covering areas as various as manufacturing, finance, commerce, trade, transportation, and real estate. According to statistics compiled by Thomas M. H. Chan, there were about 3,000 Chinese corporations in Hong Kong as of May 1988.[57] In addition, China has invested $10–12 billion in Hong Kong, which is roughly double the amount ($6 billion) that the United States has invested in the colony.[58]

In order for China to overcome the collapse of its accumulation mechanism, reduce the conspicuously large gap between its economy and those of the Asian NICs, and establish one state–two systems as a solution to unification with Hong Kong, Macao, and Taiwan, it urgently needed to transform and develop its economy. China met this challenge by reforming its traditional economic system and introducing foreign capital and technology. By conducting a reform and open policy, China sought to achieve the

Table 4-5
Trade Records between China and Hong Kong, 1961–1980 (unit: U.S.$1 million, %)

	Total trade with H.K.			Total trade with H.K. ÷ China's total trade	Total exports to H.K. ÷ China's total exports	Total imports from H.K. ÷ China's total imports	Total trade with H.K. ÷ China's total trade with non-Communist countries
		Exports	Imports				
1961	135	134	1	4.48	8.99	0.07	10.11
1962	161	159	2	6.03	40.67	0.17	12.73
1963	198	197	1	7.14	11.94	0.08	12.98
1964	265	263	2	8.23	13.77	0.13	12.50
1965	315	312	3	8.11	13.99	0.15	11.6
1966	380	377	3	8.95	15.91	0.13	12.04
1967	292	291	1	7.46	13.60	0.05	9.47
1968	311	310	1	8.22	14.76	0.05	10.56
1969	327	326	1	8.40	14.82	0.05	10.51
1970	359	354	5	8.22	15.66	0.21	10.13
1971	431	428	3	8.89	16.21	0.14	11.27
1972	513	509	4	8.52	14.80	0.14	10.68
1973	796	787	9	7.86	13.52	0.17	9.03
1974	895	876	19	6.34	12.60	0.12	7.61
1975	1,026	1,020	6	7.06	14.05	0.08	8.17
1976	1,102	1,097	5	8.30	15.99	0.08	10.08
1977	1,208	1,201	7	7.93	15.82	0.10	9.53
1978	1,489	1,469	20	6.99	15.07	0.18	8.24
1979	2,020	1,890	130	6.87	13.87	0.83	7.86
1980	3,037	2,716	321	7.46	14.87	1.64	8.31
Average				7.57			10.17

Source: State Statistical Bureau of China, 1987, p. 59.

industrial revolution which had failed to materialize under the rigid traditional system. In this sense, the period after 1978—when the reform and open policy was first adopted—can be seen as China's new industrial revolution. The first movement of this revolution was the establishment of the special economic zones.

PART II

Economic Development in Special Economic Zones

5

Development of
Special Economic Zones

More than a decade after their establishment, special economic zones are developing and changing rapidly. In this section, the role of special economic zones as export processing areas are particularly discussed.

RECIPIENTS OF FOREIGN CAPITAL AND INDUCEMENT OF INTERNAL COMPANIES

The Shenzhen Special Economic Zone is the largest recipient of foreign capital and internal companies among the special economic zones, followed by Zhuhai, Xiamen, Hainan Province, and Shantou respectively. Of the total foreign capital in Shenzhen, there were 6,922 contracts, with negotiated investments of $5.59 billion and actual investments of $2.29 billion. As of June 1989, 2,295 *SanjiGiyie* (a general term used to collectively describe mergered, joint venture, and wholly foreign companies) have extended their business to Shenzhen City (including Shenzhen and Bauanxian Special Economic Zones), or one-seventh of all foreign companies in China, one-quarter of those in Guangdong, and one-sixth in the coastal areas. In addition, there were 4,699 Sanlaiyibao corporations in Shenzhen. Their registered capital exceeded 10 billion yuan, and they formed one-sixth of all Sanlaiyibao corporations in China and one third of them in Guangdong Province. Furthermore, 3,900 internal companies were located in Shenzhen.

During the past ten years, Zhuhai had 5,090 contracts, with negotiated investment amounting to $2.36 billion, and actual investment of $820 million. In 1989, actual investment by foreign joint venture and wholly foreign companies was $53.28 million, while Sanlaiyibao invested $6.07 million. From 1980 to 1988, 883 internal companies entered Zhuhai. Shantou had 920 contracts with foreign-capital companies from 1984 to 1989, with actual investment of $154.27 million. In 1989, actual investment by foreign joint-venture and wholly foreign companies was $58.91 million, while Sanlaiyibao invested $980,000. From 1986 to 1989, 331 internal companies entered Shantou. Xiamen had 979 foreign capital contracts from 1981 to 1989, with actual investment of $668.08 million. In 1989, actual investment by foreign joint venture and wholly foreign companies was $129.8 million, while Sanlaiyibao invested $820,000. In Hainan Province, $381.23 million in foreign capital was introduced during the five years between 1985 and 1989. In 1989, actual investment by SanjiGiyie was $107.07 million. In addition, Sanlaiyibao invested $2.37 million.[1]

EMPLOYMENT EXPANSION

The sudden entry of foreign capital and internal corporations in the special economic zones greatly increased employment opportunities (see Tables 5-1 and 5-2.). Since 1979, employment has risen drastically in all five special economic zones. The expansion of jobs in Shenzhen and Shantou has been especially remarkable. These employees come not only from the permanent population, but also the floating population that do not have household registers in the area. The increase in female employees has been highest. In Shantou, for example, the number of male employees increased by 1,320% from 1984 to 1989, but the number of female employees increased by 1,570% in the same period. Women made up 55.5% of all employees in the special economic zones as of 1989. Most of the increase in employment was from temporary labor. There are three types of employment in the nonrural sector: permanent laborers (mostly from the permanent population), contract laborers (mainly from the temporary population), and temporary laborers (mostly from the floating population). Of the three types, the proportion of temporary laborers continues to increase. The increase is particularly conspicuous in the Shenzhen zone.

In contrast to the decreasing number of laborers in the rural sector, the number of laborers in the industrial, construction, and service sectors increased considerably (see Table 5-3). In Shenzhen, for example, 4,000 laborers (2.4%) of all employees (412,000) as of the end of 1989 were working in the agricultural and fishery industry, 211,800 (51.4%) in the industrial sector, and the remaining 196,200 (47.6%) in commerce, tourism, and service sectors. This distribution shows that most of the incoming population was absorbed into the industrial or service sectors. Meanwhile, the agrarian population decreased sharply in both number and proportion due to the urbanization and industrialization of the Shenzhen zone.

However, not all of the incoming population was absorbed by the nonagricultural sector. With the increase of the temporary population, a substantial portion of the labor force became engaged in the agricultural sector with contracts with landlords (commission management). Despite the decrease in size of cultivated land due to urbanization and industrialization, the volume of agricultural production increased annually by 10% on the average for ten years. This was due not only to improvements in farmland, agricultural technology, and crop variety, but also to the increased percentage of temporary population engaged in agriculture through landlord contracts. According to statistics, the number of temporary population engaged in farming, dairy cattle, pig, and poultry breeding, and fisheries was 37,700 in 1986. Just one year later, the number increased to 69,400. It must also be remembered that a

Table 5-1
Population Growth in Shenzhen and Zhuhai (unit: 10,000 persons)

	Shenzhen				Zhuhai						
	Total population in city	Total population in special zone	Temporary population in city	Temporary population in special zone	Total population in city	Permanent population in city	Male	Female	Non-agriculture	Agriculture	Temporary population in city
1979	31.41	7.09	0.15	—	36.1	36.1	18.2	17.9	6.4	29.7	—
1980	33.29	9.41	1.20	1.00	36.5	36.5	18.5	18.0	7.1	29.5	—
1981	36.69	13.13	3.30	3.30	37.1	37.1	18.9	18.2	7.8	29.4	—
1982	44.95	19.86	9.50	7.00	37.8	37.8	18.1	18.7	8.4	29.3	—
1983	59.52	28.50	19.00	12.00	38.5	38.5	19.7	18.8	9.2	29.4	—
1984	74.13	33.75	30.61	14.61	39.5	39.5	20.2	19.3	10.4	29.1	—
1985	88.13	46.98	40.29	23.79	41.2	41.2	21.1	20.1	13.5	27.6	—
1986	93.56	48.87	42.11	23.13	53.1	42.6	21.9	20.7	15.0	27.6	10.5
1987	115.44	59.96	59.84	31.27	55.4	44.2	22.8	21.4	16.5	27.7	11.3
1988	153.14	78.40	93.00	46.21	63.1	46.6	24.0	22.6	18.5	28.1	16.5
1989	191.60	102.69	126.78	66.49	71.6	48.6	25.1	23.5	20.1	28.5	23.0
Avg. annual growth rate	21.5%	30.4%	67.8%	59.4%	7.5%	3.1%	3.3%	2.8%	12.3%	-0.2%	31.0%

Sources: For Shenzhen's total city population and temporary population in city during 1979–1988, Statistical Bureau of Shenzhen, 1989, p. 89; for total population and temporary population in Shenzhen Zone for 1989, Shenzhen Special Economic Zone Yearbook, ed., 1985–1989; for Zhuhai, an interview with the staff of Zhuhai Statistics Bureau, January 4–May 15, 1991.

Table 5-2
Changes in Number of Laborers and Employees in Shantou (unit: person)

		1984	1985	1986	1987	1988	1989
Number of laborers and employees at the end of the year		2,530	6,791	12,585	20,495	27,724	36,780
	Male	1,230	2,234	7,116	8,974	12,468	16,354
	Female	1,300	2,925	5,469	11,521	15,256	20,426
Number of laborers and employees in each sector	Permanent laborers	673	1,918	3,862	4,672	5,830	6,602
	Contract laborers	1,174	1,698	2,616	3,405	4,771	7,790
	Others	683	3,175	6,107	12,418	17,123	22,338

Source: Shantou Special Economic Zone Yearbook, ed., 1984–1989.

Table 5-3
Changes in Employed Population by Industrial Sector (unit: 10,000 persons, %)

Shenzhen	1979	1980	1981	1982	1983	1984	1985	1986	1987	1988	1989	Avg. annual growth rate
Agriculture, forestry, livestock, fishery, and marine products	—	0.68	0.65	0.77	0.39	0.28	0.35	0.33	0.40	0.82	0.40	-5.7
Industry	—	0.61	0.96	1.36	2.86	4.35	5.75	7.51	12.12	16.33	21.18	48.3
Construction	—	—	0.10	0.71	2.84	3.39	2.78	2.99	2.54	3.27	3.58	56.4
Transportation and communication	—	0.21	0.28	0.70	0.46	0.74	1.29	1.44	1.48	1.59	1.73	26.4
Commerce and restaurants	—	0.55	0.87	1.60	2.25	3.85	4.43	4.62	4.39	6.28	5.93	30.2
Real estate and hotel management	—	0.03	0.08	0.43	0.44	0.75	1.55	1.95	2.80	3.43	3.61	70.3
Banking and insurance	—	0.05	0.07	0.11	0.13	0.22	0.31	0.36	0.49	0.63	0.74	34.9
Others	—	0.52	0.84	1.00	1.39	1.87	2.85	2.93	3.14	3.44	4.03	29.0

Table 5-3 (continued)

Zhuhai	1979	1980	1981	1982	1983	1984	1985	1986	1987	1988	1989	Avg. annual growth rate
Agriculture, forestry, livestock, fishery, and marine products	3.1	3.0	2.8	2.9	2.7	2.7	2.5	2.6	2.5	2.5	2.3	-3.0
Industry	0.9	1.0	1.0	1.2	1.4	1.6	2.0	2.4	3.3	4.1	5.1	19.3
Construction	0.1	0.2	0.2	0.2	0.3	0.2	0.3	0.3	0.3	0.3	0.5	15.0
Transportation and communication	0.3	0.3	0.4	0.4	0.4	0.4	0.5	0.5	0.5	0.54	0.6	7.1
Commerce and restaurants	1.0	1.1	1.3	1.5	1.6	1.9	1.7	1.9	2.0	2.3	2.7	10.3
Real estate and hotel management	0.04	0.1	0.1	0.1	0.1	0.1	0.6	0.7	0.7	0.9	1.0	59.3
Banking and insurance	0.1	0.1	0.1	0.1	0.1	0.1	0.2	0.2	0.2	0.3	0.3	17.9
Others	0.9	1.0	1.0	1.1	1.2	1.2	1.4	1.6	1.7	1.9	2.2	9.4

Table 5-3 (continued)

Shantou	1979	1980	1981	1982	1983	1984	1985	1986	1987	1988	1989	Avg. annual growth rate
Agriculture, forestry, livestock, fishery, and marine products	—	—	—	—	—	0.01	0.03	0.1	0.2	0.2	0.2	112.0
Industry	—	—	—	—	—	0.1	0.3	0.6	1.3	1.7	2.4	85.1
Construction	—	—	—	—	—	—	0.1	0.1	0.1	0.1	0.2	210.0
Transportation and communication	—	—	—	—	—	0.03	0.04	0.06	0.05	0.06	0.05	14.8
Commerce and restaurants	—	—	—	—	—	0.05	0.1	0.2	0.2	0.3	0.5	55.4
Banking and insurance	—	—	—	—	—	—	—	0.01	0.01	0.02	0.03	62.3
Others	—	—	—	—	—	0.03	0.1	0.2	0.3	0.3	0.4	111.0

Sources: Shenzhen Special Economic Zone Yearbook, ed., 1985–1990; an interview with the staff of Zhuhai Statistics Bureau, January 4–May 15, 1991; Shantou Special Economic Zone Yearbook, ed., 1979–1989.

large number of commission management cases is actually carried out by a floating population in addition to the temporary population. According to an official in the city's Department of Labor, most of the special zone's farming is commissioned to non-natives of the zone. Therefore, one can safely conclude that commission management is being conducted much more extensively than the official statistics suggest.[2]

Each special economic zone has distinct regional characteristics. In the Zhuhai zone, where tourism is a huge industry, more than half of the entire population is employed in the service sector. Although the industrial sector is prominent in the Shantou zone, the employment increase in laborers in the agricultural and fishery industry has been remarkable compared to other zones. This is closely related to the fact that Shantou has traditionally been famous for herbal medicinal plants. Its fishing industry is also flourishing. In Xiamen, the total number of laborers increased from 482,400 in 1980 to 654,900 in 1989, showing an increase of about 36% in ten years. As for the range of these laborers in industrial sectors in 1989, of the total number of 287,148 employees (excluding the number of individuals, and group/independent laborers in the rural sector), 13,049 (4.5%) were engaged in the primary industry (agriculture, fishery), 154,772 (53.8%) in the industrial sector and the remaining 119,377 in commerce, tourism, and service sectors. In the case of Hainan Province, the effect of employment expansion has been relatively small compared to other zones because of its short history as a special economic zone. In terms of industrial structure, agriculture still remains the largest sector. In 1989, primary industry (agriculture, fishery) employed 71% of all laborers, with no more than 6.6% of the population in the industrial sector.[3] The light industries sector, including the electronics, machine assembly, and textiles, made up most of the industrial sector.

GAIN OF FOREIGN CURRENCY

Most foreign currency was earned through exports (see Table 5-4). On the average, 70–80% of foreign currency earnings came from exports (Shenzhen, 57%; Zhuhai, 71.9%; Xiamen, 86.2%). The five special economic zones in 1989 produced $3.85 billion worth of exports, or 10% of the total volume of Chinese exports. Major export items were bicycles, TVs, tape recorders, telephones, and calculators.[4] In terms of net foreign currency earnings, revenues and expenditures have recently been balanced, although variation exists among the zones.

Shenzhen overimported by about $200 million in 1987 but kept a balance of revenue and expenditure in 1989. Zhuhai showed a revenue of $84.6 million and an expenditure of $182.26 million in 1987, resulting in a deficit of $97.62 million. Xiamen recorded a revenue of $139.83 million and an expenditure of $57.06 million in 1989.[5]

GROWTH OF INCOME

As shown in Table 5-5, Shenzhen showed the highest growth of income among the five special economic zones. In 1979, the city's entire income (income in budget) was 35.99 million yuan, which increased in 1989 to 1.877 billion yuan, an increase of 5,200%.[6] About 90% of this came from industrial and commercial tax revenues.[7] In

Table 5-4
Changes in Foreign Revenues and Expenditures in Shenzhen and Zhuhai (unit: U.S.$10,000)

Shenzhen	1980	1981	1982	1983	1984	1985	1986	1987	1988	1989	Avg. annual growth rate
Total foreign revenues	20,144	17,123	17,525	17,669	21,613	19,405	33,248	76,601	101,002	83,011	17.0
Revenues from exports	9,188	10,457	11,562	11,426	9,866	7,861	19,425	56,725	70,368	47,708	20.1
Revenues from the manufacturing industry	675	1,174	1,650	2,482	3,494	3,811	6,986	12,389	18,135	21,897	47.2
Revenues from nontrade businesses	10,281	5,492	4,313	3,761	8,253	7,733	6,837	7,487	12,499	13,406	3.0
Zhuhai											
Total foreign revenus	—	—	—	—	—	3,974	3,309	19,818	30,057	8,464	115.5
Revenues from exports	—	—	—	—	—	2,839	2,083	18,411	28,196	5,973	185.1
Revenues from the manufacturing industry	—	—	—	—	—	484	612	945	1,368	1,556	34.8
Revenues from nontrade businesses	—	—	—	—	—	624	614	462	493	935	17.4
Total foreign expenditures	—	—	—	—	—	3,798	5,082	19,835	37,034	18,226	89.9
Net balance	—	—	—	—	—	149	-1,773	-17	-6,977	-9,762	

Source: Interviews with the staffs of the Statistical Bureau of Shenzhen and Zhuhai Statistics Bureau, January 4–May 15, 1991.

Table 5-5
Financial Income in Special Economic Zones (unit: 10,000 yuan)

Shenzhen	1980	1981	1982	1983	1984	1985	1986	1987	1988	1989	Total
Total income in budget	3,043	8,787	9,163	15,605	29,435	62,894	74,160	76,921	124,429	187,696	592,133
Special Zone	3,043	8,787	8,339	14,403	27,490	59,646	69,898	71,716	111,904	168,370	554,197
Corporate income	75	263	686	1,877	2,383	1,897	5,010	3,668	6,233	4,120	26,212
State-run corporations income tax	—	—	—	—	—	1,727	3,079	2,596	6,042	3,878	17,322
Industry and commerce tax	2,721	8,310	8,126	13,155	26,607	59,972	65,644	67,449	109,604	164,140	525,728
Customs	1,627	6,224	3,618	6,017	14,624	23,541	24,566	25,224	39,419	43,420	188,280
Local tax	1,094	2,086	4,508	7,138	11,983	36,431	41,078	42,225	70,185	120,720	337,448
Agriculture tax	200	204	201	183	165	185	195	208	456	641	2,638
Other	47	10	150	390	280	840	3,311	5,596	8,136	18,795	37,555
Zhuhai											
Total financial income	3,652	6,696	7,647	8,944	17,308	30,333	17,231	21,723	43,750	54,530	211,814
Corporate income*	503	523	507	442	653	-1,108	-417	-718	-609	1,546	-602
Taxes	3,092	6,064	6,844	7,949	15,758	30,414	15,294	20,425	41,754	50,541	198,135
Industry and commerce tax	2,745	5,528	6,302	7,758	14,756	28,351	14,067	18,338	39,425	49,977	187,247
Agriculture tax	297	282	311	317	300	357	375	414	396	564**	3,613
Other	57	110	296	554	487	1,007	2,354	2,016	2,605	2,443	11,929

Table 5-5 (continued)

Shantou	1980	1981	1982	1983	1984	1985	1986	1987	1988	1989	Total
Total financial income	—	—	—	—	2,986.3	4,561.5	4,042.6	5,429.8	13,117.4	21,259.5	—
Corporate income	—	—	—	—	292.9	-87.0	39.6	-382.2	174.9	1,654.7	—
Taxes	—	—	—	—	779.1	2,904.0	2,257.5	5,100.1	12,196.8	18,722.4	—
Industry and commerce tax	—	—	—	—	779.1	2,904.0	2,250.4	5,071.0	12,059.0	18,334.2	—
Cultivated land-use tax	—	—	—	—	—	—	—	22.0	132.7	376.0	—
Agriculture tax	—	—	—	—	—	—	4.1	7.1	5.1	10.0	—
Province/city additional tax	—	—	—	—	1,586.4	1,641.6	1,651.3	654.0	661.6	674.0	—
Other	—	—	—	—	327.9	102.9	94.2	57.9	841.0	208.4	—

Sources: For Zhuhai and Shenzhen: Interviews with the staffs of the Statistical Bureau of Shenzhen and Zhuhai Statistics Bureau, January 4–May 15, 1991. For Shantou: *Shantou Special Economic Zone Yearbook,* ed., 1980–1989.

Notes: *Income and adjustment taxes of state-run corporations are not included. **Agriculture and cultivated land-use taxes.

1989, industry and commerce taxes collected in the Shenzhen zone came to 1.64 billion yuan, or 87.4% of city income. This increase in taxes collected implies the smooth progress of corporations. In addition, city financial management autonomy and the various sources of financial income that appeared with economic development are major factors in the increased income.

Xiamen had income of 155 million yuan in 1980, which grew by 520% to 811 million yuan in 1989. Revenue from industrial and commercial tax forms the largest portion of the income, amounting to 716.75 million yuan in 1989, 88% of the total. Hainan Province recorded income of 295.88 million yuan in 1987, which increased by 210% to 624.81 million yuan in 1989. Again, industrial and commercial tax form the largest portion of revenues, amounting to 424.86 million yuan in 1989, 86% of total income.[8]

RISE OF LIVING STANDARDS

Along with the rapid economic development, the standard of living has greatly improved. The Shenzhen zone, for example, used to be a fishing area across from Hong Kong. Since its transformation into a special economic zone, however, it is now a major industrial city with a population of 1.5 million. During the past ten years, Shenzhen's GNP grew by 48.3% annually, and GNP per resident showed an annual growth rate of 24.9% (GNP in 1989 was 9.78 billion, GNP per resident 5,600 yuan).[9] The yearly average wage of laborers in 1989 was 3,943 yuan, an increase of 580% from 1978. In addition, the yearly average income of farmers in 1989 was 1,607 yuan, an increase of 650% from 1978. Even when the different costs of living are taken into consideration, Shenzhen's income is very high compared to other areas in China.

The total amount of agricultural and industrial production in Shantou had shown a growth rate of 34.8% every year from 1984 to 1989. The total amount of agricultural and industrial production in 1989 was 917.75 million yuan. The total amount of social production in Xiamen had shown an annual growth rate of 18.46% for ten years. The total amount of social production in 1989 was 991.75 million yuan. The total amount of social production in Hainan Province in 1987 was 8.51 billion yuan and increased to 14.28 billion yuan in 1989, showing an increase of 167%.[10]

With the wage increase, the quality of life has also increased. The percentage of households with color TV, a refrigerator, and a washing machine, all signs of improvement in quality of life, is higher in Shenzhen than in Beijing or Shanghai. The percentage of households with a color TV is especially high. The rate of refrigerator and washing machine possession is also higher than in other areas, which means that housework is being reduced in Shenzhen sooner than in other areas (see Table 5-6). There is no doubt that all five zones have made drastic economic advancements. The development of Shenzhen has been especially conspicuous.

The vitalization of currency circulation and private businesses have contributed to the improvement in citizens' standard of living. However, these gains have been followed by negative side-effects, such as smuggling and black-marketing of products manufactured by foreign-capital companies. These are big problems for an area whose industrial development is dependent on the protection of its domestic industry and a regulated foreign currency.

Table 5-6
Ownership of Consumer Goods per 100 Households (unit: each)

	Shenzhen 1988	Beijing 1987	Shanghai 1987	Guangzhou 1987	Hangzou 1987
Automobile	184	210	87	192	236
Sewing machine	62	72	97	93	86
Wristwatch	195	238	298	290	281
Electric fan	300	109	144	299	216
Color television	99	58	44	57	209
Black & white television	11	71	77	62	83
Refrigerator	93	72	62	59	73
Washing machine	84	83	49	74	58
Tape recorder	91	118	111	76	85
Camera	47	56	31	23	19
Air conditioner	9	0.1	0	0	0
Motorcycle	4	1.9	0.6	1	0

Source: China Reseach Center, 1989, p. 46.

6

Introduction of Foreign Capital and Its Effect on Employment Expansion and Wage Gain

There are two different opinions regarding the effects of investment of foreign capital on the economic growth of developing countries. The positive opinion holds, first, that foreign capital accelerates economic growth by making up for disparities between domestic consumption and domestic production, between pure investments and domestic savings, and between values of imported goods and services (including payment for production factors) and values of exported goods and services (including gain of production factors). Second, introduction of foreign capital changes the industrial structure to become more capital intensive, boosts labor productivity and wages, and evens out the income distribution. Third, it expands employment. This is particularly important to a country that worries about unemployment and overpopulation, especially incomplete employment in the rural sector. Finally, foreign capital investment stimulates investment in other industries by creating demands which provides an opportunity to increase the entire domestic investment. The negative opinion holds that increased dependency on foreign capital prevents the formation of capital by domestic savings and stresses the subsidiary company's dependency on the parent company and worsens the international balance of payments by paying interest and dividends.

As previously mentioned, the purpose of the special economic zones was to achieve economic development through the introduction of foreign capital.[11] This chapter discusses the extent to which foreign capital contributed to growth in the special economic zones and the role of foreign capital in employment expansion and wage gain.

CURRENT STATUS OF THE INTRODUCTION OF FOREIGN CAPITAL TO SPECIAL ECONOMIC ZONES

Change in the Introduction of Foreign Capital

Three factors must be discussed regarding the introduction of foreign capital to the special economic zones: loans, direct investment, and leases (see Table 6-1.).

Loans make up only a small portion of total foreign capital. From 1980 to 1989, Shenzhen Special Economic Zone reserved foreign capital worth $2.6 billion, of which loans made up 26.2%. Loans make up a smaller portion of foreign capital than in other countries (see Table 6-2) because loans were introduced much later than direct investment. Most necessary funds were supported by the state in the early stages of development. However, as state support declined and direct investment in sectors such as resource development, transportation, and basic construction failed to satisfy expectations, the city government had to take out foreign loans. The investment fund was large, the repayment period was long, and the burden of risk was heavy. Also, for policy purposes, direct investment was given priority over loans. This was based on the idea that direct investment brought not only funds but also technology, business management methods, and market extension techniques, while foreign loans only provided funds. Direct investment was also much safer because both partners (the foreign country and China in case of a merger, and the foreign country in case of 100% foreign capital) shared the business burden. The Xiamen zone started using foreign capital in the form of foreign loans relatively early. As of 1989, two-thirds of Xiamen's total debt was borrowed from foreign banks ($764.60 million) and 82.93% of the debt was long-term.[12] Foreign loans formed most of the foreign debt until 1989. Xiamen relied so heavily on loans compared to other zones because, as the only zone in Fujian Province, it was granted early autonomy.

The Shenzhen and Shantou zones actively used foreign capital in the form of leases, because leasing has the advantage of saving funds when the period of use (i.e., seasonal production) is relatively short, or when the renovation of facilities is required due to the rapid advance of scientific technology. Direct investment in the Shenzhen zone has been slowly falling since 1986. This phenomenon is closely reviewed later, but the main reasons behind it are wage increases, difficulties in labor management, and nonmaintenance of basic facilities such as water and electricity. Direct investments by wholly foreign companies have recently been increasing drastically. This reflects the fact that foreign corporations want 100% ownership because this type of investment is easier for them to manage than mergers or joint ventures. Considering its situation, China has to attract foreign capital actively. Investment by wholly foreign companies is expected to increase as the special economic zones attract foreign corporations.

The special economic zones are fiercely competing with each other to attract foreign-capital companies. For example, a doll manufacturing company (with 100% Korean capital, 350 employees, and yearly production volume of $2.5 million) currently located in Zhuhai originally obtained a business permit from the Shenzhen municipal government to enter the zone under the condition that it would export 70%

Table 6-1
Changes in Introduction of Foreign Capital (unit: U.S.$10,000)

Shenzhen	1980	1981	1982	1983	1984	1985	1986	1987	1988	1989	Total 1980–1989
Total of actually usable foreign capital	2,657	11,098	6,690	11,941	22,624	32,427	48,401	39,380	39,439	43,411	258,068
Loans	—	—	—	—	1,962	13,585	10,860	12,436	14,430	15,563	68,836
Direct investment	2,336	8,618	5,750	11,187	18,437	17,651	36,080	26,486	23,870	23,144	177,559
Merger	252	1,073	1,093	1,777	7,819	6,939	4,916	8,176	9,048	16,286	57,379
Joint venture	1,891	5,427	3,823	6,077	5,976	10,065	30,079	17,342	7,873	5,716	94,269
Wholly foreign	193	2,118	834	3,333	4,642	647	1,085	968	6,949	5,142	25,911
Leases	321	1,342	940	754	2,225	1,191	1,461	458	1,139	704	10,535

Zhuhai	1980	1981	1982	1983	1984	1985	1986	1987	1988	1989	Total 1980–1989
Total of actually usable foreign capital	1,575	1,377	5,649	2,938	12,694	9,104	7,568	6,963	21,762	16,947	86,577
Loans	—	—	—	—	—	3,759	2,591	3,088	16,174	11,012	36,624
Direct investment	1,065	1,308	5,536	2,593	12,457	5,262	4,518	3,382	4,740	5,328	46,189
Merger	—	172	200	800	958	752	1,032	1,528	1,808	1,550	8,800
Joint venture	1,065	1,136	5,336	1,793	11,490	4,510	3,486	1,854	2,559	2,516	35,745
Wholly foreign	—	—	—	—	9	—	—	—	373	1,262	1,644
Leases	510	69	113	345	237	83	459	493	848	607	3,764

Table 6-1 (continued)

Shantou		Total 1981–1983	1984	1985	1986	1987	1988	1989	Total 1984–1989
Total of actually usable foreign capital		152.7	779.3	783.2	1,177.8	2,270	3,440	6,977	15,580.0
Loans		—	—	—	—	—	—	988	988.0
Direct investment		152.7	779.3	729.9	800.3	1,773	2,274	5,891	12,400.2
	Merger	29.19	127.0	432.0	69.8	221	506	1,817	3,202.0
	Joint venture	17.01	382.6	128.7	417.3	1,164	850	1,109	4,068.61
	Wholly foreign	106.5	269.7	169.2	313.2	388	918	2,965	5,129.6
Leases		—	—	53.3	377.5	497	1,166	98	2,191.8

Xiamen		Total 1981–1985	1986	1987	1988	1989	Total 1981–1989
Total of contract base foreign capital		50,978	4,873	13,359	42,876	77,034	189,120
Loans		3,719	2,114	7,688	10,936	6,307	30,764
Direct investment		47,259	2,759	5,671	15,564	51,449	122,702
	Merger	26,837	2,198	3,193	1,971	9,200	34,199
	Joint venture	18,097	401	628	1,160	454	20,740
	Wholly foreign	2,325	160	1,850	12,433	46,346	63,114
Other		—	—	—	16,376	19,278	34,654

Table 6-1 (continued)

Hainan Province	1980	1981	1982	1983	1984	1985	1986	1987	1988	1989	Total 1980–1989
Total of actually usable foreign capital	28	109	83	438	1,784	2,643	3,259	911	12,771	16,097	38,123
Loans	—	—	—	200	313	244	—	—	526	5,153	6,436
Direct investment	10	109	83	192	1,162	2,095	3,073	893	11,421	10,707	29,745
Merger	—	—	83	25	96	606	462	165	2,283	5,436	9,156
Joint venture	10	109	—	167	1,066	1,489	2,611	728	2,314	784	9,278
Wholly foreign	—	—	—	—	—	—	—	—	6,824	4,487	11,311
Other	18	—	—	46	309	304	186	18	824	237	1,942

Source: Shenzhen Special Economic Zone Yearbook, ed., 1985–1990; interview with the staff of Zhuhai Statistics Bureau, January 4–May 15, 1991; Lin Wuru, ed., 1990, p. 351; Shantou Special Economic Zone Yearbook, ed., 1990, pp. 327–28; Xiamen Special Economic Zone Yearbook, ed., 1990, pp. 327–28; Statistical Bureau of Hainan, 1990, p. 604.

Table 6-2

Percentage of Loans in Foreign Capital as of 1981 (unit: U.S.$1 million, %)

	Korea	Singapore	Hong Kong	Mexico	Brazil
Loan*	19,964 (94.3)**	1,318 (14.9)	1,739 (35.8)	42,642 (83.4)	43,999 (71.6)
Direct foreign investment	1,206 (5.7)	7,520*** (85.1)	3,114 (64.2)	8,459*** (16.2)	17,480*** (28.4)
Total	21,170 (100)	8,838 (100)	4,853 (100)	51,101 (100)	61,479 (100)

Source: Cha Dongse, 1986, p. 76.

Notes: *Loan for more than 1 year supply. **( ) = percentage. ***Supply of 1980.

of its production and sell the remaining 30% in the Chinese domestic market. When a contract was about to be drafted, however, the Shenzhen government refused to permit the 30% domestic sales. It would allow the Korean company to conduct its business activities only under the condition that it export all of its products. However, in negotiating with the Zhuhai municipal government, the company was able to obtain a business permit that would allow it to sell 30% of production in the Chinese domestic market. Zhuhai agreed to this concession because it still had a relatively small number of foreign companies and wanted to actively attract foreign investments.

Changes in Foreign Capital of Industrial Sectors

Table 6-3 shows the status of foreign capital in each industrial sector in the special economic zones. Investments in real estate, tourism, traffic, transportation, commerce, and services were relatively high in the early stages of development, but have been slowly decreasing. For example, real estate in the Shenzhen zone received the highest portion of foreign capital, as much as 40% until 1982, when it began to decline. Conversely, the proportion of industry has been rising sharply. As of 1989, the industrial sector received 57%, $251.48 million, of the total investment of $434.11 million. The commerce and restaurants sector took 30% out of the total investment until 1984, but since then its portion has been slowly decreasing and is currently no more than 3.5% of the total.

The industrial sector in the Zhuhai zone received only 7% of foreign capital in 1980, but reached 90% in 1988. In the Shantou zone, the industrial sector received 81.7% of foreign capital until 1988. The shares of traffic, transportation, commerce, and services were high in the early stages of development, but they slowly decreased. Compared to other zones, the high level of investment in the agriculture and marine products sector in the Shantou zone is notable. In the Xiamen zone, the industrial sector receives the highest level of foreign capital, as in the other zones. Until 1989, the industrial sector occupied 58% of all foreign investment. The share of the real estate and services sector was relatively high (26% of total foreign investment until 1989) in comparison with other zones, primarily because Xiamen was originally a resort area. Foreign investment in the real estate, tourism, and service sector is also high in Hainan Province because its beautiful scenery has earned it the title, "Asia's Hawaii."

One reason the real estate, commerce, and restaurant sector occupied a large portion of foreign investment in the early stages of development was to solve the problem of the balancing of foreign currency. Article 9 of the Business Administration Law of China and Foreign Country Joint Venture Company of the People's Republic of China recommends that "raw materials, fuels, and accessories needed by merged corporations be procured in the Chinese domestic market, but merged corporations can directly procure these materials with foreign currency it gained itself."[13] Merged corporations do try to purchase raw materials and accessories from the domestic market, when it is possible. However, most corporations must depend on imported accessories and raw materials because purchasing these items on the domestic market carries limitations in terms of quality and payment schedules. If the procedure depends on imports, necessary foreign currency must be gained through exports, but exports are not easily achieved. Thus this problem of balancing foreign capital can be a burden on corporations in the beginning stages. Accordingly, most foreign corporations enter sectors that do not present this problem, such as hotels, restaurants, and real estate (e.g., apartment construction).

Shifts in the Introduction of Foreign Capital by Country

Shenzhen Special Economic Zone

The introduction of foreign capital to Shenzhen Special Economic Zone, by country, is shown in Table 6-4.

The absolute amount of investment from Hong Kong continues to increase every year, but its proportion of all foreign investment is decreasing every year. That is, in the early developmental stages, from 1979 to 1984, investment from Hong Kong was worth H.K.$16.4 billion, or 90.3% of all foreign currency invested up to that point in Shenzhen Special Economic Zone (H.K.$18.15 billion based on the negotiated amount).[14] However, in 1988 investment from Hong Kong amounted to $1.81 billion (based on the actual investment amount), or only 71.6% of all foreign investment. In terms of size, Hong Kong investments were small, worth H.K.$600,000 on average.[15] The reason for this decline was an increase in investments from other countries, such as Japan.

Starting in 1989, Taiwanese investments increased dramatically. Taiwanese investments in 1989 in Shenzhen Special Economic Zone were the second largest after Hong Kong with 28 corporations.[16] In addition, some Hong Kong corporations conduct investments from Taiwan, even though they are under Hong Kong names. If these cases are included, Taiwanese investments in the Shenzhen zone are much larger than official statistics would indicate. Taiwanese investments in China are most active in the Xiamen zone. The background to this dramatic increase can be explained by two factors. The first is the entry, due to rising wages and labor shortages in Taiwan, of Taiwanese corporations in search of cheap production sites. The second is the entry of

Table 6-3
Changes in Foreign Capital in Industrial Sectors in Each Special Economic Zone (unit: U.S.$10,000)

Shenzhen	1980	1981	1982	1983	1984	1985	1986	1987	1988	1989	Total 1980–1989
Agriculture, forestry, livestock, fishery, and marine products	10	34	22	—	38	73	122	231	39	140	709
Industry	1,016	4,075	2,820	5,200	8,065	6,363	31,547	24,444	26,103	25,148	134,780
Construction	1,110	3,836	2,509	4,908	2,747	3,580	3	226	45	53	19,017
Traffic, transportation, and communication	65	226	148	273	881	1,457	413	400	877	1,071	5,811
Commerce and restaurants	344	1,261	873	1,149	5,243	1,216	960	387	1,063	1,530	14,026
Real estate and services	65	226	148	216	1,665	4,249	2,965	454	4,594	4,664	19,226
Other	48	98	170	95	3,985	15,489	12,391	13,238	8,718	10,805	65,037
Zhuhai											
Agriculture, forestry, livestock, fishery, and marine products	—	5	10	5	64	126	55	21	136	199	621
Industry	—	—	420	483	2,962	3,102	3,818	2,429	4,520	4,868	22,602
Construction	—	—	—	—	112	48	24	6	50	118	358
Transportation and communication	71	175	320	878	3,901	130	7	32	10	10	5,605
Commerce and restaurants	9	137	174	214	316	207	178	28	24	22	1,309
Real estate, tourism, and services	984	946	4,604	1,013	5,077	1,645	436	866	—	90	22,195
Other	1	45	10	—	25	4	—	—	—	21	105

Table 6-3 (continued)

Shantou	Total 1981–1983	1984	1985	1986	1987	1988	Total 1981–1988	Hainan Province	1989
Agriculture and marine products	—	3	41	216.68	260	1,350	1,870.68	Agriculture, forestry, livestock, fishery, and marine products	678
Industry	114.2	329	360	554.37	1,760	1,970	5,087.57	Industry	4,241
Traffic and transportation	—	416	240	—	5	7	668.0	Construction	711
Commerce and services	38.5	7	84	404.2	245	34	812.7	Traffic, transportation, and communication	611
Other	—	25	59	2.56	—	79	—	Commerce and restaurants	614
								Banking and insurance	1,991
								Real estate and services	4,791
								Other	2,187

Total 1980–1989

Xiamen	Frequency of negotiation	Total negotiated investment (U.S.$10,000)
Agriculture	36	4,677
Industry	478	113,179
Construction	21	1,386
Traffic and transportation	14	3,147
Commerce and restaurants	28	3,136
Real estate	91	50,887
Other	8	10,883
Total	676	194,415

Sources: Shenzhen Special Economic Zone Yearbook, ed., 1985–1990; interview with the staff of Zhuhai Statistics Bureau, January 4–May 15, 1991; for Shantou: Lin Wuru, ed., 1990, p. 351; Statistical Bureau of Hainan, 1989; Xiamen Special Economic Zone Yearbook, ed., 1980–1989.

Note: Zhuhai and Xiamen include only direct investments.

Table 6-4
Changes in Foreign Capital by Country (unit: U.S.$10,000)

Shenzhen	1980	1981	1982	1983	1984	1985	1986	1987	1988	1989	Total 1980–1989
Hong Kong	—	—	—	—	—	—	—	25,632	28,198	28,729	181,454 (65)**
Japan	—	—	—	—	—	—	—	9,291	14,561	10,004	41,033 (15.77)
United States	—	—	—	—	—	—	—	3,101	294	1,143	9,981 (3.57)
Italy	—	—	—	—	—	—	—	29	10	166	3,905 (1.40)
Singapore	—	—	—	—	—	—	—	247	146	1,177	3,027 (1.08)
France	—	—	—	—	—	—	—	1,194	501	3,399	2,300 (0.82)
England	—	—	—	—	—	—	—	6	5	112	1,976 (0.70)
Germany	—	—	—	—	—	—	—	18	201	—	1,813 (0.64)
Canada	—	—	—	—	—	—	—	899	150	16	286 (0.50)
Other*	—	—	—	—	—	—	—	32	1,063	357	29,253 (10.45)

Zhuhai	1980	1981	1982	1983	1984	1985	1986	1987	1988	1989	Total 1980–1989
Hong Kong	628	602	448	2,230	7,724	1,166	3,873	1,406	3,428	4,005	25,510
Macao	437	706	5,088	363	4,733	2,477	396	1,933	1,263	1,205	18,601
Singapore	—	—	—	—	—	—	—	—	8	78	86
Japan	—	—	—	—	—	1,619	249	10	—	—	1,878
United States	—	—	—	—	—	—	—	—	31	2	33
Italy	—	—	—	—	—	—	—	—	10	—	10
Canada	—	—	—	—	—	—	—	33	—	38	71

Table 6-4 (continued)

Hainan Province	1980	1981	1982	1983	1984	1985	1986	1987	1988	1989
Hong Kong	28	—	—	—	—	2,050	—	911	10,522	14,411
Taiwan	—	—	—	—	—	—	—	—	—	356
Japan	—	—	—	—	—	60	—	—	1,011	798
Thailand	—	—	—	—	—	—	—	—	359	130
Singapore	—	—	—	—	—	217	—	—	122	43
United States	—	—	—	—	—	1	—	—	198	246
Germany	—	—	—	—	—	—	—	—	162	113
Other	—	—	—	—	—	315	—	—	367	—
Total	28	—	—	—	—	2,643	—	911	12,771	16,097

Xiamen

1980–1989

	Frequency of negotiations	Negotiated investments ($10,000)		Frequency of negotiations	Negotiated investments ($10,000)
Hong Kong and Macao	382	135,288	Thailand	2	400
Taiwan***	175	23,385	Canada	1	81
United States	26	7,933	Germany	3	2,906
Japan	19	4,983	Italy	2	70
Singapore	43	9,551	Other	5	2,912
Philippines	17	6,866	Total	676	194,415
Korea	1	40	Taiwan****	227	60,877

Sources: Zheng Tianlun and Chen Zhuohua, eds., 1990, pp. 252–53; interviews with the staffs of the Statistical Bureau of Shenzhen and Zhuhai Statistics Bureau, January 4– May 15, 1991; Xiamen Special Economic Zone Yearbook, ed., 1990, p. 329; Statistical Bureau of Hainan, 1980–1989.

Notes: * Most investments are by Taiwan. ** ( ) = %. *** Direct investment in Xiamen. **** Includes indirect investment through a third country.

affiliates or subcontract corporations following their parent corporations. According to my research, many Taiwanese corporations entered China because of the second factor. Two cases are introduced here.

Case 1: Tokyo Bartz Industry Corporation is a Japanese company that produces electronic goods worth 10.5 billion yen yearly, with capital of 900 million yen. This company entered Taiwan and established the Taiwanese Sanjia Electronic Company (a wholly Japanese-owned company) in 1971. In February 1988, the Bartz Industry Corporation founded the Tokyo Yuanjian Youxian Company in the Shantou zone and started production there with an investment of H.K.$10 million (Bartz invested 90% and the Chinese partner invested 10%). In the beginning, it imported accessories from its subsidiary company in Taiwan, but the production unit cost became too high due to a rise in the unit cost of imports, resulting from wage increases, a shortage of labor, and an increase in transportation expenses. Accordingly, it stopped importing accessories from Taiwan, and its subsidiary company also entered China and established a sub-subsidiary company. Tokyo Yuanjian Youxian Company could thus buy accessories at low prices through this grandson company. Currently, this sub-subsidiary company is located in the Shenzhen zone and mainly produces motors with 1,000 employees. Some of the production is supplied to Tokyo Yuanjian Youxian Company, and the remainder is exported to Hong Kong, Taiwan, Korea, and the United States.

Case 2: Saitou Toy Company, a wholly Japanese-owned company with capital of 12 million yen, makes dolls in Shenzhen with 1,000 employees. This company produced dolls in Korea and Taiwan from 1970 to 1987. Since it began production in China, it has imported all raw materials from subcontracting corporations in Korea and Taiwan. However, with rising production costs in Korea and Taiwan, the parent company encouraged these subcontracting companies to establish companies in China, to reduce transportation expenses and take advantage of low-cost Chinese labor.

Zhuhai Special Economic Zone

Hong Kong had the largest investment in Zhuhai, as it did in Shenzhen. Zhuhai also had much more investment from Macao compared to other zones. Investment from Macao in 1988 equaled 22% of all foreign investment in Zhuhai.

Although investments from Hong Kong and Macao made up over 95% of all investment, individual investments from these countries were generally small. The average size of investment from Hong Kong was about $650,000 and from Macao no more than $370,000.[17] This suggests that most foreign corporations entering Shenzhen were labor-intensive, small- or medium-sized companies centered in Hong Kong or Macao.

Shantou Special Economic Zone

Most foreign capital in Shantou also came from Hong Kong or Macao. Among 142 joint venture and wholly foreign companies in 1988, 130 (92%) were from Hong Kong or Macao.[18] In addition, three Thai companies, four Singaporean companies, and one company each from the United States, Japan, England, Pakistan, and Panama entered this zone.

Xiamen Special Economic Zone

Hong Kong was the largest investor in Xiamen, as in other zones, but its proportion in Xiamen was the lowest among the five zones. However, the average Hong Kong investment was worth $2.1 million, the highest among the five zones. Taiwanese investments made up 25% of all foreign investment from 1980 to 1989. However, this figure represents only direct investment from Taiwan. If indirect investments through third countries, such as Hong Kong, are included, the figure goes up to 33% of the number of investments and 43% of the value of the investment. The reason for this large investment is that Xiamen is closest to Taiwan, and most Taiwanese are from Fujian Province. Taiwanese investments also tend to be labor-intensive, small- or medium-sized companies. The average investment is worth about $1.23 million.

Hainan Province Special Economic Zone

Hong Kong had the largest investment share with 70% of all foreign investment in Hainan Province in 1989, however, because Hainan Province, like Xiamen, is geographically far from Hong Kong, this represented the lowest level of Hong Kong investment compared to other areas. Another feature of foreign investment in Hainan Province was that this zone had relatively large investments from Southeast Asian countries, such as Thailand and Singapore. In 1988, investments from Southeast Asian countries made up 16% of all foreign investment in Hainan. This may have been due to investments by overseas Chinese living in the Southeast Asian region.

Although some differences exist among the five zones, capital from Hong Kong plays the leading role. Furthermore, these Hong Kong corporations are generally labor-intensive, small- and medium-sized companies. In zones other than Shenzhen, major investing countries (excluding Hong Kong) are Macao in the Zhuhai zone, Taiwan in Xiamen, and Southeast Asian countries in Hainan Province. Shantou Special Economic Zone has the worst conditions in terms of geographical location. In Shantou, the majority of investments come from overseas Chinese who have relatives living there. Differences in levels of investment can be said to result from the geographical distance between zones and foreign countries.

EFFECTS ON ENLARGEMENT OF EMPLOYMENT

To accurately analyze the enlargement of employment, the effects of foreign loans and direct investment need to be analyzed separately. However, since statistical data on the expansion of employment from foreign loans is not yet available, only the effects on expansion of employment from direct investment is analyzed here.

Changes in the number of workers employed by foreign-capital companies in the special economic zones from 1983 to 1989 are shown in Table 6-5. As of 1989, a total of 120,000 laborers were employed by foreign-capital companies in Shenzhen, or 30% of all laborers. This represents 16% for Zhuhai, 50% for Shantou, 10.6% for Xiamen, and 0.8% for Hainan Province. In addition, the average annual rate of increase in employment in foreign-capital companies in Shenzhen was 53.3% from 1983 to 1989. This far exceeded the average annual rate of 20.1% in companies owned by the people and 25.9% for collective ownership companies during the same period.[19] Foreign-capital companies in Zhuhai showed an average annual rate of increase in employment of 41.1% from 1985 to 1989. During the same period, companies owned by the people showed a rate of increase of 9.57%, and collective ownership companies showed a rate of 1.95%.[20] In Shantou from 1984 to 1989, foreign-capital companies recorded an average annual increase in employment of 73%, 108% for companies owned by the people, and 94% for collective ownership companies. The rate of employment increase in foreign-capital companies was higher in Shantou than in other special economic zones, but lower than the rates for companies owned by the people and collective ownership companies.[21] Foreign-capital companies in Xiamen recorded an average annual rate of increase in employment of 40.8% from 1985 to 1989.[22] In Hainan Province from 1985 to 1989, foreign-capital companies recorded an average annual rate of increase in employment of 369%, 1.52% for companies owned by the people, and -1.66% for collective ownership companies.[23] The number of laborers employed by different countries is shown in Table 6-6. Hong Kong companies employed 80% of all laborers in foreign-capital companies in Shenzhen. The next largest employers were Japan, the United States, and Singapore.

Of foreign-capital companies by industrial sector, technology industries have the biggest effects on employment. In 1988, 71.8% of all employees in foreign-capital companies in Shenzhen,[24] 62.9% in Zhuhai,[25] and 88.3% in Xiamen[26] were employed in technology industries.

Overall, investments by foreign companies are concentrated in technology industries, especially in labor-intensive areas such as electricity, electronics, textiles, and clothing. From the perspective of employment expansion this is a desirable pattern for the Chinese. The concentration in these areas suggests that the primary purpose of foreign investments was access to cheap labor.

The five special economic zones, Shenzhen, Xiamen, Zhuhai, Shantou, and Hainan Province, in order of diminishing magnitude, have all seen employment expansion. These rankings match those for size of foreign investment and are also related to geographical distance from the zones to strong foreign investors.

In terms of employment growth, the rate of increase in foreign-capital companies was higher than in Chinese collective ownership companies and companies owned by the people in all zones, except Shantou. The reason for this was that foreign-capital companies usually came into the special economic zones to launch new businesses requiring a fresh supply of labor.

The rate of employment created by foreign-capital companies among all employees in each special economic zone, in decreasing order of magnitude, was Shantou, Shenzhen, Xiamen, and Hainan Province. This reflects the size of foreign investment

Table 6-5
Changes in Number of Employees in Corporations with Different Ownerships

Shantou (unit: person)	1984	1985	1986	1987	1988	1989	Avg. annual growth rate (%)
Companies owned by the people	828	6,791	12,585	20,495	27,724	13,835	108
Collective ownership companies	414	2,968	6,034	8,915	11,260	4,716	94
Foreign-capital companies	1,288	858	2,106	3,814	5,559	18,229	73
Total	2,530	10,617	20,735	33,224	44,543	36,780	

Zhuhai (unit: person)	1985	1986	1987	1988	1989	Avg. annual growth rate (%)
Companies owned by the people	72,427	78,677	87,458	96,924	104,563	9.57
Collective ownership companies	17,896	18,625	20,221	20,431	19,250	1.95
Foreign-capital companies	5,893	8,827	12,027	17,060	23,328	41.10
Total	96,216	106,129	119,706	134,415	147,141	

Xiamen (unit: person)	1985	1986	1987	1988	1989	Avg. annual growth rate (%)
Companies owned by the people	112,254	115,081	120,704	123,910	124,473	2.57
Collective ownership companies	64,403	61,627	68,224	65,921	67,142	3.1
Foreign-capital companies	7,940	11,591	15,778	19,362	30,652	40.8
Other	3,736	2,881	3,375	3,525	2,567	-7.1
Total	188,333	191,180	208,081	212,718	224,834	

Hainan Province (unit: person)	1985	1986	1987	1988	1989	Avg. annual growth rate (%)
Companies owned by the people	883,500	—	905,700	928,700	940,700	1.52
Collective ownership companies	92,300	—	90,600	90,200	87,900	-1.66
Foreign-capital companies	442	—	501	5,596	9,209	369.00
Other	3,658	—	5,199	1,704	2,091	-1.1
Total	979,900	—	1,002,000	1,026,200	1,039,900	

Table 6-5 (continued)

Shenzhen (unit: 10,000 persons)	1983	1984	1985	1986	1987	1988	1989	Avg. annual growth rate (%)
Companies owned by the people	10.10	14.09	16.84	18.97	22.04	28.04	30.34	20.1
Permanent laborers	8.19	10.24	10.98	11.98	12.37	13.12	14.33	9.8
Contract laborers	0.84	1.54	1.79	2.14	2.68	3.95	3.95	29.4
Temporary laborers	1.07	2.31	4.07	4.85	6.99	10.88	12.06	49.7
Collective ownership companies	1.22	2.15	2.60	2.68	3.55	4.53	4.85	25.9
Permanent laborers	1.01	1.71	0.67	0.51	0.58	0.63	0.50	-11.1
Contract laborers	0.08	0.19	0.09	0.16	0.22	0.26	0.24	20.1
Temporary laborers	0.13	0.25	1.84	2.01	2.75	3.64	4.11	77.8
Foreign-capital companies	0.93	0.90	2.50	3.33	6.47	8.54	12.09	53.3
Permanent laborers	0.64	0.32	1.08	1.21	1.57	2.00	2.61	26.4
Contract laborers	0.12	0.22	0.70	0.95	1.72	2.21	2.47	65.5
Temporary laborers	0.17	0.36	0.72	1.17	3.18	4.33	7.01	85.9
Total	12.25	17.14	21.94	24.98	32.06	41.11	47.01	

Sources: Shenzhen Special Economic Zone Yearbook, ed., 1985–1990; interview with the staff of the Zhuhai Statistics Bureau, January 4–May 15, 1991; Shantou Special Economic Zone Yearbook, ed., 1984–1989; Xiamen Special Economic Zone Yearbook, ed., 1990, p. 171; Statistical Bureau of Hainan, 1990, pp. 124, 128.

Table 6-6
Foreign-Capital Companies in Shenzhen, 1988

	No. of companies (cases)	Total production in technological industry (10,000 yuan)	Exports (10,000 yuan)	No. of employees	Labor productivity (yuan/person)
Hong Kong	337 (87.98)	385,761 (71.02)	237,030 (68.15)	49,258 (80.23)	78,314
Japan	19 (4.96)	93,831 (17.28)	74,601 (21.45)	7,093 (11.55)	132,287
United States	11 (2.87)	35,708 (6.57)	27,563 (7.93)	2,807 (4.57)	127,211
Singapore	6 (1.57)	16,835 (30.9)	5,301 (1.52)	1,102 (1.79)	152,702
Thailand	3	8,835	1,871	508	173,917
Oceania	3	1,045	619	137	76,227
Philippines	1	649	341	220	29,500
Sri Lanka	1	320	320	192	16,667
Taiwan	1	108	80	65	16,615
England	1	60	60	12	50,000
Total	383 (100)	543,152 (100)	347,786 (100)	61,394 (100)	

Source: Wong Pui Yee, 1989, p. 23.

Note: ( ) = percentage.

in each special economic zone. Shantou had relatively little foreign investment compared to the other zones, but foreign capital played an important role in employment in Shantou. However, the overall contribution by foreign capital to employment expansion in the zones was not very significant. Foreign-capital company employment amounted to only 30% of the total, even in Shenzhen, with the largest number of labor-intensive foreign corporations, and not more than 15.8%, 10.6%, and 0.8% in the Zhuhai, Xiamen, and Hainan Province zones, respectively. There are three reasons for the relatively small contribution: (1) China did not attract as much foreign capital as originally expected, (2) corporations that entered the zones did not reinvest heavily, and (3) the production technology possessed by foreign-capital companies was relatively inappropriate for increasing employment.

Many criteria can be used in judging whether production technology is effective in increasing employment, but the capital equipment ratio has been chosen here. The capital equipment ratio is an index which represents how much one employee uses a company's facilities, that is, utilization of capital facilities by one employee. If this ratio is high, the company's production technology is evaluated as capital-intensive. Theoretically, only companies of the same industry type should be compared with each other. However, these calculations include all types of industry due to the limited data available. The capital equipment ratio of foreign corporations in each special economic zone is shown in Table 6-7. Capital equipment ratios are in an overall state of suspension or reduction although figures differ for each zone. These ratios were high in the early stage because investment in machines was high. Most investment was in real estate, commerce, and services where the employment absorption capability was lower than in technological industries. This is best reflected in Shenzhen Special Economic Zone. Shantou has the lowest capital equipment ratio among the five zones. This indicates that foreign corporations here were mostly labor-intensive. Ranked in order of decreasing capital equipment ratios, are Shantou, Xiamen, Shenzhen, Zhuhai, and Hainan Province.

The capital equipment ratio of companies owned by the people is higher than that of collective ownership companies. This is because most collective ownership companies are in rural areas, which have more labor-intensive industrial sectors than urban areas. Overall, the capital equipment ratios of companies owned by the people and collective ownership companies have been gradually increasing. The special economic zones can be ranked according to rising capital equipment ratios by (1) companies owned by the people: Shenzhen, Zhuhai, Xiamen, Hainan Provinces, and (2) collective ownership companies: Shenzhen, Zhuhai, Xiamen, Hainan Provinces. With the exception of Shantou, the capital equipment ratios (of companies owned by the people and collective ownership companies) are almost parallel to the level of industrialization of the zones.

As shown in Table 6-7, the difference between the capital equipment ratio of foreign corporations and Chinese companies owned by the people and collective ownership companies has been decreasing, but still remains large. The disparity between the capital equipment ratios of foreign corporations and Chinese collective ownership companies is particularly large. This suggests that foreign corporations make much greater use of capital-intensive technologies than Chinese corporations. In comparing the averages of the past ten years, the gap has varied from a factor of 2.2 to 3.8. The lower the level of industrialization in an area, the larger the difference.

EFFECTS OF THE WAGE GAIN

Direct investment brings in foreign currency. Generally, gaining foreign currency through direct investment is manifested through such factors as wages, taxes, or rents for land or buildings. Data is only available for wages, so this is the only factor that can be discussed. Fortunately, wages have the largest weight in measuring the gain of foreign currency through direct investment. Total wages by ownership type in each special economic zone is shown in Table 6-8.

As of 1989, foreign-capital companies in Shenzhen Special Economic Zone were paying total wages of 464.4 million yuan, or 29.6% of the total wages paid in the zone.[27] This represents an increase of about 350% in six years from 12% in 1983.

Table 6-7
Changes in Capital Equipment Ratio by Different Ownership Type

Shantou	1984	1985	1986	1987	1988	1989	Avg. annual growth rate (%)
Companies owned by the people (A)	1.57	1.38	1.00	1.01	1.43	2.23	1.43
Collective ownership companies (B)							0.66
Foreign-capital companies (C)	0.60	0.52	0.61	0.64	0.77	0.84	0.66
C/A*	0.38	0.38	0.61	0.63	0.54	0.38	0.49
C/B**	—	—	—	—	—	—	—
Xiamen							
Companies owned by the people (A)	—	0.48	0.55	0.65	0.76	0.91	0.67
Collective ownership companies (B)	—	0.07	0.08	0.09	0.12	0.14	0.1
Foreign-capital companies (C)	—	1.78	1.83	1.68	2.22	2.17	1.93
C/A*	—	3.7	3.3	2.5	2.9	2.3	2.9
C/B**	—	25.4	22.8	18.6	18.5	15.5	20.2
Hainan Province							
Companies owned by the people (A)	0.03	0.07	0.10	0.13	0.17	0.23	0.12
Collective ownership companies (B)	0.01	0.04	0.05	0.07	0.11	0.14	0.07
Foreign-capital companies (C)	—	1.23	—	1.62	3.02	3.36	2.30
C/A*	—	17.5	—	12.4	17.7	14.6	15.6
C/B**	—	30.7	—	23.1	27.4	24.0	26.3

Table 6-7 (continued)

Shenzhen	1980	1981	1982	1983	1984	1985	1986	1987	1988	1989	Avg. annual growth rate (%)
Companies owned by the people (A)	0.21	0.51	0.78	0.97	1.07	1.27	1.27	1.28	1.35	1.64	1.03
Collective ownership companies (B)	0.07	0.015	0.19	0.54	0.74	0.99	1.17	1.18	1.22	1.30	0.75
Foreign-capital companies (C)	—	—	—	3.90	6.59	3.69	4.23	2.80	2.64	2.24	2.88
C/A*	—	—	—	4.0	6.1	2.9	3.3	2.1	1.9	1.3	3.1
C/B**	—	—	—	7.2	8.9	3.7	3.6	2.3	2.1	1.7	4.2
Zhuhai											
Companies owned by the people (A)	0.08	0.15	0.26	0.26	0.52	0.81	0.90	1.01	1.19	1.34	0.66
Collective ownership companies (B)	0.11	0.14	0.21	0.26	0.27	0.30	0.35	0.43	0.66	0.77	0.32
Foreign-capital companies (C)	—	—	—	—	—	4.78	3.70	3.00	2.39	2.63	3.3
C/A*	—	—	—	—	—	5.9	4.1	2.9	2.0	1.7	3.3
C/B**	—	—	—	—	—	15.9	10.5	6.9	3.6	3.0	6.65

Sources: Shenzhen Special Economic Zone Yearbook, ed., 1985–1990; interviews with the staffs of the Statistical Bureau of Shenzhen and Zhuhai Statistics Bureau, January 4–May 15, 1991; Shantou Special Economic Zone Yearbook, ed., 1984–1989; Xiamen Special Economic Zone Yearbook, ed., 1990; Statistical Bureau of Hainan, 1990.

Notes: * C/A = foreign capital companies (C) ÷ companies owned by the people (A). ** C/B = foreign capital companies (C) ÷ collective ownership companies (B).

Table 6-8
Changes in Total Wage by Ownership Type (unit: U.S.$10,000)

Shenzhen	1983	1984	1985	1986	1987	1988	1989
Total wage	13,689	30,705	46,070	53,625	71,027	119,989	156,795
Ownership by the people	10,770	24,902	33,552	38,826	46,596	75,667	95,707
Collective ownership	1,256	2,974	4,009	4,482	6,355	9,937	11,272
Foreign capital	1,663	740	—	9,739	17,558	32,820	46,436
Other	—	2,089	—	578	518	1,565	3,380
Zhuhai							
Total wage	—	—	15,693	18,124	23,599	34,639	47,271
Ownership by the people	—	—	11,439	13,235	16,874	24,330	32,426
Collective ownership	—	—	3,063	3,131	4,130	5,390	5,822
Foreign capital	—	—	1,191	1,758	2,596	4,919	9,022
Shantou							
Total wage	—	204	802	1,637	3,188	6,181	10,380
Ownership by the people	—	89	349	830	1,297	2,236	3,416
Collective ownership	—	28	119	195	510	1,167	1,223
Foreign capital	—	97	334	612	1,380	2,778	5,741

Table 6-8 continued

Xiamen	1983	1984	1985	1986	1987	1988	1989
Total wage	—	—	24,707	29,384	35,422	46,742	61,505
Ownership by the people	—	—	15,306	19,057	21,582	28,598	35,612
Collective ownership	—	—	7,857	8,005	10,541	12,459	16,020
Foreign capital	—	—	1,544	2,322	3,299	5,685	9,873
Hainan Province							
Total wage	—	—	97,401	—	122,089	140,358	168,152
Ownership by the people	—	—	88,621	—	112,713	129,128	153,969
Collective ownership	—	—	8,324	—	8,524	10,069	11,341
Foreign capital	—	—	49	—	75	893	2,310
Other	—	—	407	—	776	267	532

Sources: Shenzhen Special Economic Zone Yearbook, ed., 1985–1990; interviews with the staff of the Zhuhai Statistics Bureau, January 4–May 15, 1991; Shantou Special Economic Zone Yearbook, ed., 1984–1989; Xiamen Special Economic Zone Yearbook, ed., 1990; Statistical Bureau of Hainan, 1990.

However, in addition to wages, foreign-capital companies paid social welfare contributions worth 25% of wages to the Department of Labor of the Shenzhen municipal government. Including these social welfare payments, the total wage bill paid by foreign-capital companies in 1989 was 580.5 million yuan. As of 1989, the wage bill paid by foreign-capital companies in Zhuhai was 90.2 million yuan. This amounted to 19% of total wage payments, a 250% increase from the 7.5% wage share in 1985. As in Shenzhen, with the addition of social welfare payments (25% of the basic wage), the bill totaled 112.8 million yuan. In Shantou it was 57.4 million yuan, or 55.3% of the total and 71.8 million including social welfare payments. In Xiamen it was 98.7 million yuan, 16.1% of the total in Xiamen, and 135.3 million with social welfare payments.[28] In Hainan Province it was 23.1 million yuan, or 1.3% of the total in Xiamen and 28.8 million with social welfare. Overall, the introduction of foreign capital did not significantly affect the wage gain in the special economic zones. Relatively high proportions are seen in Shantou and Shenzhen, but in other zones the proportion is around 10%, and in Hainan Province it is only 1.3%.[29]

One additional note in the effects of the wage gain is that the share in total wages paid by foreign-capital companies in the special zones is almost the same as their share in the number of laborers employed. This means that there are only small differences in wages between foreign-capital companies and other companies (companies owned by the people and collective ownership companies). As shown in Table 6-9, the average wage at foreign-capital companies is highest, but the difference from the average wage in companies owned by the people is no more than 100 yuan. There is a greater difference in wages between foreign-capital companies and collective ownership companies, but the proportion of laborers working in collective ownership companies is small, so there are no noticeable effects.

Although there is no big difference in wages, many people want to be employed by foreign corporations for the following reasons: (1) foreign corporations offer more overtime than domestic Chinese companies; (2) most foreign corporations pay for overtime in Hong Kong dollars, which can be exchanged for yuan above the official exchange rate on the black market; and (3) foreign corporations offer better working conditions.

Table 6-9
Changes in Average Annual Wage of Laborers/Employees by Ownership Type in Shenzhen Special Economic Zone (unit: yuan, person)

	1983	1984	1985	1986	1987	1988	1987	Average annual growth rate (%)
Ownership by the people	1,610	2,363	2,588	2,624	2,789	3,455	4,014	15.1
Collective ownership	1,495	1,859	2,000	2,113	2,392	2,769	2,760	5.7
Foreign capital	1,714	1,773	—	2,637	3,024	4,169	4,158	15.9
Average	1,610	2,266	2,524	2,568	2,798	3,543	3,919	14.8

Source: Shenzhen Special Economic Zone Yearbook, ed., 1985–1990.

7

Industrial Structure and Improvement of International Balance of Payments and Foreign Capital

INDUSTRIAL STRUCTURE

Foreign capital accelerates the growth of capital-intensive industries and industrial restructuring by supplementing insufficient domestic capital. As the supply of capital increases, interest rates decrease and capital-intensive industries are promoted. Foreign captital brought relatively large improvements in industrial structure in Shenzhen and Shantou. In the case of Zhuhai, however, foreign capital did not make as large a contribution because foreign capital investment in Zhuhai's industrial sector was lower. The same holds true for Xiamen and Hainan Provinces, where foreign investment was concentrated in real estate and services. (Foreign investments in real estate and services in Shenzhen made up 7.4% of foreign investment from 1980 to 1989, and 27%, or 400% more, in Xiamen.)[30] The effects of the introduction of foreign capital on industrial structure are shown in Table 7-1.

Shenzhen Special Economic Zone

Agriculture decreased from 9.4% of Shenzhen's industrial structure in 1980 to 0.6% in 1989, while industry increased from 18.9% in 1980 to 62.9% in 1989. The percentage of construction, which formed a high 47.2% in the beginning, gradually decreased to 22.7% in 1989. The percentage of commerce slipped from 16.5% in 1980 to 10.8% in 1989. Since the rate of increase in industry was high relative to other sectors, the shares of other sectors in the total decreased, although they increased in absolute terms.

Although many domestic companies entered Shenzhen from all parts of China, foreign capital contributed most to Shenzhen's high level of industrialization. As examined, 52% of foreign capital invested (including foreign loans and direct investments) from 1979 to 1989 was in the industrial sector. As a result, production by

Table 7-1
Total Production Value by Industrial Sector (unit U.S.$10,000, %)

Shenzhen	1980	1981	1982	1983	1984	1985	1986	1987	1988	1989	Average annual growth rate (%)
Agriculture	2,550 (9.4)	3,220 (5.0)	4,057 (3.4)	2,007 (1.0)	5,748 (1.6)	5,011 (0.9)	7,621 (1.3)	12,946 (1.6)	17,146 (1.2)	11,115 (0.6)	17.8
Industry	5,121 (18.9)	20,111 (31.1)	26,291 (22.4)	58,928 (30.6)	129,919 (35.2)	209,428 (35.4)	279,172 (47.9)	453,742 (57.6)	862,157 (61.5)	1,092,292 (62.9)	81.5
Construction	12,796 (47.2)	30,033 (46.5)	66,475 (56.5)	90,203 (46.8)	147,980 (40.0)	253,252 (42.8)	179,057 (30.8)	176,086 (22.4)	292,986 (20.9)	393,433 (22.7)	46.3
Transportation and communication	2,156 (8.0)	2,513 (3.9)	3,464 (3.0)	8,073 (4.2)	15,418 (4.2)	21,178 (3.6)	22,072 (3.8)	23,640 (3.0)	334,965 (2.5)	52,563 (3.0)	42.6
Commerce	4,490 (16.5)	8,767 (13.5)	17,333 (14.7)	33,434 (17.4)	70,194 (19.0)	102,548 (17.3)	94,293 (16.2)	120,651 (15.4)	194,963 (13.9)	187,905 (10.8)	51.4
Total	27,113 (100)	64,644 (100)	117,620 (100)	192,645 (100)	369,259 (100)	591,417 (100)	582,215 (100)	787,065 (100)	1,402,197 (100)	1,737,308 (100)	58.8
Zhuhai											
Agriculture	28,471 (37.3)	30,892 (34.2)	31,117 (30.9)	32,321 (27.4)	33,922 (21.7)	36,303 (15.9)	41,319 (17.9)	44,439 (14.4)	81,405 (14.8)	83,337 (12.3)	14.1
Industry	23,178 (31.3)	24,038 (26.6)	26,730 (26.6)	37,151 (31.5)	51,302 (32.8)	64,205 (28.2)	80,647 (34.9)	142,321 (46.1)	308,437 (56.3)	420,135 (62.2)	41.4
Construction	4,713 (6.2)	9,260 (10.2)	14,505 (14.4)	17,531 (14.7)	38,324 (24.5)	81,504 (35.7)	71,020 (30.7)	77,199 (25.0)	90,182 (16.4)	82,524 (12.3)	44.5
Transportation and communication	1,066 (1.4)	1,833 (2.0)	2,030 (2.0)	2,366 (2.0)	3,230 (2.1)	4,057 (1.8)	3,274 (1.0)	5,092 (1.6)	13,611 (2.5)	24,001 (3.5)	48.2
Commerce and restaurants	18,961 (24.8)	24,411 (27.0)	26,185 (26.1)	28,919 (24.4)	29,427 (18.9)	41,969 (18.4)	34,669 (14.9)	39,978 (12.9)	54,685 (10.0)	65,486 (9.7)	16.2
Total	76,389 (100)	90,434 (100)	100,567 (100)	118,108 (100)	156,295 (100)	228,038 (100)	231,379 (100)	308,849 (100)	548,320 (100)	675,483 (100)	29.0

Table 7-1 (continued)

Hainan Province	1980	1981	1982	1983	1984	1985	1986	1987	1988	1989	Average annual growth rate (%)
Agriculture	—	—	—	—	126,800 (49.53)	306,100 (45.73)	355,200 48.62	412,400 (48.45)	576,200 (48.6)	644,700 (45.13)	45.0
Industry	—	—	—	—	70,500 27.54	164,900 (24.63)	176,700 (24.13)	215,000 (25.26)	312,600 (26.37)	389,600 (27.27)	46.5
Construction	—	—	—	—	22,000 (8.59)	108,000 (16.25)	103,300 (14.19)	101,300 (11.90)	142,300 (12.0)	224,400 (15.71)	96.5
Traffic, transportation, and communication	—	—	—	—	11,100 (4.34)	26,400 (3.94)	29,400 (4.03)	42,200 (4.96)	44,900 (3.79)	50,800 (3.56)	33.7
Commerce	—	—	—	—	25,600 (10.0)	63,200 (9.45)	66,000 (9.03)	80,300 (9.43)	109,600 (9.24)	119,000 (8.33)	43.6
Total	—	—	—	—	256,000 (100)	669,400 (100)	730,700 (100)	851,200 (100)	1,185,600 (100)	1,428,500 (100)	49.4

Sources: Shenzhen Special Economic Zone Yearbook, ed., 1985–1990; interviews with the staffs of the Statistical Bureau of Shenzhen and Zhuhai Statistics Bureau, January 4–May 15, 1991; Statistical Bureau of Hainan, 1990, p. 79.

Notes: ( ) represents the component ratio. Amounts for Shantou were calculated based on 1980 constant prices. Shantou's total industrial production is exclusive of rural industrial production.

foreign-capital companies occupied more than 64% of total industrial production as of 1989.[31]

Zhuhai Special Economic Zone

In Zhuhai Special Economic Zone, the share of agriculture fell from 37.3% in 1980 to 12.3% in 1989. On the other hand, the share of industry rose from 31.3% in 1980 to 62.2% in 1989. In 1985 when construction was running full-scale, it constituted 35.7% of Zhuhai's industrial structure, but slowly fell to 12.3% as of 1989. The commerce/restaurants sector formed 27% in 1981, but only 9.7% in 1989.

From 1979 to 1989, the percentage of industry in Zhuhai increased and reached a high level. Of course, foreign capital played an important role. In fact, 48.9% of all foreign capital introduced from 1979 to 1989 (only direct investment) was put into the industrial sector. As a result, more than 36% of total industrial production in Zhuhai was by foreign-capital companies as of 1989.[32]

Shantou Special Economic Zone

In the Shantou industrial structure of 1984, of total production (32.11 million yuan), primary industry formed 1.44%, secondary industry 17.52%, and tertiary industry 81.04%. In tertiary industry, the development of commerce and restaurants was especially remarkable, forming 98.4% of tertiary industry and 79.77% of total production. This suggests that the commerce/restaurant sector occupied most of total industrial production until 1984. Since then, with steady development, total production in 1988 was 3,100% of 1984 levels, and the percentages of primary, secondary and tertiary industries changed to 5.55%, 63.35% and 29.1%, respectively. In secondary industry, the development of the industrial sector was especially conspicuous, forming 97.76% (628.75 million yuan) of secondary industry and 62.23% of total production.[33] Investments in the industrial sector made up 88% of foreign capital introduced from 1981 to 1988. As a result, as of 1989, 83.6% of total industrial production in Shantou was by foreign-capital companies.[34]

Xiamen Special Economic Zone

In Xiamen, agriculture formed 14.1% of total production in 1980, which decreased to 3% in 1989. Industry also decreased from 69.6% in 1980 to 57% in 1989. However, production in other sectors, which had formed 16.1% of total production in 1980, increased by about 250% to 39.9% of total production in 1989. The percentage of industry in the total industrial sector has remained largely unchanged over the last 10 years. This is closely related to the nature of foreign capital invested in Xiamen, which has been significant in non-industrial sectors, such as real estate and services (27% of the total contract-based investment for 1980–1989). As of 1989, 48.35% of total industrial production was with foreign capital.[35]

Hainan Province Special Economic Zone

The Hainan Province industrial structure from 1980 to 1988 is shown in Table 7-1. Agriculture formed 49.53% of total production in 1984, decreasing to 45.13% in 1989. Meanwhile, industrial production slowly increased from late 1980 when Hainan Province became a special economic zone, to 3.89 billion yuan by 1989, or 550% of the 1980 level. However, the percentage of industrial production in total production remained largely unchanged. This percentage was low because foreign investment in Hainan Province was mainly in real estate, public utilities, tourism, and services. In 1989, 26.7% of foreign capital was invested in the industrial sector, the lowest of the five special economic zones. Foreign-capital companies composed 12.8% of total industrial production in Hainan Province in 1989.[36]

EFFECTS ON EXPORTS

The introduction of foreign capital to the special economic zones has greatly increased exports, but it is difficult to say how much, especially regarding indirect exports. Therefore, the export results of foreign-capital companies and their share in total exports in the special economic zones are examined in this section.

Foreign-capital companies in Shenzhen exported goods worth $258.24 million in 1986, 35.6% of total, and $1.01 billion in 1989, 46.6% of total. In Zhuhai, foreign-capital companies recorded exports worth $31.39 million in 1987, 11.5% of total city exports, increasing to $130.21 million in 1989, or 35.6%. In Shantou the 1985 figure was $20.48 million, 36.7% of total exports, increasing to $148.89 million in 1989, or 49.7%. In Xiamen foreign-capital companies exported $18.17 million in 1985, 11.0% of total, increasing to $181.76 million in 1989, or 28.1% (see Table 7-2). In Hainan Province 1987, foreign-capital companies exported $1.35 million, or 1.1% of total volume. In 1988, this increased to $1.6 million, only 0.5% of the total exports.[37] As shown in Table 7-3, the industrial and mining sector was responsible for 73.4% of total export volume in Shenzhen in 1989. It is estimated that foreign-capital companies made up at least 60% of total industrial and mineral exports.[38]

Areas most affected by foreign capital exports are Shenzhen (46.6%) and Shantou (49.7%). However, as the figures show, in terms of total export volume, foreign capital has not significantly affected exports. There were three major reasons for this: first, the size of the foreign capital influx was not substantial; second, it was mainly invested in real estate and services, that is, sectors unrelated to exports; and third, a significant portion of foreign-capital company production is not exported, but sold in the Chinese domestic market. Of these reasons, the most significant is the third. This subject is discussed more closely in the section on the international balance of payments.

INTERINDUSTRIAL RELATIONSHIP EFFECTS

Foreign capital also had important effects on inter-industrial relationships, in terms of how much raw material or intermediate material is purchased from the Chinese

Table 7-2
Exports and Imports of Foreign-Capital Companies (unit: U.S.$10,000)

	1984	1985	1986	1987	1988	1989
Shenzhen						
Total exports	—	—	72,652 (100)	141,354 (100)	184,949 (100)	217,400 (100)
SanjiGiyie*	—	—	25,824 (35.6)	50,709 (35.9)	55,601 (30.1)	101,408 (46.6)
Total imports	—	—	112,144 (100)	114,430 (100)	159,328 (100)	157,831 (100)
SanjiGiyie	—	—	64,426 (57.50)	51,090 (44.70)	52,617 (33.10)	87,385 (55.4)
Zhuhai						
Total exports	—	—	7,072 (100)	27,372 (100)	42,105 (100)	36,508 (100)
Commissioned processing	—	—	729 (10.3)	949 (3.5)	1,395 (3.3)	1,874 (5.1)
SanjiGiyie	—	—	1,029 (14.6)	2,190 (8.0)	5,148 (12.2)	11,147 (30.5)
Total imports	—	—	14,260 (100)	16,445 (100)	21,520 (100)	16,450 (100)
SanjiGiyie	—	—	6,066 (42.5)	5,783 (35.2)	6,462 (30.3)	6,887 (41.9)
Shantou						
Total exports	449 (100)	5,591 (100)	7,358 (100)	17,802 (100)	29,816 (100)	29,939 (100)
Commissioned processing		1,239 (22.2)	1,372 (18.6)	2,897 (16.3)	4,000 (13.3)	2,620 (8.7)
SanjiGiyie	286 (63.7)	809 (14.5)	1,719 (23.4)	4,596 (25.8)	7,740 (26.0)	12,269 (41.0)
Total imports	2,580 (100)	6,699 (100)	4,460 (100)	12,532 (100)	29,993 (100)	32,066 (100)
SanjiGiyie	845 (32.8)	621 (9.2)	1,258 (28.2)	2,906 (23.2)	6,452 (21.5)	8,490 (26.8)
Xiamen						
Total exports		16,527 (100)	16,374 (100)	26,107 (100)	57,607 (100)	64,678 (100)
SanjiGiyie		1,817 (11.0)	1,516 (9.3)	4,184 (16.0)	8,428 (14.6)	18,176 (28.1)
Total imports		27,870 (100)	11,464 (100)	15,469 (100)	29,778 (100)	32,450 (100)
SanjiGiyie		11,263 (40.4)	4,522 (39.4)	4,014 (25.9)	9,014 (30.3)	4,586 (14.1)

Sources: Zheng Tianlun and Chen Zhuohua, eds., 1990, pp. 254–55; interviews with the staffs of the Statistical Bureau of Shenzhen and Zhuhai Statistics Bureau, January 4–May 15, 1991; Shantou Special Economic Zone Yearbook, ed., 1984–1989; Xiamen Special Economic Zone Yearbook, ed., 1990, p. 324.

Notes: ( ) represents the component ratio. *SanjiGiyie means foreign direct investment including merger, joint venture, and wholly foreign.

Table 7-3
Exports by Industrial Sector in Shenzhen (unit: U.S.$10,000, %)

	1986	1987	1988	1989
Total Exports	72,652 (100)	141,354 (100)	184,949 (100)	217,400 (100)
Industrial and mineral products	43,586 (60.10)	103,175 (73.00)	127,985 (69.20)	159,682 (73.4)
Agricultural products	16,465 (22.70)	25,351 (17.9)	39,729 (21.50)	32,071 (14.8)
Commissioned processed products	9,780 (13.50)	12,068 (8.50)	14,888 (8.00)	20,702 (9.5)
Other	2,721 (3.70)	760 (0.60)	2,349 (1.30)	4,973 (2.3)

Sources: Zheng Tianlun and Chen Zhuohua, eds., 1990, pp. 254–55; interview with the staff of the Statistical Bureau of Shenzhen, January 4–May 15, 1991.

Note: ( ) represents the component ratio.

domestic market for use by foreign capital companies and by companies investing directly in China. When foreign capital is invested in a certain industry and used to purchase raw materials in the Chinese domestic market, demand for these materials increases and greatly contributes to the development of the industry that generates the materials. Through this demand-creating process, foreign capital strengthens the attraction of investment in the entire nation.

The inter-industry relationship effects that accompany the introduction of foreign capital in each special economic zone are examined here. Because statistical data on corporations using foreign loans are unavailable, only direct investment by foreign corporations is analyzed here.

Foreign-capital companies in Shenzhen (see Table 7-4) imported $644.26 million worth of goods in 1986, increasing to $873.85 million in 1989. However, their share of total imports over the same period decreased from 57.5% to 55.4%. In Zhuhai they imported $60.66 million of goods in 1986, increasing to $68.87 million in 1989. Their share of total imports decreased from 42.5% to 41.9%. In Shantou foreign-capital company imports increased by 1,000% from $8.45 million in 1984 to $84.9 million in 1989. However, their share in total imports decreased over the same period from 32.7% to 26.4%. In Xiamen foreign-capital company imports also increased by about 1,000% from 1985 to 1989. Unlike the others, their share of the total increased over the same period from 10.9% to 28.1%.

Foreign-capital company share of total imports in all zones except Xiamen, has been gradually decreasing, that is, despite the increase in investment by foreign-capital companies, their imports of raw materials for production have been gradually decreasing. Because total production of foreign-capital companies has not been reported, their reliance on imports for exports is estimated through the import/export reliance ratio,

Table 7-4
Exports and Imports by Ownership Type (unit: U.S.$10,000, %)

Shenzhen	1980	1981	1982	1983	1984	1985	1986	1987	1988	1989	Total 1986–1989
Total exports	—	—	—	—	—	—	72,552 (100)	141,354 (100)	184,949 (100)	217,428 (100)	613,283 (100)
State-run companies	—	—	—	—	—	—	13,332 (18.4)	22,773 (16.1)	37,084 (20.1)	31,646 (14.6)	104,835 (17.0)
Guangdong Province-run companies	—	—	—	—	—	—	1,876 (2.6)	5,939 (4.2)	6,984 (3.7)	4,320 (2.0)	19,029 (3.1)
City-run companies and others	—	—	—	—	—	—	31,520 (43.3)	61,933 (43.8)	85,370 (46.1)	80,054 (36.8)	258,877 (42.0)
Foreign-capital companies	—	—	—	—	—	—	25,824 (35.6)	50,709 (35.9)	55,601 (30.1)	101,408 (46.6)	233,542 (37.9)
Total imports	—	—	—	—	—	—	112,144 (100)	114,430 (100)	159,328 (100)	157,831 (100)	543,733 (100)
State-run companies	—	—	—	—	—	—	10,210 (9.1)	19,814 (19.3)	26,918 (16.9)	21,602 (13.7)	78,544 14.4
Guangdong Province-run companies	—	—	—	—	—	—	1,368 (1.2)	3,106 (2.7)	5,152 (3.2)	2,580 (1.6)	12,206 (2.3)
City-run companies and others	—	—	—	—	—	—	36,140 (32.2)	40,424 (35.3)	74,587 (46.8)	46,264 (29.3)	197,415 (36.3)
Foreign-capital companies	—	—	—	—	—	—	64,426 (57.5)	51,090 (44.70)	52,671 (33.1)	87,385 (55.4)	255,572 (47.0)

Table 7-4 (continued)

Zhuhai	1980	1981	1982	1983	1984	1985	1986	1987	1988	1989	Total 1986–1989
Total exports	1,309.9 (100)	1,880.7 (100)	2,098.9 (100)	2,448.8 (100)	2,319 (100)	3,337.3 (100)	7,072 (100)	27,372 (100)	42,105 (100)	36,508 (100)	216,451.1 (100)
Foreign trade-specializing corporations	1,127.7 (86.0)	1,628.7 (86.6)	1,854.1 (88.3)	2,061.2 (84.2)	1,803 (77.7)	2,791.7 (83.7)	3,862 (56.6)	10,466 (38.2)	11,444 (27.2)	3,973 (10.9)	41,011.4 (32.4)
Local export and import corporations	—	—	—	—	—	—	1,452 (20.5)	13,767 (50.3)	24,118 (57.3)	19,414 (53.2)	58,751.0 (46.5)
Commissioned processing companies	182.2 (14.0)	252 (13.4)	244.8 (11.7)	387.6 (15.8)	516 (22.3)	545.6 (16.3)	729 (10.3)	949 (3.4)	1,395 (3.3)	1,974 (5.4)	7,175.2 (5.7)
SanjiGiyie*	—	—	—	—	—	—	1,029 (14.6)	2,190 (8.0)	5,148 (12.2)	11,147 (30.5)	19,514.0 (15.4)
Total imports	625 (100)	1,250 (100)	1,643 (100)	4,241 (100)	4,524 (100)	11,158 (100)	14,260 (100)	16,445 (100)	21,520 (100)	16,450 (100)	92,116 (100)
Foreign trade-specializing corporations	625 (100)	1,250 (100)	1,643 (100)	4,241 (100)	4,524 (100)	2,276 (20.4)	2,139 (15)	1,924 (11.7)	1,826 (8.5)	691 (4.2)	21,139 (22.9)
Local export and import corporations	—	—	—	—	—	8,882 (79.6)	6,055 (42.5)	8,738 (53.1)	13,232 (61.5)	8,872 (53.6)	45,779 (49.7)
SanjiGiyie	—	—	—	—	—	—	6,066 (42.5)	5,783 (35.2)	6,462 (16.0)	6,887 (41.9)	25,198 (27.4)

Sources: Zheng Tianlun and Chen Zhuohua, eds., 1990, pp. 254–55; interviews with the staffs of the Statistical Bureau of Shenzhen and Zhuhai Statistics Bureau, January 4–May 15, 1991.

Notes: ( ) represents the component ratio. *SanjiGiyie means foreign direct investment including merger, joint venture, and wholly foreign.

which indicates how much foreign-capital companies rely on imports of raw materials for production of exports (see Table 7-5). The import/export reliance ratio in Shenzhen decreased from 249% in 1986 to 86% in 1989 and in Zhuhai from 590% to 60%. In Shantou, the ratio decreased by 20% from 1984 to 1989. In Xiamen, it decreased from 619% in 1985 to 27% in 1989.

Foreign-capital companies have higher import/export reliance ratios than other ownership companies. This means that the procurement rate of accessories in the domestic market by foreign-capital companies is lower than that by other ownership companies. For example, in Shenzhen, the imports/exports reliance ratio of foreign-capital companies was 91.6% in 1989, while for state-run companies it was 68.2%, Guangdong Province-run companies 59.7%, and Shenzhen City-run companies 57.9%. This suggests that foreign-capital companies rely more on imports of raw and intermediate materials to produce a unit of the export product.

SUMMARY

The interindustrial relationship effects of foreign-capital companies are: (1) foreign-capital companies' import/export reliance ratio is higher than that of Chinese internal companies in the special economic zones, with the exception of Shantou; (2) the special economic zones can be arranged according to decreasing import/export reliance ratios as Xiamen, Shantou, Shenzhen, and Zhuhai; and (3) the overall import/export reliance ratios are gradually decreasing. This suggests that the procurement rate for raw and intermediate materials in the Chinese domestic market by foreign-capital companies is increasing.

However, one should take note of the sources of raw and intermediate materials for foreign-capital companies. According to my research, when foreign-capital companies purchase raw or intermediate materials in the Chinese domestic market, most are traded among the foreign-capital companies themselves. Accordingly, even though the materials are supplied by the domestic market, the purchase actually affects imports because the foreign-capital companies that sell the raw materials to other foreign-capital companies import the raw materials from overseas. The inter-foreign-capital company trade relationship is shown in Figure 7-1.

Furthermore, when the foreign-capital companies that sell the raw materials are located in other areas, the amount of imports is not revealed. Here are two cases.

Case 1: Company A, an electronics corporation which mainly manufactures color televisions, was established through mergers of Hong Kong, Chinese, and Korean firms. This company purchases accessories in the following manner: (1) it imports 60–70% of parts for products to be exported and procures the remainder in the Chinese domestic market; (2) for products to be sold in China, it imports 30–40% of parts and buys the remainder in the Chinese domestic market. In practice, however, more than 80% of the accessories procured in China are supplied by other foreign-capital companies in China. Purchases from wholly Chinese companies, mostly packaging materials (such as boxes and instruction manuals), make up only 20%.

Table 7-5
Reliance on Imports for Exports by Ownership Type

Shenzhen	1984	1985	1986	1987	1988	1989
State-run companies	—	—	0.76	0.87	0.61	0.68
Guangong Province-run companies	—	—	0.72	0.52	0.75	0.59
City-run companies and others	—	—	1.14	0.65	0.87	0.58
SanjiGiyie*	—	—	2.49	2.78	0.94	0.86
Zhuhai						
Foreign trade-specializing corporations	—	—	0.55	0.18	0.16	0.17
Local export and import corporations	—	—	4.1	0.63	0.59	0.46
SanjiGiyie	—	—	5.9	2.64	1.25	0.60
Shantou						
SanjiGiyie	2.96	0.77	0.73	0.63	0.83	0.69
Other	10.6	1.71	0.75	0.93	1.30	1.57
Xiamen						
Foreign trade-specializing corporations	—	0.10	0.02	0.03	0.05	0.03
Engineering export and import corporations	—	1.48	—	0.43	0.34	0.58
Province-run export and import corporationns	—	0.45	—	1.47	0.48	0.09
City-run export and import corporations	—	6.10	3.35	1.39	0.49	0.71
SanjiGiyie	—	6.19	2.98	0.96	1.07	0.27

Sources: Zheng Tianlun and Chen Zhuohua, eds., 1990, p. 254; interviews with the staffs of the Statistical Bureau of Shenzhen and Zhuhai Statistics Bureau, January 4–May 15, 1991; Shantou Special Economic Zone Yearbook, ed., 1984–1989; Xiamen Special Economic Zone Yearbook, ed., 1990, p. 324.

Notes: Reliance on imports for exports = imports ÷ exports. *SanjiGiyie means foreign direct investment including merger, joint venture, and wholly foreign.

Case 2: Company B, a Hong Kong firm, established two corporations in Shenzhen Special Economic Zone. One is Company C (a wholly foreign company) located in Shakou, and the other is Company D established with 50% investment by a Chinese corporation. Company D purchases 26% of its accessories for products to be exported from the domestic market, but most of the purchased accessories are from foreign-capital companies (including Company C) in China. If accessories in China are supplied in this manner, foreign-capital companies may not induce significant inter-industry relationship effects, although the importing of raw materials may be added value from assembling products.

EFFECTS OF INTERNATIONAL BALANCE OF PAYMENTS

Analyzing the effects of foreign capital inflows on the current account balance is very complex and carries many difficulties, because it is necessary to gain an understanding of export effects, import effects, import replacement effects, and the remittance of interest and profits. Furthermore, for a more accurate analysis, the increase in imports resulting from increased incomes further resulting from the introduction of foreign capital must also be considered. However, statistical data necessary for this analysis has not been published, and is treated here as x.

The effects on the international balance in the zones, excluding Hainan Province, are summarized below. As shown in Table 7-6, the international balance turned into a surplus for the most part around 1988–1989 (Shenzhen-1988, Zhuhai-1989,

Figure 7-1
Inter-Foreign-Capital Company Trade Relationship

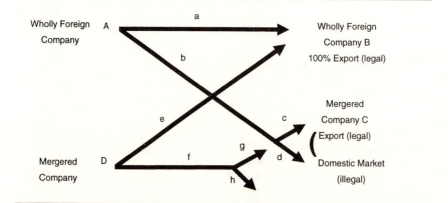

Note: For *a, b, c, e, f, g,* and *h,* there is no problem because the products made with accessories supplied by Companies A and D are exported. In addition, products made with accessories purchased from the mergered Company D can be sold in China. A problem occurs in the case of *d* when products made with accessories supplied by Company A are sold in China, because it is illegal for a foreign-capital company to sell its products in the Chinese domestic market. However, such illegal sales frequently occur. Company D wants to purchase accessories from Company A, even though it knows it is illegal, because the prices are lower than imports and it can save time and freight costs.

Shantou-1985, Xiamen-1989). This turning point differed according to the size of profit remittances. The international balance was in a deficit because imported raw materials and many products made with imported raw materials were sold in the Chinese domestic market instead of being exported. To examine this problem more accurately, however, the following two factors must be considered. First, the magnitude of imports of capital materials, including production machines, is not significant. Imports of capital materials into Shenzhen Special Economic Zone in 1988 formed 26.6% of all imports by foreign-capital companies. Second, because the proportion of raw materials used in the production of exports differs according to the item, it is hard to make generalizations. However, according to my research, the price of exported goods made by foreign-capital companies generally breaks down into 60% for raw materials, 20–30% for wages and overall expenses, and 10–20% for profits.

Accordingly, the calculation of the effects on the actual international balance of foreign-capital companies in the special economic zones with these two factors in mind is shown in Table 7-7.

The actual international balance for foreign-capital companies in three special economic zones, excluding Shantou, turned into a surplus in 1989. Until 1988, considerable amounts of raw or intermediate materials imported by foreign-capital companies were sold in the Chinese domestic market instead of being exported. The balance changed early in Shantou because 88% of investment by foreign-capital companies in Shantou was in the industrial sector, and Shantou has many wholly foreign companies that are obligated to export 100% of their products.

In summary, the size of foreign capital introduced to the special economic zones has not met expectations. The capital equipment ratio per worker at foreign-capital companies in the zones was higher than for Chinese companies, and the foreign-capital companies did not greatly expand employment (30% in Shenzhen, 15.8% in Zhuhai, 10.6% in Xiamen, and 0.8% in Hainan Province). Nor did foreign-capital companies greatly improve the industrial structure, because while they invested the most in the industrial sector, a lot of their investments went into real estate and services (64% of total city industrial production in Shenzhen, 36.0% in Zhuhai, 63.3% in Shantou, 48.35% in Xiamen, and 12.8% in Hainan Province). With respect to the effects on international balances, foreign-capital companies sold a great deal of raw materials and products in the Chinese domestic market up to 1989, legally or otherwise, and earned great profits. Considering all these factors, it is no exaggeration to say that foreign-capital companies in the special economic zones owe their success to China's strong protection.

Table 7-6
Changes in Effects on International Balance of Foreign-Capital Companies (unit: U.S.$10,000)

	1984	1985	1986	1987	1988	1989
Shenzhen						
Total exports	—	—	28,824	50,709	55,601	101,408
Total imports	—	—	64,426	51,090	52,671	87,385
Remittance of profits	—	—	x	x	x	x
Effects of international balance	—	—	-(38,602 + x)	-(381 + x)	2,930 - x	14,023 - x
Zhuhai						
Total exports	—	—	1,029	2,190	5,148	11,147
Total imports	—	—	6,066	5,783	6,462	6,734
Remittance of profits	—	—	x	x	x	x
Effects of international balance	—	—	-(5,037 + x)	-(3,593 + x)	-(1,314 + x)	4,413 - x
Shantou						
Total exports	286	809	1,719	4,596	7,740	12,270
Total imports	845	621	1,258	2,906	6,452	8,490
Remittance of profits	x	x	x	x	x	x
Effects of international balance	-(559 + x)	188 - x	461 - x	1,690 - x	1,288 - x	3,780 - x
Xiamen						
Total exports	—	1,817	1,516	4,184	8,428	18,176
Total imports	—	11,263	4,522	4,014	9,014	4,586
Remittance of profits	—	x	x	x	x	x
Effects of international balance	—	-(9,446 + x)	-(3,006 + x)	170 - x	-(586 + x)	13,590 - x

Source: Calculations based on Tables 7-3 and 7-4.

Note: x = data not available. Effects of international balance = exports - (imports + remittance of profits).

Table 7-7
Effects on Actual International Balance of Foreign-Capital Companies (unit: U.S.$10,000)

Shenzhen	1984	1985	1986	1987	1988	1989
Total exports	—	—	15,494	30,425	33,360	60,844
Total imports	—	—	51,540	40,872	42,136	48,675
Remittance of profits	—	—	x	x	x	x
Effects of international balance	—	—	-(36,046 + x)	-(10,447 + x)	-(8,776 + x)	12,169 - x
Zhuhai						
Total exports	—	—	617	1,314	3,088	6,688
Total imports	—	—	4,852	4,626	5,169	5,387
Remittance of profits	—	—	x	x	x	x
Effects of international balance	—	—	-(4,235 + x)	-(3,312 + x)	-(2,081 + x)	1,301 - x
Shantou						
Total exports	171	485	1,031	2,757	4,655	7,362
Total imports	676	496	754	2,324	5,161	6,792
Remittance of profits	x	x	x	x	x	x
Effects of international balance	-(505 + x)	-(11 + x)	277 - x	433 - x	-(517 + x)	570 - x
Xiamen						
Total exports	—	1,090	909	2,510	5,056	10,905
Total imports	—	9,010	3,617	3,211	7,211	3,210
Remittance of profits	—	x	x	x	x	x
Effects of international balance	—	-(7,920 + x)	-(2,708 + x)	-(701 + x)	-(2,155 + x)	7,695 - x

Source: Calculations based on Tables 7-3 and 7-4.

Note: x = data not available. Effects of international balance = exports - (imports + remittance of profits).

8

Investments by the Central, Provincial, and Municipal Governments

Clearly foreign capital was not the only factor in bringing about economic growth in the special zones. Investment by the central government, loans from the various financial agencies in China, investment by provincial and municipal governments, advantages derived from being a transit trade area, and geographical proximity to Hong Kong were also important factors.

INVESTMENTS BY THE CENTRAL, PROVINCIAL, AND MUNICIPAL GOVERNMENTS

The degree of investment by central, provincial, and municipal governments in industrial sectors in the special economic zones is uncertain. Unfortunately, the only data available is the amount of funds raised for investment in basic construction. Therefore, this index is used to analyze the amount of investment by the nation, province, and city. Data on the sources of funds invested in basic construction in each special economic zone from 1980 to 1989 are shown in Table 8-1. Basic construction investment in Shenzhen Special Economic Zone consisted of 37.3% corporate funds and financial investment by the municipal government, 21% foreign capital, the balance coming from other sources in China. The state invested in 34% of the total basic construction in Zhuhai. More than half of the funds for the basic construction investment in Shantou, Xiamen, and Hainan Provinces came from other Chinese sources.

Over time, in all five special economic zones, state funding was reduced and investment by municipal and corporate capital filled the gap. However, more than 50% of basic construction funding continues to come from other Chinese provinces and cities, even though ten years have passed since the special economic zones were established.

Table 8-1
Source of Funds for Investment in Basic Construction (unit: 10,000 yuan)

Shenzhen	1980	1981	1982	1983	1984	1985	1986	1987	1988	1989	Total 1980–1989
Total	11,294	26,508	58,673	83,642	147,369	260,108	184,759	204,702	338,319	432,370	1,738,744
Central government	2,697	2,007	4,303	4,319	2,086	4,285	4,957	2,724	2,699	1,118	31,265
Domestic financial agencies (loans)	697	3,062	19,491	31,167	59,118	48,389	25,635	35,818	53,289	49,839	326,505
Foreign capital	4,956	13,533	16,785	22,212	26,498	36,065	34,656	34,474	52,079	135,622	379,669
Municipal government (Shenzhen)	923	3,192	5,863	7,399	20,727	44,047	33,928	26,632	37,392	57,904	235,007
Funds of department of province/city (except for Shenzhen)	1,209	2,430	5,560	6,603	14,991	37,842	30,233	25,048	41,389	4,786	170,091
Funds of private companies in Shenzhen	812	1,994	4,779	8,272	20,533	68,174	28,376	64,950	87,012	129,036	413,985
Internal corporations	—	290	1,892	3,383	806	17,376	17,672	—	13,392	—	—
Other	—	—	—	287	2,580	4,397	9,649	18,278	51,249	45,013	186,264

Table 8-1 (continued)

Zhuhai	1980	1981	1982	1983	1984	1985	1986	1987	1988	1989	Total 1980–1989
Total	4,522	8,456	11,722	13,654	36,212	81,618	72,685	79,001	94,318	87,679	492,992
Central government	1,533	909	1,292	1,350	2,215	1,334	1,325	3,204	4,229	—	—
Domestic financial agencies (loans)	43	1,933	2,968	3,616	16,448	22,511	20,930	24,499	25,241	—	—
Foreign capital	405	633	1,616	3,081	6,415	21,404	21,697	11,437	15,757	—	—
Funds of private companies	2,261	4,983	5,846	5,486	10,382	34,186	24,252	36,897	44,318	—	—
Other	—	—	—	121	752	2,185	4,481	2,964	4,773	—	—
Shantou											
Total	—	—	—	—	4,537	11,007	12,687	19,821	41,613	89,664	—
Central government	—	—	—	—	—	—	494	1,149	1,120	2,763	—
Domestic financial agencies (loans)	—	—	—	—	2,633	6,390	5,143	6,807	11,992	32,965	—
Foreign capital	—	—	—	—	1,304	1,286	3,024	7,637	13,558	26,809	—
Funds of private companies	—	—	—	—	—	2,024	2,184	3,594	14,225	22,027	—
Financial investment	—	—	—	—	600	1,307	1,842	632	718	5,099	—

Table 8-1 (continued)

Xiamen	1980	1981	1982	1983	1984	1985	1986	1987	1988	1989	Total 1980–1989
Total	—	—	—	—	—	—	—	—	98,463	129,972	—
Central government	—	—	—	—	—	—	—	—	11,158	8,297	—
Domestic financial agencies (loans)	—	—	—	—	—	—	—	—	33,985	36,364	—
Foreign capital	—	—	—	—	—	—	—	—	5,763	13,616	—
Funds of private companies	—	—	—	—	—	—	—	—	25,322	43,048	—
Other	—	—	—	—	—	—	—	—	22,235	28,017	—
Hainan Province											
Total	34,228	34,170	36,024	32,705	58,027	100,557	100,376	76,663	18,162	199,754	780,666
Central government	20,421	13,350	13,141	14,051	19,196	24,303	24,038	22,125	22,826	22,112	195,563
Domestic financial agencies (loans)	871	2,509	4,632	8,684	14,574	24,184	21,155	13,118	26,004	43,318	159,049
Foreign capital	159	524	791	37	3,648	7,885	9,521	6,687	7,291	29,480	66,023
Funds of private companies	12,777	17,187	17,460	9,807	18,152	38,803	42,987	32,742	47,627	86,422	323,964
Other	—	—	—	126	2,457	5,382	2,675	1,991	4,414	18,422	35,467

Source: Shenzhen Special Economic Zone Yearbook, ed., 1985–1990; interviews with the staffs of the Statistical Bureau of Shenzhen and Zhuhai Statistics Bureau, January 4–May 15, 1991; Shantou Special Economic Zone Yearbook, ed., 1984–1989; Xiamen Special Economic Zone Yearbook, ed., 1990; Statistical Bureau of Hainan, 1990, p. 79.

INVESTMENTS BY INTERNAL COMPANIES IN THE SPECIAL ECONOMIC ZONES

The entry of internal companies into the zones was one of the most important factors in sustaining their economic progress. These corporations entered from other Chinese provinces and cities, having funding and/or business connections with corporations in areas outside the zones. It must be noted that the central government, with its belief that "the nation supports the special zones and special zones work for the nation," played a significant role in encouraging the entry of internal companies into the special zones.

Shenzhen Special Economic Zone

By the end of 1989, 3,900 internal companies had entered Shenzhen Special Economic Zone[39] from twenty-eight provinces, cities under the direct control of the government, and independent districts (excluding the Xi Zang independent district); as well as about 40 departments, bureaus, and corporations from the central government. They had total negotiated investments of 9.5 billion yuan, with actual investments of 3.6 billion yuan. These companies made up one-third of all corporations in the city. Of these firms, 58.9% were in the industrial sector. The major sectors for domestic corporations included machinery, 23.6%; light industries, 17%; electronics, 15.9%; petroleum and chemicals, 9.8%; services, 8.6%; textiles, 5.9%; clothing, 5.7%; and food products, 3.9%. The total industrial production by domestic companies in 1989 was worth 3.9 billion yuan, or 36% of total industrial production in the city. Domestic companies also produced 35% ($740 million) of total exports in the city.[40]

Other Special Economic Zones

By the end of 1983, only 6 internal companies had entered Zhuhai from central area departments, the twenty-eight provinces, cities under the direct control of the government, and independent districts, but this figure increased to 883 by the end of 1989, or one-third of all corporations in the zone. Of these, 450 were internal independent corporations. Negotiated investments by these internal corporations amounted to 1.8 billion yuan. In 1988, total industrial production by internal corporations was worth 550 million yuan, or 20% of all industrial production in the city. These internal corporations earned profits of 200 million yuan, 100 million of which was paid to the city government as taxes. Exports from these internal corporations brought in 70% of total foreign currency earned in the city.

From 1986 to 1988, 339 internal corporations entered Shantou from each department of the central area and twenty-eight provinces/cities under the direct control of the government/independent districts, with negotiated investments worth 242.4 million yuan and actual investments of 134.93 million yuan. Internal corporations were responsible for 25.5% of total industrial production in the city from 1984 to 1989.[41] Over 80% of the 367 internal companies in Shantou were in the industrial and business sectors as of June 1988. Among these companies, many had a three-part investment structure (Chinese-Chinese-Foreign). In 1989, 43 companies were of this investment type, with an actual investment of $11.73 million.

City statistical data on internal corporations in Xiamen is unavailable. In 1989, there were 1,020 internal corporations in Xiamen, with total investment worth 760 million yuan. In addition, 100 local government liaisons were established. Exports by internal corporations in 1989 were worth $125 million, recording a growth rate of 19.0% from the previous year. This amounted to 20% of the total export volume in the city.[42]

OTHER FACTORS

Indirect factors that made possible the economic development in the special economic zones include geographical proximity to Hong Kong and advantages gained from being a transit trade area connecting Hong Kong and mainland China. Shenzhen's geographical proximity to Hong Kong attracted 28.17 million visitors from Hong Kong and Macao in 1988. A direct train running between Guangzou and Jiulong three times daily carries 10 million tourists from Hong Kong and Macao every year. The entry of foreign tourists to Shenzhen dramatically increased the demand for housing facilities, restaurants, shopping malls, and recreational facilities. Foreign currency earned from these tourists over the past ten years exceeded 2.18 billion yuan (see Table 8-2).

After establishment as a special economic zone, Zhuhai developed a close economic relationship with Hong Kong and Macao. At the same time many foreign tourists including overseas Chinese visited Zhuhai. About 245,000 foreign tourists and overseas Chinese brought in 233.03 million yuan worth of foreign currency in 1989. This was a 940% increase in the number of tourists, and a 15,754% increase in foreign currency earnings compared to 1980 (26,100 foreign tourists and foreign currency earnings of 1.48 million yuan), before the special economic zone was established.

A total of 135,700 tourists visited Shantou between 1981 and 1989. Foreign currency earned from these tourists equaled 136.84 million yuan. In 1989 alone, this figure amounted to 50.45 million yuan, or an improvement of 45% from the previous year. A total of 138,505 foreign tourists visited Xiamen in 1989, bringing with them foreign currency earnings of 113.52 million yuan. This was an increase of 400% from over 29.06 million yuan earned in 1984. From 1984 to 1989, tourist income amounted to 360.75 million yuan.[43] A total of 110,473 foreign tourists visited Hainan Province in 1989, and 77.8% of these tourists were from Hong Kong, Macao, or Taiwan. Tourism income from these foreign tourists amounted to 44.3 million yuan.[44]

A by-product of the special economic zones' proximity to Hong Kong is smuggling. Smuggled items are transported by sea in great quantity into the zones, escaping the surveillance of coast guards. Foreigners, including those from Hong Kong, who come to visit the zones daily by the thousands (100,000 during holidays) provide another channel for smuggling. Huge bundles of duty-free items (such as liquor, tobacco, clothing, and electric home appliances) are hand-carried into the zones by foreigners, which are then sold in private stores to customers who come from all parts of the country.

With some variations over time, about 20% (20.4% in exports and 17% in imports) of total exports, on average, was produced by trade corporations belonging to either the central government or Guangdong Province.[45] Tens of thousands of people from all parts of China visit Shenzhen every day to shop. Accordingly, most of the goods imported by the city-run trade corporations are consumed by customers from other parts of China, not by the residents of Shenzhen. These customers buy commodities in Shenzhen and resell them at higher prices in internal areas. According to my research, many private stores sell to such customers. Purchase of electronic products by internal customers in Shenzhen, are legally limited to one item per customer. In addition, each purchased product must be accompanied by a receipt. However, these laws are often ignored. Internal customers often buy several miniature products, such as cameras and tape recorders, which can be easily concealed, and rarely encounter problems when they leave Shenzhen. (Shenzhen's exports and imports from 1986 to 1989 are provided in Table 7-2). In Zhuhai from 1986 to 1989, 35.4% of exports was processed through the state-run trade corporation. However, the actual percentage of the total trade is considered to be higher, as in Shenzhen. In Xiamen, the volume of trade by monopoly in 1988 was $38.33 million, forming 4.3% of total exports. This increased to $70.53 million in 1989, amounting to 7.2% of the total export volume.[46]

Accurate statistical data on special economic zones as transit trade areas is not available. Nonetheless, this is a very important factor in understanding the nature of special economic zones and remains an area to be studied.

Table 8-2
Foreign Tourists and Foreign-Capital Earnings (unit: 10,000 persons, 10,000 yuan, foreign currency convertible note)

Shenzhen	1980	1981	1982	1983	1984	1985	1986	1987	1988	1989	Avg. annual growth rate (%)
Number of tourists	0.14	0.48	1.91	42.67	55.79	77.85	73.53	84.65	103.94	100.58	107.7
Foreigners	0.07	0.10	0.09	0.38	4.16	3.49	2.63	4.11	4.47	5.78	63.3
Overseas Chinese	—	—	0.01	0.23	0.20	0.15	0.30	0.30	0.56	0.60	—
Tourists from Hong Kong, Macao, and Taiwan	0.07	0.38	1.81	42.06	51.43	74.21	70.60	80.24	98.87	94.24	122.7
Foreign currency earnings from tourists	134	340	545	12,687	16,139	21,351	31,031	40,532	47,731	47,658	92.1
Income from products	69	245	361	11,361	12,659	14,124	21,850	30,220	32,564	27,906	94.8
Income from consumption of products	—	—	—	9,837	10,912	10,669	17,439	24,782	25,755	19,609	—
Income from consumption of food	—	—	—	1,524	1,747	3,455	4,411	5,438	6,809	8,297	—
Income from labor	65	95	184	1,326	3,480	7,227	9,181	10,312	15,167	19,752	88.7

Table 8-2 (continued)

Zhuhai	1980	1981	1982	1983	1984	1985	1986	1987	1988	1989	Avg. annual growth rate (%)
Number of tourists	2.61	4.80	6.40	13.90	28.96	29.80	34.30	40.30	38.30	24.50	—
Foreigners	1.10	1.60	3.54	5.82	7.82	6.36	1.52	1.20	0.60	0.70	—
Overseas Chinese	0.01	0.01	0.03	0.10	0.30	0.37	0.05	0.10	0.03	0.02	—
Tourists from Hong Kong, Macao, and Taiwan	1.50	3.19	2.83	7.98	20.84	23.07	32.73	39.00	37.67	23.78	—
Foreign currency earnings from tourists	148	620	1,377	5,193	25,405	13,520	21,975	23,524	32,262	23,303	—
Shantou											
Number of tourists	—	—	—	—	1.2	1.3	1.1	3.5	3.3	2.5	—
Foreigners and overseas Chinese	—	—	—	—	0.3	0.5	0.7	2.0	1.6	1.3	—
Foreign currency earnings from tourists	—	—	—	—	—	536	1,308	2,953	3,482	5,045.3	—

Sources: Shenzhen Special Economic Zone Yearbook, ed., 1985–1990; interviews with the staffs of the Statistical Bureau of Shenzhen and Zhuhai Statistics Bureau, January 4–May 15, 1991; Lin Wuru, ed., 1990, p. 377; Shantou Special Economic Zone Yearbook, ed., 1984–1989.

PART III

Corporate Structure and Transfer of Technology and Managerial Techniques

9

Supply of Labor

In general, industrial structure comprises agriculture, industry, commerce, and services. Analysis here centers on corporate industrial structure, because the industrial sector occupies an absolute proportion in terms of corporate structures in the special economic zones.[1] One particular problem that must be analyzed is whether the industry-centered corporate structure introduced with the establishment of the zones was able to bring about the transfer of advanced technology and managerial techniques as expected. Many theories deny the effectiveness of transfer of technology and management techniques, taking into consideration the negative effects caused by the entry of foreign-capital companies into developing countries. They include: double-structured economy, interruption of domestic industrial development, unequal income distribution, weakening of national technical development efforts, unbalanced distribution of resources, decline in entrepreneurship, and political as well as economic subordination. Unfortunately, these problems are very difficult to quantify. Nevertheless, they are approached from five perspectives: supply of labor, fostering of manpower, production management, forward and reverse related effects, and business achievements, that is, the transfer is examined by analyzing overall corporate production activities, working conditions, the effects of these conditions on laborers, corporate business achievements, and the problems that have been encountered. The analysis centers on Shenzhen Special Economic Zone, because the number of corporations in Shenzhen is the highest, and the structure of these corporations is similar to that of corporations in the other zones. My research found no big difference in corporate structures among the five special economic zones. Differences are noted whenever necessary.

INTRODUCTION TO SUBJECT COMPANIES

Various types of corporations, including foreign-capital firms, exist in the special economic zones. The analysis of the subject companies is based on the classifications provided in Figure 9-1, and an outline of the subject companies is provided in Table 9-1.

Types of Business Entry by Foreign Companies

It was previously noted that a company in a special economic zone that exports 100% of its products is classified as having 100% independent ownership, while a company that wants to sell its products in the Chinese domestic market is classified as having mergered ownership. However, this is not necessarily true in all cases. Many mergered companies export 100% of their products. The main examples are Companies E, M, and K.

When a company considers entering China, the choice between 100% independent ownership or mergered ownership is closely related not only to the issue of exporting versus domestic sales but also to the issue of business management efficiency. For example, Company M in Shantou exports 100% of its products, but it has mergered ownership, with 90% of its capital from Japan and 10% from China. Since businesses with 100% foreign ownership can run into a lot of friction in China, many foreign firms like Company M opt for 10% Chinese capital and let the Chinese partner take care of such problems.

Many Korean companies that entered the special zones did so by either mergered ownership with a Chinese company or, in the case of 100% foreign capital, by

Figure 9-1
Classification of Subject Companies

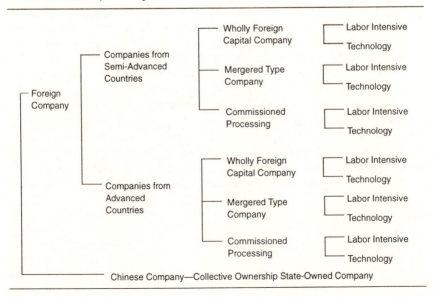

Chinese Company—Collective Ownership State-Owned Company

Table 9-1
Outline of Subject Companies

	Companies from semi-advanced countries					
	Wholly foreign-capital companies				Mergered companies	
	Labor intensive			Technology intensive	Labor intensive	Technology intensive
Company	A	B	C	D	E	F
Location	Shenzhen	Zhuhai	Xiamen	Shenzhen	Shenzhen	Shenzhen
Establishment date	October 1988	April 1990	January 1989	February 1989	August 1989	May 1984
Investment	Hong Kong: 100%	Korea: 54.55% Hong Kong: 45.45%	Korea: 100%	Korea: 100%	Korea: 50% China: 50%	Korea: 20% Hong Kong: 20% China: 60%
Purpose	Low wages; close to Hong Kong	Low wages; trade expansion with China; Korean government's policy on northern areas	Low wages; future market opening; raw materials supplier	Low wages	Future market opening; low wages; close to Hong Kong	Future market opening; low wages; most open city in China
Capital	H.K.$12 million	U.S.$2.01 million	U.S.$400,000	—	U.S.$145,000	U.S.$6 million
Size (unit: m²)	3,000	6,880	5,000	2,000	880	2,000
Items produced	Wigs	Dolls	Tents	Computer parts	Bags	Televisions

Table 9-1 (continued)

	Companies from advanced countries					
	Commissioned processing company	Wholly foreign-capital companies			Mergered companies	
	Labor intensive	Labor intensive	Technology intensive		Labor intensive	Technology intensive
Company	G	H	I	J	K	L
Location	Shenzhen	Shenzhen	Shenzhen	Zhuhai	Shenzhen	Shenzhen
Establishment date	December 1987	April 1988	March 1989	January 1990	March 1990	July 1984
Investment	China: land Hong Kong: machinery, capital	Japan: 100%	Japan: 100%	Japan: 100%	U.S.: 50% China: 30% Hong Kong: 20%	Japan: 50% China: 50%
Purpose	Low wages; sufficient labor; GSP advantage	Low wages; sufficient labor; close to Hong Kong	Tax advantage; future market opening	Low wages; sufficient labor; contribution to transfer of technology to China; employment expansion	Low wages; market opening	Market opening
Capital	U.S.$1 million	13 million yen	H.K.$104 million	U.S.$20 million	U.S.$1 million	U.S.$10 million
Size (unit: m^2)	8,600	Factory (4-story building), dormitory (6-story building)	42,000	1,800	2 6-story buildings	4-story building
Items produced	Dolls	Dolls	Calculators, motors, audio speakers	Camera lenses	Dolls	Televisions, tape recorders, cabinets

Table 9-1 (continued)

	Companies from advanced countries			Chinese companies		
	Mergered company	Commissioned processing companies		State-owned companies		Collective ownership company
	Technology intensive	Labor intensive	Technology intensive	Labor intensive	Technology intensive	Labor intensive
Company	M	N	O	P	Q	R
Location	Shantou	Shenzhen	Shenzhen	Shenzhen	Shenzhen	Shenzhen
Establishment date	February 1988	July 1984	November 1989	December 1987	March 1982	August 1989
Investment	Japan: 90% China: 10%	China: building, land Japan: machinery, capital	China: building, land Japan: machinery, capital	China: 100%	China: 100%	China: 100%
Purpose	Low wages; sufficient labor; future market opening	Sufficient labor; low wages; tax benefits; close to Hong Kong	Low wages; lenient pollution regulations; request from major customer*	—	—	Export increase; introduction of advanced technology; tax benefits; maintained basic construction; easy business management**
Capital	U.S.$100 million	10 million yen	50 million yen	2.22 million yuan	10 million yuan	1 million yuan
Size (unit: m²)	6,600	4,215	3,300	3,000	10,000	880
Items produced	Various coils for domestic electric appliances	Wallets, handbags	Printers and printer cables, final controlling elements for computers	Dolls	Acoustic equipment	Women's blouses

Source: Interviews with the managers of each company, January 4–May 15, 1991. To protect privacy, companies are listed A–R.

Notes: *The Japanese Electric Company, this company's largest customer, requested that it extend its business to China. Originally, the Japanese company planned to enter China, but the negative political climate prevented this plan; therefore, it requested that company O enter China and produce its products there. **Because most laborers in Shenzhen are temporary, it is always possible to fire them. In addition, companies within the Shenzhen Economic Zone are not responsible for employees' living conditions as are companies in the internal areas. Thus, it is much easier to conduct business in Shenzhen than in the internal areas.

mergered ownership with a Hong Kong company. This is because it was very risky for a wholly Korean-capital company to enter China before the establishment of official diplomatic relations between the two countries. (This research was conducted before such relations were established.) For example, Company E produces bags as a mergered company with 50% Chinese capital and 50% Korean capital. Before entering China, it contracted about $50,000 of production to a Chinese company for six months to test the feasibility of conducting business in China. Subsequently, it decided to extend its business in China. Although this company exports 100% of its products, it decided to become a mergered company because of potential problems during production in China, and because of political instability resulting from the lack of formal diplomatic relations between Korea and China.

However, there were Korean companies that entered China as wholly foreign-capital companies despite the political instability. For example, Company C produces tents in Xiamen as a wholly Korean-capital company. Before entering Xiamen, this company provided academic scholarships for local residents to bolster its local image. It continues to provide scholarships of about 30,000–40,000 yuan to the No. 6 Xiamen Middle School and Xiamen University. After establishing good public relations with residents and the local government through this scholarship system, the company began consultations with the Xiamen municipal government about doing business in Xiamen. The Xiamen municipal government welcomed the proposal and formally committed itself to active cooperation with the Korean company. The scholarship system was continued after Company C's entry into the city, and the No. 6 Xiamen Middle School chose Company C as an on-the-job training school and sends its senior students there to train before graduation. Students who excel can continue to work at the company after graduation. This company also hires outstanding graduates of Xiamen University as manager trainees.

However, few Korean companies enter China as wholly foreign-capital companies using this type of community contribution. Most companies opt for mergered ownership with Chinese or Hong Kong companies.

Companies entering China as a mergered company with a Hong Kong partner often experience friction in the business relationship. Company A originally entered China as a mergered company with 50% Korean capital and 50% Hong Kong capital, but the Hong Kong partner bought out the Korean ownership and now operates the company as a wholly Hong Kong-capital company. The original plan had been drawn up under the original company presidents, who maintained a friendly relationship. However, friction increased after the sons of the original presidents took over management. This ultimately led to the takeover by the Hong Kong partner. A Hong Kong company spokesperson explains, "The Korean partner had a factory of about 100 employees in Korea. Even though the Korean customers' orders were limited, the Korean partner emphasized the importance of its company in Korea over the interests of the company in China. Therefore, we had to take over the Korean capital."[2]

The causes of the friction are plain, but it is hard to judge which side was right. Many Korea–Hong Kong mergered companies in the special economic zones experience this kind of friction. Companies B in Zhuhai and G in Shenzhen experienced similar problems. The Korean company G first entered China in the form of a merger with a Hong Kong company. Company G plans to take over its Hong Kong partner in the near future, however, because of constant friction between the two firms. Founded in 1987, the company was operated by the Hong Kong partner for the first two years, during which it experienced continuous deficits. It may be reasoned that this was because the company was in its beginning stages. However, it is argued that the problem lay in the faulty business management of the Hong Kong company. According to Company G's Korean manager, the Hong Kong company was not thorough in hiring employees, employing inexperienced sewing machine operators when experienced operators were necessary, and rarely offering training programs for its employees. In addition, employees' working conditions were totally neglected. About 400 sewing machines were placed on the same floor of the building, and labor productivity could not help but decline considerably during the hot summer months. Because of the Hong Kong firm's unsatisfactory management style, the Korean partner had to participate directly in the management of the company. (There are no more Hong Kong managers now.) Company G currently recruits only experienced machine operators. It places laborers from the same hometown in the same working unit. This strategy is designed to increase labor productivity by stimulating camaraderie among the workers. Working conditions have improved. The Korean manager claims that productivity has speedily increased due to improved management.

However, Korean companies are not the only ones experiencing friction in relationships with Hong Kong companies. Company H started as a mergered company with 50% Japanese capital and 50% Hong Kong capital. However, the Japanese partner took over the Hong Kong half, and the company is now a wholly Japanese-capital company. The Japanese company president explained that "the Hong Kong company had a short-term vision about its investment. It wanted returns on its investment as soon as possible. However, our Japanese company invested in China with a somewhat longer-term vision. Thus, there was a great deal of friction over business management." This kind of incompatibility is also found in the Japanese companies I and N.

Background to the Entry of Foreign Companies

Foreign companies do not necessarily extend their businesses into China for purely economic reasons (low wages, sufficient labor supply, and market opening). Sentiments concerning family and race are also a major reason for the entry of foreign companies. In the case of Company A, its Hong Kong president was originally from Shanghai, and most of his relatives still resided there. He extended his business into China because he felt that he could entrust management of the company, including labor management, to his relatives and thus financially support them through his company in China. Korean company B extended its business into China to financially support ethnic Koreans living in China through jobs, a move based on racial sentiments. Other examples of familial and racial motivations for extending business into China can be found in Company J, whose president has a special affection for China because he was born there, and Company G, which plans to hire as many Korean-Chinese people as possible.

Selection of Location for Business Extension

Geographical proximity to Hong Kong is one of the biggest advantages that Shenzhen offers to foreigners seeking to do business in the special economic zones. Shenzhen is a convenient location for suppliers, since delivery time to and from Hong Kong is low. When raw materials are urgently needed, they can be purchased in Hong Kong. In addition, Shenzhen has many more skilled laborers and managers than other areas and is convenient for foreigners because it is the largest city among the special economic zones. Company O explains, "We chose a convenient place for Japanese people to live because they would be transferring technology for some time in that area. When we are far from Hong Kong, there can be many difficulties for us as foreigners. Therefore, we chose Shenzhen, which is close to Hong Kong, and lets us visit Hong Kong whenever necessary."

Foreign companies have their own reasons for extending their business into other special economic zones. For example, Zhuhai has the advantage of good environment. Company B explains why it chose to establish itself in Zhuhai: "Shenzhen is convenient for bringing in and taking out raw materials, but it has bad environmental conditions and a serious pollution problem. Zhuhai has a better environment than Shenzhen. Although it is less convenient for exports and imports than Shenzhen, this does not pose that great a problem." Company J explained that "we finally chose Zhuhai after inspecting five areas in Shanghai, Xiamen, Beijing, Dalian, and Zhuhai over twenty days. All the locations in China had a high population density. However, Zhuhai was different. It was attractive from the perspective of living environment, which is an important consideration since technicians from our country have to live in China until the technology transfer is completed."

Another important motive for foreign companies in moving to Zhuhai and other areas was avoiding competition from other companies in their own country. For example, Company C said that "by entering Xiamen, we were able to avoid competition from other Korean companies." Company M had the same motive for entering Shantou. Each city's promotional activities to entice foreign-capital companies are also important factors for the entry of foreign-capital companies (Companies B, C, G, Z, and M).

SUPPLY OF LABOR

With respect to the supply of labor in the special economic zones, the following features are shared by the subject companies (see Table 9-2).

Age

The average age of all employees was twenty, regardless of investment type, or whether the companies were foreign or Chinese. The average age of employees in Company J in Zhuhai (twenty-six) and Company L in Shenzhen (twenty-eight) was exceptionally high relative to other companies. Company J, a Japanese firm, manufactures cameras. It hired college graduates, especially professionals from across China,

Table 9-2
Employment of Labor in Each Company

	A	B	C	D	E	F
No. of employees	520	150	350	462	80	640
Sex Female	70%	70%	71%	90%	81%	70%
Male	30%	30%	29%	10%	19%	30%
No. of clerks	20	6	10	6	4	90
Average age	21	19–21	22.6	20	19–20	19–22
Education					(number of persons)	
Elementary	80%	25%	20%	20%	2	
Middle	15%	60%	40%	70%	67	40%
High		14%	30%			50%
High school & higher	5%			10%	10	
2-year college						
4-year college		1%	10%			10%
Hometown	Guangdong: 50% Others: 50%	Guangdong; 40%; Liaoling: 20%; Hunan: 10%; Anhui: 10%; Sichuan: 10%; Jiangsi: 10%	Most from rural areas near Xiamen except 20 Korean-Chinese	Guangdong: 60% Others: 40%	(number of persons) Guangdong: 71; Heilongjian: 5; Henan: 2; Hunan: 1; Jiangsi: 1	Laborers—Guangdong: 90%; Others: 10% Managers— Guangdong: 10%; Others: 90%
Recruiting method	Newspapers; posters; friend's introduction; experience not considered, but preferred for managers	Direct hiring of people seeking jobs; indirect hiring through city Department of Labor	Newspapers; posters; friend's introduction	Newspapers; posters; friend's introduction; experience preferred for managers	Newspapers; posters; friend's introduction; experience required for sewing machine operators and managers	40% from newspapers; posters; friend's introduction; 60% from indirect hiring through city Department of Labor
Employment type						
Fixed		15%	5%	5%		20%
Temporary	100%, 2-year contract	85%, 1-year contract	90%, 1-year contract	95%, 1-year contract	100%, renew every year after 3-year contract	80%, renew every year after 2-year contract

Table 9-2 (continued)

	G	H	I	J	K	L
No. of employees	904	850	3,440	600	296	1,591
Sex Female	90%	88%	83%	65%	85%	48%
Male	10%	12%	17%	35%	15%	52%
No. of clerks	20	15	236	—	10	128
Average age	—	18–23	21.7	18	18–22	27–28
Education						
Elementary	20%	10%	25%		65%	4%
Middle	50%	85%			30%	30%
High			70%	85%		40%
High school & higher	30%	5%			5%	
2-year college						
4-year college			5%	15%		26%
Hometown	(number of persons) Guangdong: 400 Hunan: 200 Others: 304	Hunan: 50% Fujian: 25% Guangdong: 25%	Guangdong: 90% Others: 10%	Guangdong: 85% Others: 15%	(number of persons) Guangdong: 212 Others: 84	Guangdong: 80% Others: 20%
Recruiting method	Primarily hiring through public corporations' management council; sometimes direct hiring	Laborers: newspapers; posters; friend's introduction; sewing machine operators up to 23 years old Managers: newspapers; posters; friend's introduction	Hiring through city's Department of Labor; over 18 years old, vision over 1.0, height over 155cm, free use of hands and legs	Laborers: high school teachers' recommendations Managers: newspapers	Newspapers; posters; friend's introduction	Newspapers; posters; friend's introduction
Employment type	(number of persons)				(number of persons)	(number of persons)
Fixed	3	15%	25%	70%	4	637
Temporary	901, 1-year contract	85%, 1-year contract	75%: 25%, 3-year contract; 50%, 1-year contract	30%, renew contract every year after 5-year contract	292, 1-year contract	954: 50%, 1-year contract

Table 9-2 (continued)

	M	N	O	P	Q	R
No. of employees	1,050	800	390	220	380	153
Sex Female	98%	75%	97%	92%	75%	80%
Male	2%	25%	3%	8%	25%	20%
No. of clerks	—	19	—	—	—	—
Average age	20.5	20	19	20	22	20
Education			(number of persons)			
Elementary	—	50%	327	—	—	—
Middle	—	30%	—	—	—	—
High	—	—	10	—	—	—
High school & higher	—	20%	10	—	—	—
2-year college	—	—	10	—	—	—
4-year college	—	—	10	—	—	—
Hometown	—	(number of persons) Guangdong: 787 Others: 15	Guangdong: 50% Others: 50%	Guangdong: 40% Others: 60%	Guangdong: 98% Others: 2%	Others: 100%
Recruiting method	Newspapers; posters; friend's introduction	Hiring through city's Department of Labor	Laborers: private introduction College graduates: newspapers	Newspapers; posters; friend's introduction; indirect hiring through city's Department of Labor	Hiring through city's Department of Labor	Hiring through city's Department of Labor and Shanxi provincial government
Employment type		(number of persons)				
Fixed	98%	4		5%	33%	
Temporary	2%	797, 1-year contract	100%, 1-year contract	95%, 3-year contract	67%, 1-year contract	100%, 1-year contract

Source: Interviews with the managers of each company, January 4–May 15, 1991. To protect privacy, companies are listed A–R.

because the production of cameras requires a relatively high level of education and high-level management skills compared to other manufacturing fields (e.g., textiles). In addition, Company J emphasized not only technical, but also managerial skills in hiring employees for management. Accordingly, personal leadership, experience, and age were important qualifications. A field manager explained that not only management abilities, but also age, is very important in junior management employees. This is considered to be deeply related to the Japanese management system that emphasizes seniority over ability. At Company L, a mergered company, the average age of employees in the manufacturing department (of tape recorders) is also high because its current partner was once a commissioned processor of radios, and most of its employees have been working there for more than ten years. However, the TV manufacturing department in Company L is relatively new, so the average age of its employees is only twenty-two to twenty-three.

With the exception of these two cases, the average age of laborers is low. There are two main reasons. First, most companies entering the special economic zones are assembly factories which do not require skilled labor. Therefore, hiring young unskilled people is advantageous in terms of labor costs. Second, because most workers are hired on a temporary basis, they face many restrictions in working in the special economic zones for an extended period. On average, most workers return to their hometown after working two to three years. It is practically impossible for them to come back to the special economic zones after marriage.

Gender

With some differences according to the company, female laborers tend to outnumber males. As previously mentioned, most companies in the special economic zones are assembly factories. Women are preferred over men in such companies because it is believed they are able to endure tedious and difficult assembly-line work better than men.

These young women have many worries. Their biggest worry concerns marriage. Because they do not have urban household registers, they must eventually go back home. (They may legally stay for unlimited periods of time, however, if they are willing to endure the disadvantages temporary laborers face: distribution of food, unstable job and housing arrangements, absence of education and welfare facilities.) However, they rarely return to their hometown because they become accustomed to the city life that the special economic zones offer. To be able to live permanently in the special economic zone, they must marry men who have household registers in the zone. However, marriage between a woman having a rural household register and a man having an urban household register is rare because children automatically become registered to the mother's rural address when such a couple gets married. Because the Chinese take the location of the household register very seriously, this system prevents many such marriages from taking place. This restrictive system drives many young female laborers to a life of pleasure and consumption. This problem surrounding marriage is one of the biggest social problems in the special economic zones.

Education

The level of worker education is higher in technology-intensive companies than in labor-intensive companies because although such industries (such as electronics) tend to have simple assembly procedures, some foreign language ability is necessary in learning instructions and recognizing the names of parts. Also, the processes are more complicated than in, say, doll manufacturing. Accordingly, these factors are considered when hiring laborers and companies set educational qualification at the middle school level. Electronics manufacturing companies researched here explained that they emphasize education as a company policy, although they cannot openly discuss such matters because educational qualifications are regarded as discriminatory.

Furthermore, there is a disparity between companies located in the special economic zones and those located outside. A mere 2.5% of workers in Company E, located in a special economic zone, have only elementary school level education whereas 80% of workers in Company A, located outside the special economic zone, are not educated beyond elementary school. Companies E and A are both labor-intensive companies. The reason for this gap is the closely related hiring method and the attitudes of the labor service companies in hiring laborers. Company A is outside the zones, so it can recruit workers freely. Workers cannot enter the zones freely, but they can freely approach the areas surrounding them. On the other hand, Company E is in a special economic zone and must hire workers through the city's Labor Service Company which gives entry priority to highly educated people. According to Professor Chen Zhuohua, of the Department of Special Economic Zones Studies at Shenzhen University, the city's Department of Labor tests the quality of laborers who enter the zone. Therefore, although people may be from the same rural areas, those who enter the zones tend to be more educated. Accordingly, their wages are higher. In contrast, laborers working outside the zone have lower educational levels and lower wages.

Even among the special economic zones, there are differences in the level of worker education. For example, Companies A and C are both wholly foreign-owned labor-intensive companies located in special economic zones. Company A in Shenzhen hires workers from rural areas across China, centered in Guangdong Province. It cannot hire all of the fixed laborers in Shenzhen because there are too many factories in Shenzhen. On the other hand, Company C in Xiamen can recruit all the workers it needs from Xiamen or nearby rural areas because Xiamen lags behind Shenzhen economically and thus has fewer companies. Because the labor market conditions are different, Company C can hire laborers with relatively high levels of education.

Companies I and J are direct examples of educational differences arising in different areas. Both are wholly Japanese-owned companies manufacturing electronic products. Company I's factory is located in Shakou, the most advanced industrial area within Shenzhen Special Economic Zone. From 1983 (when the factory was first established) to 1986, 100% of its laborers were high school graduates. However, as more factories were built in Shakou, the demand for labor increased and it became harder to hire high school graduates. Therefore, Company I had to make up for the shortfall with workers from rural areas in Guangdong Province who had no family register in Shenzhen. As a result, the educational level of workers dropped. Company J, on the other hand, entered Zhuhai Special Economic Zone in 1990. The supply of labor in Zhuhai was larger than in Shenzhen. Therefore, Company J was able to hire all of its laborers from Zhuhai with high school diplomas, even though it entered China later than Company I. Moreover, relatively high-performing graduates were hired through teachers' recommendations and the company's own tests.

Residence

The vast majority of laborers in Shenzhen Special Economic Zone come from Guangdong. This is not only because the zone is located in Guangdong Province, but because of local government restrictions on employing people from outside the province. Companies may hire only technicians, interpreters, and others with special skills from outside the Guangdong region and even their numbers are restricted.

For example, Company E, a shoe manufacturer, employed five workers from outside Guangdong Province out of a total of 80 laborers. Company K had 56 non-Guangdong residents out of 296 laborers. If the number of outside laborers exceeds a given limit, companies must negotiate with the local Department of Labor. However, most companies in practice hire outside laborers beyond the limit because laborers from Guangdong Province quit in proportionally greater numbers than outside laborers. Laborers from Guangdong Province tend to have lower levels of education than outside laborers. Their hometowns are also closer to their workplace than for outside laborers, so it is easier for them not only to stop working and return to their hometowns, but also to come back. For laborers outside the province, however, once they quit it is not easy to return to their hometowns, find another job within the zone, or return to the zone once they have left. Moreover, Guangdong laborers have more connections at nearby factories. If they hear about a place paying higher wages from their friends or relatives, they immediately quit their present job to work there. Companies experience difficulties if labor turnover is too rapid. For these reasons, some companies hire outside laborers beyond the legal limit, even bribing officials of the Department of Labor in the process. A typical example is Company R, a domestic company with 100% Chinese capital, which entered Shenzhen Special Economic Zone from Shanxi Province. When it first began operations, most of its laborers were from Guangdong Province. However, their turnover rate was too high, so the company forced them to resign and brought in laborers from Shanxi Province. These new laborers rarely quit because they had come to the zone from so far away.

This practice is common among labor-intensive Chinese companies that were established relatively late (e.g., Company P). However, companies outside the special economic zone have a higher percentage of outside laborers than those in the zones, even in Shenzhen. Guangdong laborers form 88%, 90%, 90%, and 80%, respectively, of the total labor at Companies E, F, I, and L, all located in the special zones. On the other hand, they only form 50%, 60%, and 25% of labor at Companies A, D, and H, located outside the zone. Furthermore, commissioned processing companies located in the special zones have higher percentages of Guangdong Province laborers. Company N in the special zones employs 98% Guangdong Province laborers. On the other hand, Companies G and O only employ 44% and 50% of them, respectively.

When an area is transformed into a special economic zone, the industrial center moves from agriculture to industry. The largest portion of the farming population in the special economic zone is therefore formed by temporary farmers who do not have a household register in the zone and are there for a temporary stay until they can find new industrial jobs. In Shenzhen, for example, over 95% of the farmers are temporary farmers. A social problem that recently appeared as a result of the industrial shift from agriculture to industry is the formation of urban slums. Several factors led to the formation of slums: a large number of temporary farmers, a sudden increase in private stores, an increase in the number of temporary laborers, less thorough supervision of social conditions by public safety agencies, and unrestricted hiring/firing. The formation of this slum-dwelling class has not yet become an issue, but it will surely become a big social problem in the near future. Along with temporary farmers, illegal laborers and people who do not return to their homes after they leave the factory also live in these urban slums.

HIRING METHODS

Companies mergered with foreign firms and Chinese companies in the special zone can hire laborers through either the direct or indirect method. In principle, different hiring methods are used by companies of different ownership types, but practically all companies, regardless of ownership type, use a blend of these two methods.

Direct Hiring

A company directly hires laborers, including occasional work seekers, and reports hirings to the local Department of Labor. Foreign-capital companies (wholly foreign-capital companies and mergered companies) in the special zones hire laborers by this method. However, a wholly foreign-capital company generally hires laborers through the Labor Service Company in the city.

Indirect Hiring

Prospective workers receive permits from the Department of Labor of a given area to visit that area for employment tests. Wholly foreign-capital companies outside the special zones recruit using this method.

A new trend in indirect hiring is for companies to provide the Department of Labor with certain requirements and conditions vis-à-vis the laborer's hometown, the number of laborers needed, and the skills required, and the department hires laborers accordingly receiving a commission of 3% of the wages. Recently, the Department of Labor has been encouraging foreign-capital companies to use this method because the commissions are a big source of income. Previously, when companies hired laborers through the indirect method, the department received its commission once only upon signing of the contract between company and labor. Under the new method, companies pay commission monthly.

Temporary Employment

Most laborers are employed on a temporary basis. While their family registers are in their hometowns, laborers work in the special economic zone under 1–2 year contracts. This applies not only to foreign-capital companies but also to Chinese companies. Companies P, Q, and R are good examples. By industry, labor-intensive companies employ a higher percentage of temporary laborers than technology-intensive companies. The labor-intensive companies A, E, and H employ 100% temporary laborers, while the technology-intensive companies F, I, and L employ 80%, 75%, and 60%, respectively. This may be because people with family registers in the special economic zones, considering the future of industrial development, prefer technology-intensive companies to labor-intensive ones.

The percentage of permanent laborers in Shantou, Zhuhai, and Xiamen is higher than in Shenzhen. Companies B (10%), C (10%), J (70%), and M (98%) are good examples. This is because not as many companies enter these zones. Chinese technology-intensive companies have a higher percentage of permanent laborers than foreign-capital companies. For example, wholly foreign-capital Company I employs 25% of permanent laborers, while Company Q, a Chinese company with only one-ninth the work force of Company I, employs 33%. Despite the relatively low wages, laborers prefer Chinese companies to foreign-capital companies for a number of reasons. They have greater future development potential and they are more secure. Unlike foreign companies, who may withdraw from China if the economy slows down, Chinese companies are more likely to continue operating even in hard times. Moreover, permanent laborers are less likely to get fired in state-run Chinese companies. Company Q for example has a policy of hiring as many temporary laborers as possible because they are easier to fire than permanent laborers. State-run Chinese companies also provide housing allowances for permanent laborers which most workers obtain upon marriage. Foreign-capital companies do not. Of these reasons, this last is the most decisive in preferring state-run Chinese companies.

10

Fostering Manpower

This chapter examines how corporations foster labor in the special economic zones. The problem is approached from two perspectives: (1) working conditions and (2) education and training programs. The outline for fostering manpower in companies investigated for this research is provided in Table 10-1.

WORKING CONDITIONS

Workdays tend to be long and holidays tend to be few. Breaks in the workday are generally for meals only (e.g., fifteen minutes in the morning and fifteen minutes in the afternoon at a technology-intensive company). Despite the long days, employees work hard, with piped music to speakers to raise morale. Such work practices are very much related to China's large industrial labor reserve and the fact that because they do not have family registers workers can generally work only for two to three years even when they want to work longer. Moreover, young workers, who make up most of the work force, desire longer hours to earn more money. While long hours benefit the companies, they are not without problems. Many workers quit before their contracts expire because the work is difficult, and tired workers often make defective products.

Despite laborious working conditions, the absentee rate is low since nonattendance is directly linked to pay. For example, laborers in Company A lose three-days' pay if they are absent for one day and do not receive full-duty pay (a bonus paid for perfect attendance) if they are late even once. (Full-duty pay for a month is 2 yuan or H.K.$20 for three months.) Arrival and departure times are checked six times a day (morning, before lunch, after lunch, before dinner, after dinner, and after overtime work), and no excuses are accepted for absence. Company B has the following wage policy. For a full week of work, a day of paid leave is given. Accordingly, for twenty-six full days of work, excluding Sundays, calculated as four weeks of work, four days of paid leave is given. Full-duty pay is added, adding one more day's wages. Thus, a total of thirty-one

Table 10-1
Fostering Manpower of Each Company

	A	B	C	D	E	F
Workday	8 hrs. + 3–4 hrs. overtime, 1 shift	8 hrs. + 2–3 hrs. overtime, 1 shift	8 hrs. + 3 hrs. overtime, 1 shift	8 hrs. + 3 hrs. overtime, 2 shifts, 24-hr. operation	8 hrs. + 4 hrs. overtime, 1 shift	8 hrs. + 3–4 hrs. overtime, 1 shift
Workdays per year	326; no work on New Year's day, holidays, 2 Sundays a month	300	310	365	290	295
Uniforms	No	No	Yes (shirts and pants)	Yes	No	Yes (shirts)
Absenteeism	Very low	Under 1%	2–3 persons per day	1%	3–4 persons per day	3%
Turnover	Over 30%	Over 15%	Over 25%	Over 30%	Over 30%	—
Unionization	Yes	Yes	Yes	Yes	Yes	Yes
Training	On-the-job training; Management skill training for foremen and floor supervisors for 4 hrs. Newcomers only assisted on shop floor for first 3 months	On-the-job training; Newcomers only assisted on shop floor for first 3 months; 10 workers sent to Korea for skill training	On-the-job training; Newcomers only assisted on shop floor for first 3 months	On-the-job training; Training for pre-employees for 1–3 weeks—they are employed only if they pass the skill test (half of them pass)	On-the-job training	On-the-job training; On-site training whenever new models are introduced

Table 10-1 (continued)

	G	H	I	J	K	L
Workday	8 hrs. + 5–6 hrs. overtime, 1 shift	8 hrs. + 5–6 hrs. overtime, 1 shift	8 hrs. + overtime, 1 shift	8 hrs. + overtime, 1 shift	8 hrs. + 3 hrs. overtime, 1 shift	8 hrs. + overtime, 1 shift
Workdays per year	310	330	No work on Sundays and holidays	295	310	295
Uniforms	No	No	Yes	No	No	Yes (shirts)
Absenteeism	20 persons per month	Low	Low	Low	Low	3%
Turnover	Over 30%	Over 30%	Over 30%	Low	40%	—
Unionization	Yes	Yes	Yes	Yes	Yes	Yes
Training	Training for 1 week before employment; on-the-job training by foremen after being allocated	On-the-job training; Newcomers only assisted on shop floor for first 3 months	On-the-job training for first 3 months; orientation by each shop floor	Managers sent to foreign countries for training; trainers are invited from Japan	Selected by the test score in each area	On-the-job training; Managers sent to Japan for training

Table 10-1 (continued)

	M	N	O	P	Q	R
Workday	8 hrs. + overtime, 1 shift	8 hrs. + overtime, 1 shift	8 hrs. + 2 hrs. overtime, 1 shift	8 hrs. + overtime, 1 shift	8 hrs. + overtime, 1 shift	8 hrs. + 4 hrs. overtime, 1 shift
Workdays per year	310	No work on Sundays and holidays	No work on Sundays and holidays	No work on Sundays and holidays	—	—
Uniforms	Yes (shirts)	Yes (shirts)	Yes (shirts)	No	Yes (shirts)	No
Absenteeism	2%	4%	1%	3%	Low	1%
Turnover	30%	—	Over 30%	Over 30%	Most temporary workers leave in 2–3 years	Most workers leave in 2–3 years
Unionization	Yes	Yes	Yes	Yes	Yes	Yes
Training	On-the-job training: Managers take 2-hour class training	On-the-job training: Managers sent to evening college (company pays half of tuition from the second year)	On-the-job training: Trainers from Japan teach foremen	On-the-job training	Basic skill training for first week, then on-the-job training. Managers have special training for 3 months a year (10 hrs. per week intensively)	Hire only skilled workers; on-the-job training if necessary

Source: Interviews with the managers of each company, January 4–May 15, 1991. To protect privacy, companies are listed A–R.

paid working days are calculated. Furthermore, female workers are given one-day paid menstruation leave, so their total work month equals thirty-two paid days. However, if a worker takes a day off, she loses four days' pay (1 day of nonattendance, 1 day of paid leave, 1 day of full-duty, and 1 day of menstruation leave). If a worker is absent for two days, three days, four days, she loses pay for six days, eight days, ten days, respectively. In addition, other allowances are all affected by absences. The Chinese Company Q reduces its subsidy by 20% for one day of absence and 50% for a two-day absence. If a worker is absent for more than two days, she is dismissed.

Since absences have such serious consequences, workers try to avoid them at all costs. Labor unions exist, but have no teeth. Laborers can be fired at the employers' discretion, without recourse even for unjust dismissals. Yet there is little friction between employers and laborers and that friction is usually due to misunderstanding between management and labor. For example, there were two disputes about wages in Company G. One arose from a misunderstanding by laborers. They thought the basic wage of 160 yuan was too low, thinking that the public management office (a public employment agency or broker in the industrial area) should pay them H.K.$600, the amount it received from companies for each laborer rather than the 160 yuan that workers were receiving. The laborers thought that the company was exploiting them because their wage was lower than that received by laborers working for companies that did not belong to the public management office. Even though the company explained the wage payment structure precisely and sufficiently to the laborers, they did not understand. Thus, the company had to increase wages after negotiating with the public management office. Company K paid about 100 yuan higher than other companies because it did not know about the wage structure in China at the outset. However, as the company's economic performance deteriorated over time, it decreased its wage to the level paid by other companies. Fifty sewing machine operators quit as a result. These two situations described above, however, are extremely unusual cases. In most cases, laborers have to follow the employer's policies.

With respect to working conditions, the turnover rate of laborers is high, amounting to an annual average of 30%. The cause seems to be the family register problem, which allows nonprovincial workers to work in special economic zones for a limited time. Inferior working conditions are another cause. A laborer from the Northeast area working at Company A says, "Work is very hard. I endure it by rationalizing that I am earning money. I do not express my suffering. When I arrive at the company in the morning, I do not want to sit in front of a sewing machine. However, I operate the machine with the thought that I can go back home after I earn a lot of money if I just bear it."

Many methods have been suggested to reduce the high job turnover rate. For example, Company C requires laborers to deposit 20 yuan out of their monthly wage for two years. When the two-year contract expires, it returns the two-year savings of 480 yuan to the laborers. If they leave before the contract ends, however, they forfeit their deposits. Company A also retains 20 yuan a month for an educational fee for eight months. If laborers leave the company before the two-year contract is completed, the educational fee is not repaid to them. Company I selects one person from each manufacturing department and sends the person to Japan once a year to receive overseas training. If the person leaves the company within five years after returning from Japan, the laborer must pay back to the company the entire cost of the trip.[3] Company H tries to reduce the turnover rate by giving a bonus after the lunar New Year's Day to those who return to the company after the holiday. This is because many workers tend to leave the company at this time. The bonus covers transportation expenses to each worker's hometown plus a sum based on length of employment with the company: over 1 year, 100% (of a month's wages); six months, 50%; three months, 30%; two months, 15%.

Chinese companies also try to reduce the labor turnover rate. For example, at the time of hiring, Company R requires from laborers a deposit of 300 yuan, which is not returned if they leave the company within one year. Although this and other harsh methods practiced by Chinese companies violate Chinese labor laws they are common occurrences. Small-group and company activities are rarely conducted except in large companies (like Company I) or those with a special interest in them (like Company B). Few companies provide a suggestion box for employees to express their opinions. The president of Company A said, "We had a suggestion box before, but nobody used it. We therefore judged that the box was unnecessary and got rid of it." However, laborers asserted that they made many suggestions, but that these were not answered and so they stopped using the box, thinking it was only a decoration.

EDUCATIONAL SYSTEM

Most companies' education programs focus on on-the-job training (OJT). No company offers special education programs or facilities. Training is generally conducted on the job. For example, Company I uses different colored lamps on the production line corresponding to different job positions (foremen, heads, and laborers). A red lamp, for example, designates an intensive training area for laborers.

It is not easy for the Chinese to go to a foreign country, so overseas education programs for employees are rarely offered and those that are tend to be nonproductive, turning into sightseeing tours rather than educational experiences. For example, Company I sends one employee from each department to Japan for an education program. The schedule includes sightseeing, quality control training, field trips to factories, and leadership training. However, most of the time is spent sightseeing. Such overseas trips only stimulate other employees to go on such "education" programs rather than gain technical training. These programs exacerbate the shortage of labor in the mother company. In the case of Company M, one employee from each department is sent to Japan for six months of training. Thirty-two employees had been sent to Japan at the time of writing. In contrast to other companies, M offered a long-term program to more employees in a move to make up for the shortage of labor in the mother company in Japan. The Chinese employees work either in the office for China-related affairs or in the production line of the factory. There are several reasons why overseas generally do not focus on manpower:

1. The work itself is so difficult that it requires training through education programs. Therefore, the three-month educational training for new employees is futile, as most companies in zones

are simple assembly companies. Companies can fire laborers during the training period, and do not need to pay the social welfare (25% of the basic wage) that must be paid to the local Department of Labor when contracts are made with laborers after the trial period. Companies want to use this period as advantageously as possible because new laborers do the same work that experienced laborers do. At Company B, the daily wage during the trial period for new laborers is 5.2 yuan, of which they must pay 100 yuan per month to the company for meals.

2. The laborers work an average of two to three years, so education programs prove to be a meaningless investment. Each company has various methods to increase the retention rate of laborers.

3. Companies generally recruit experienced people, especially labor-intensive companies. Company E hires managers separately from laborers and recruits experienced sewing machine operators for its production field. Companies G and D also recruit laborers and managers separately. One reason why managers are hired separately is related to the diversity of dialects in China. In Japanese Company I, only those who speak Mandarin (China's official language) are selected as team heads and foremen. According to Company I's Japanese field manager, leaders have to speak Mandarin to be able to communicate freely with all the laborers, who usually come from various dialect areas. Companies P and R hire skilled laborers from the beginning.

11

Production Management

This chapter examines production management, which includes the following factors: type of management organization, job rotation for laborers, promotion systems, and quality control management. A summary of subject companies is given in Table 11-1. They have the following features.

MANAGEMENT ORGANIZATION

In foreign-capital companies, the management of technology is generally performed by foreigners. This is necessary because of China's inexperience in this area. However, the number of foreign skilled laborers is decreasing. For example, each production department of Company A is divided into eight divisions, and each division is headed by a foreman. In the past all foremen were foreigners, but they have been replaced by Chinese workers with over two years of experience. This reduction of foreign skilled laborers reflects some transfer of technology by foreign companies to China. One reason why companies want to reduce the number of foreign skilled laborers is the expense of bringing them to China. In the case of Company C, which decreased its complement of foreign skilled laborers from 14 to 6, expenses for the 14 foreigners was almost the same as that for 400 Chinese laborers. Accordingly, the company taught the skills to Chinese workers as early as possible. Another reason is the difficulty in finding foreign skilled laborers who want to work in China.

Companies M and D place one Japanese and one Chinese foreman in each production department to teach the technology to the Chinese as early as possible. Companies from advanced countries put more efforts in the transfer of technology than those from semiadvanced countries. For example, Companies B and H, which manufacture the same products, employ 8 and 4 foreign skilled laborers, respectively. The former employs 160 Chinese laborers, while the latter employs 820. Therefore, the ratio of Chinese employees to foreign skilled laborers is 20:1 for Company B and

Table 11-1
Production Management in Each Company

	A	B	C	D	E	F
Introduction of production skills	Education by Hong Kong skilled laborers	Education by Hong Kong and Korean skilled laborers	Education by Korean skilled laborers	Education by Korean skilled laborers	Education by Korean skilled laborers	Education by Hong Kong and Korean skilled laborers
Management organization	3 executives under the Hong Kong president (1 is Chinese and 2 are foreigners); all production managers are foreigners	3 departments under Korean president; production manager is Korean; manager is Korean-Chinese; half of foremen are foreigners	3 managers of production departments are foreigners; all foremen are Chinese	President, production manager, quality management manager are Korean; 5 production department managers are Chinese	Superintendent is Korean-Chinese; 2 foreign technology advisors; 4 production department managers are Chinese	President is Chinese; vice-president is Korean; production managers are Chinese; Korean skilled laborers are expected to be invited
Job rotation	Offered to foremen and those in higher positions	No	No	After passing test, laborers move to next stage	Yes	Sometimes offered to foremen or those in higher positions
Promotion	Ability-oriented	Ability-oriented	Ability, number of years worked, and rate of attendance are considered	Those with specified number of years worked and ability can test for promotion	Ability-oriented	In the past, decided by usual judgment, but seniority system to be adopted in the future
Power of managers at middle level	Foremen have leadership; general manager for each department recommends personnel matters	Foremen do technology education, production management and check on lateness, early leaving, and nonattendance	Foremen do technology education, production management, and check on lateness, early leaving, and nonattendance	Foremen do technology education, production management, and check on lateness, early leaving, and nonattendance	Foremen do technology education, production management, and check on lateness, early leaving, and nonattendance	Foremen do only advisement management
Quality control (QC) management	Each production department has 1 inspector (wages are based on production)	One inspector in each division inspects during production process and again before packing	2-4-8 system	3 inspections for final assembled products	1 inspector in each production department	Inspection division in insertion and assembly lines; 4-hour inspection for final products (sound quality and frequency)
Rate of defective production	3%	High during production; low in final product	3%	—	Higher than Korea	3%

Table 11-1 (continued)

	G	H	I	J	K	L
Introduction of production skills	Education by Hong Kong skilled laborers	Education by Japanese, Korean, and Taiwanese skilled laborers	Education by Japanese skilled laborers	Education by Korean skilled laborers	Education by Japanese skilled laborers	Education by Korean skilled laborers
Management organization	President and vice-president are foreigners; middle-level managers are Chinese	President and quality manager are Japanese; design manager is Korean; production department managers are Chinese	Among 52 foreigners (26 Japanese and 26 from Hong Kong), most are technology teachers; 4 Japanese and 4 from Hong Kong are in management department	President and director are Japanese; director of manufacturing is Chinese; 4 managers in manufacturing are Japanese	President, vice-president, and director of design development are foreigners	13 foreigners (6 Japanese and 7 from Hong Kong)
Job rotation	No	Offered only for potential managers	Offered only for potential managers	Offered to foremen and those in higher positions; senior managers are hired and educated separately	No	No
Promotion	Ability-oriented; separate hiring for sewing machine operators and management departments	Experience, technology skills, working attitude, and loyalty to company are considered	Ability-oriented	Seniority and ability-oriented, but former is emphasized (managers must have strong leadership abilities)	Ability-oriented	Ability-oriented
Power of managers at middle level	Foremen do advisement management, reward and personnel rights (hiring and firing)	Foremen do advisement management, home leave, reward, and personnel rights (hiring and firing)	Foremen do advisement management	Foremen do advisement management and personnel rights	Foremen do advisement management and personnel rights (hiring and firing); personnel department checks number of laborers	Foremen do advisement management and personnel rights
Quality control management	General inspection in quality control department based on standards set by president	Each production department has 1 inspector	No difference from Japan in machinery inspection; product appearance inspection more strict than in Japan	Frequent check of work and accessories based on Japanese work standards; 5 inspections during production	Inspector in each division; 4 inspectors in sewing machine dept.; 2 in final inspection dept.; president oversees last inspection	Quality control education once a month; inspection during production more important than final inspection
Rate of defective production	10% during production; 2% in final product	Average 15% depending on items	High during production; low in final product	Initially 5%, currently 2%	3% in final product	High during production

Table 11-1 (continued)

	M	N	O	P	Q	R
Introduction of production skills	Education by Japanese skilled laborers	Education by Japanese technology teacher	Education by Japanese and Korean skilled laborers	Development and management employees recruited from Shanghai (skilled in doll production)	90% Chinese technology	Recruited from Shantou Province
Management organization	3 superintendents are Japanese skilled laborers; 1 Japanese and 1 Chinese manager in each department	President and 1 technology teacher are Japanese	President is Japanese; 1 Japanese and 1 Chinese manager in 7 departments	No foreigners; no different from foreign companies in organization	No foreigners; no different from foreign companies in organization, but repair and QC departments are separately organized	No foreigners; no different from foreign companies in organization
Job rotation	All begin as laborers and are promoted when ability is recognized by working in various departments; all managers are Japanese	Offered only for potential managers	No	Offered to foremen and those in higher positions	No	No; however movement can occur depending on the products
Promotion	Performance results, personality, and intelligence most important; inexperienced laborers hired	Ability-oriented; inexperienced laborers are hired	Ability-oriented; separate hiring of laborers and managers	Ability-oriented; experienced managers are recruited from outside companies	Ability-oriented; senior managers are recruited from outside companies	Ability-oriented; laborers hired by each department
Power of managers at middle level	Foremen do advisement management and personnel rights (hiring and firing)	Foremen do advisement management	Foremen do advisement management and personnel rights	Foremen do advisement management	Foremen do advisement management	Foremen do advisement management
Quality control management	2 inspections during production; final inspection shortly before shipment	Each production department has inspection; final inspection shortly before shipment; defective products (5%) are sent to Japan and remanufactured	Quality control education 30 minutes per day first month; special education 1 hr. per week for quality control professionals; 20 inspectors each for arrival and shipment; 50 inspectors for manufacturing dept.	Inspectors in each production department	4 inspectors in insertion line; 2 inspectors in assembly line; 1 inspection in technology department	Inspectors in each production department
Rate of defective production	15% during production	High rate; overall quality 80% of Japanese products	15% during production	20% during production; 5% in final product	30% during production; 3% in final product	—

Source: Interviews with the managers of each company, January 4–May 15, 1991. To protect privacy, companies are listed A–R.

205:1 for Company H. The number of foreign skilled laborers in Company H, a Japanese-capital company, is low because it has to spend a lot to bring Japanese skilled laborers to China. (Company H also employs two Korean skilled laborers.)

JOB ROTATION

Job-rotation is not practiced, except at management level. Company J offers special leadership programs to thirty specially recruited managers, including a two to three month overseas program in Japan. On the other hand, it fixes ordinary laborers to specific jobs to increase productivity. In addition, the company believes that when a laborer leaves the line, production will not be interrupted because there are many laborers who do the same job.

Many Japanese companies, knowing little about labor conditions in China at the time, initially conducted job rotation using ordinary laborers as they did in Japan. However, they gradually discontinued the practice when a significant number of laborers left their jobs before acquiring all the needed skills. Subsequently, they offered job rotation only to long-term laborers and to managers. Company I is a typical case. Companies in Shenzhen show a lower rate of job rotation than those in other special economic zones. Even though they are in the same electric industry, Companies J and M are more active in conducting job rotation than Companies I and L. The former have more fixed laborers and lower job-turnover rates than the latter. The management and labor of Companies J and M seem to trust each other, and their employees are willing to work in their companies for a long time. Companies J and M also try to foster manpower as early as possible by teaching skills to their laborers. There is no difference in job rotation with respect to industries, but in terms of company size, small companies tend to offer job rotation more than large companies. Corporate preference for experienced laborers tends to affect the use of job rotation.

PROMOTION SYSTEMS

With respect to promotion, an ability-oriented system is preferred to a seniority system. Employers in the special economic zones feel that the bad habit of idleness may arise under a seniority system. However, Japanese companies emphasize the seniority system more than companies from other countries. This is related to the traditional Japanese business management system. In the case of Company H, it does not hire experienced employees. Instead, it hires inexperienced laborers and places them in appropriate departments while teaching them many skills during a three-month trial period. When a laborer is judged not to be proper for his department, he is sent to another department. In promotion, experience, skill, work attitude, health, and loyalty to the company (e.g., not complaining about working overtime) rather than one's abilities are emphasized in promotions. Personality is especially stressed. Some older Japanese companies emphasize ability rather than seniority. This is exhibited in Company I. A manager at this company explained that this policy results from their experience, which showed that adoption of a seniority system causes a decrease in productivity due to a high job turnover rate. Since so many laborers prove to be short-term employees, an ability-oriented system is better for the increase of productivity than a seniority system.

Technology-intensive companies tend to adopt the seniority system more than labor-intensive companies. This is because technology-intensive companies are larger, have more fixed laborers, and the rate of retention is higher. Managers explain that the seniority system not only increases performance results but also improves management affairs, including relations between senior and junior laborers. Companies F and J exemplify such a case.

In terms of authority, most foreign-capital companies offer middle-level managers not only leadership status but also the power to punish tardiness and absence, arrange home leave, and hire and fire personnel. On the other hand, Chinese companies offer only leadership status to foremen. Regarding this, the president of Company Q said, "All power must be given to the president. Otherwise, the company's system of order becomes chaotic. If foremen are given power, laborers will not listen to the president and they, together with the foremen, will secretly plot against the president. This cannot be excused. Most of all, the president's authority must be respected."

This type of management by presidential decree does not easily apply to foreign-capital companies. Because the president is a foreigner, it is not easy for him to understand the Chinese due to different languages, customs, and values. Managers in the special economic zones say that the president should have power to a certain level but has to leave the rest to middle-level managers.

QUALITY CONTROL MANAGEMENT

Each company experiences difficulties in quality control management. The method of quality control management directly affects product quality and company profits. Here are two representative attempts to improve quality control. Company M offers quality control training programs to managers from the level of team head and higher. Each program covers one topic and takes place weekly for three consecutive months. The officials are first divided into three teams. Each team makes up a name for itself and states the objective(s) of the team. A team head is elected who is given some authority. The team then holds a meeting which all laborers must attend, during which they are given an opportunity to express their opinions. After going through the ideas presented by the laborers, one problem area is selected for analysis and solution. Each team analyzes the problem, formulates measures to solve the problem, and puts them into practice. If the results prove to be effective, the measures are implemented throughout the entire factory. Company C adopted the "2-4-8" system. Under this system, the factory superintendent checks the factory twice daily and gives orders to leaders. Leaders check their line four times a day and give orders to foremen. Foremen check on work performance eight times a day and train laborers. Factory laborers mainly do simple assembly work while check-ups are made in the production department. However, the defect rate is a lot higher than in the parent company, which is mainly due to the small number of skilled laborers and quality inspectors, lack of quality control training, and a dirty working environment.

Various systems have been tried to reduce defects, but most companies usually do not produce the expected results. For example, Company H has set up regulations to produce a cleaner working environment and disciplines employees who violate them. These regulations include "Don't waste," "Don't blow your nose while working," and "Don't bring food into the working place." However, these regulations did not bring about visible results because habitual behaviors cannot be corrected in a day.

12

Forward- and Reverse-Related Effects

The summary of where each of the subject companies procures production facilities, technology, and raw materials, and to whom it sells its products is provided in Table 12-1.

SUPPLY OF PRODUCTION FACILITIES, TECHNOLOGY, AND RAW MATERIALS

Foreign-capital companies totally depend on imports for their production facilities because most of their products are for exports. However, Companies P, Q, and R, Chinese companies, purchase most of their machines and technology in China. When they sell their products made with raw materials and machines and technology procured in China, they have no problems. However, the products are not competitive enough for the export market. Foreign-capital companies have to depend on imports of machines and accessories to produce popular items for overseas markets.

With regard to this, the following factors should be considered. First, the quality of machines made in China does not satisfy the needs of foreign-capital companies. Second, bringing used machines from the company's home country is less expensive than purchasing new ones in China, shortening the time to reach the break-even point. By doing this, corporate tax can be reduced. The practice of inflating the price of used machines is not discussed openly, but multinational companies commonly do this. In addition, it is advantageous for mergered companies when they complete a contract with Chinese companies. Furthermore, Sanlaiyibao prices the machines at a high price when renting them.

Most skilled laborers are brought from the company's home country to train local laborers in production technology. Because production facilities are brought from the company's home country, Chinese laborers do not know how to use them in the beginning, and finding an expert in China is not easy. In addition, foreign and Chinese

Table 12-1
Forward- and Reverse-Related Effects of Each Company

	A	B	C
Status of production facilities	100% imported from Korea	100% imported from Korea	100% imported from Korea
Supply of raw materials	100% imported from foreign countries	Boxes purchased in China; other materials imported	Initially, 100% imported from Korea; currently, some raw materials–zippers, webbing, thread, boxes, poles—purchased from mergered companies. Percentage of materials imported varies according to export market (Japan, 70%; U.S., 50%; Europe, 60%)
Sales	100% of women's wigs exported to the U.S.; 50% of doll's wigs exported to U.S.; 50% to other countries	30% of sales permitted for the Chinese domestic market, but 100% exported (U.S., 40%;; Germany, 60%)	100% exported (Japan, 20%; U.S., 60%; Europe, 20%)

	D	E	F
Status of production facilities	100% leased from Singapore	90% imported from Korea; 10% imported from Japan	Imported from Japan, Taiwan, Hong Kong, partly from China
Supply of raw materials	100% of slinder imported from Korea; 100% of magnetic wire, bobbins, tubing imported from Japan; 100% of epoxy imported from U.S.	Boxes purchased in China; other materials imported	Exports: 70% imported; 30% purchased in China Domestic market: 40% imported from Hong Kong, Japan, Korea; 60% purchased in China from mergered companies
Sales	100% exported to Korea	30% of sales permitted for the Chinese domestic market, but 100% exported to U.S.	70% exported; 30% domestic market (all OEM production)

	G	H	I
Status of production facilities	100% imported from Korea	Of all sewing machines, 100 are imported from Japan and the others from Hong Kong	100% imported from Hong Kong and Japan
Supply of raw materials	Boxes purchased in China; other materials imported	Boxes purchased in China and sometimes thread and cotton; other materials imported from Hong Kong, Korea, and Taiwan	Boxes imported from mergered companies; all other materials except packing materials imported from Korea, Singapore, Japan
Sales	100% exported (U.S., 30%; Europe, 70%)	100% exported (Japan, 60%; U.S., 40%)	100% exported

Table 12-1 (continued)

	J	K	L
Status of production facilities	100% imported from Japan	100% imported from Korea	100% imported from Japan
Supply of raw materials	100% imported from Japan	95% imported from Korea; 5% from China (boxes, thread)	Exports: 26% purchased in China Domestic market: 40% purchased in China; boxes purchased from Chinese companies (excluding mergered companies)
Sales	90% exported; 10% domestic market	70% exported; 30% domestic market	100% exported (Japan, 80%; Korea, Taiwan, Singapore, 20%)

	M	N	O
Status of production facilities	100% imported from Japan	Initially, imported from Japan; currently, from Taiwan	Imported from Hong Kong and Japan
Supply of raw materials	Initially, imported from Japan; currently, from Taiwan	100% imported (Japan, 70%; Others, 30%)	Boxes purchased in China; other materials imported (Japan, 30%; Hong Kong, 50%; Taiwan, Korea, 20%)
Sales	100% exported (Japan and Europe, 50%; U.S., 50%)	100% exported (Japan, 70%; Europe, U.S., Hong Kong, 30%)	100% exported (30% of printers' bodies to U.S.; 70% of printers' bodies to Japan and ASEAN; most accessories to Europe)

	P	Q	R
Status of production facilities	Sewing machines purchased in China; others are imported	90% from China; 10% from Japan	50% from China; 50% imported
Supply of raw materials	50% imported; 50% purchased in China	Integrated circuits imported from Japan; others from China	100% from China
Sales	Most sold in domestic market	100% sold in domestic market	Most exported to Hong Kong

Source: Interviews with the managers of each company, January 4–May 15, 1991. To protect privacy, companies are listed A–R.

companies use different production methods and different raw materials although they manufacture the same products. Company A, which produces wigs, brought skilled laborers from Korea in the beginning because it was very hard to find skilled laborers in China.

Wholly owned foreign-capital companies and Sanlaiyibao depend on imports for most of their raw materials. For example, Company A relies on imports for all raw materials: (1) nets, vinyl laces, and nylon tapes from Korea, and (2) vinyl boxes and other kinds of boxes from China. Synthetic fiber is imported from Japan (90%) and Taiwan (10%). Mergered companies procure some of their accessories in China, but more than half comes from other mergered companies. For exported goods, Company F imports 70% of its accessories and buys the remaining 30% in China. For goods to be sold in the domestic market, it imports 40% of the raw materials and buys 60% in China; 80% of imported raw materials are from Hong Kong. Major accessories such as integrated circuit and brown pipes are from Japan and Korea, respectively.

Cabinets and condensers are bought in China, but more than half of them come from foreign-owned mergered companies. Company L buys 26% of raw materials for export goods and 40% for domestic sales in China, but most raw materials are purchased from mergered companies located in China. Only packaging materials such as boxes and manuals are purchased from pure Chinese companies.

PRODUCT SALES

Most products of foreign-capital companies are exported. This is an improvement from the early stages when sales in the domestic market were high. This means that products manufactured in China, based on low production expenses, including low wages and skilled labor, have become competitive in international markets. Despite an increase in exported goods, most companies are interested in expanding their sales into the Chinese market. For example, most companies are selling raw materials imported under a tax exemption for producing export goods in China, although it is prohibited, because they can make profits in the amount of the tax that they don't pay. This is possible because audits to detect misuse of imported raw materials and exported goods are neglected and corruption prevails.

13

Business Achievements

In this chapter, companies' labor productivity and business problems are examined. The outline of subject companies is provided in Table 13-1.

WAGE SYSTEM

The average monthly wage of laborers is about 400—500 yuan, two to three times higher than in other areas of China, although this differs according to business type, working hours, type of job, and nationality of the company. Even in the Shenzhen area, there is a monthly wage gap of over 100 yuan between the special economic zone and outside areas and a further gap of 100 yuan between Shenzhen and other special economic zones.

According to regulations, laborers are entitled to 150% of the basic wage for weekday overtime and 200% for Sundays. However, according to my findings, these regulations are practically ignored. Overall, laborers tend to work more overtime because the pay for overtime work is often in foreign currency. If laborers exchange the foreign currency into yuan in the black market, they increase their income.[4] For example, Company G pays laborers a basic wage of H.K.$600 a month to the public management office. However, the allowances for overtime work are paid directly to laborers, bypassing the public management office and its commission charge. Sometimes, overtime work allowance can actually be higher than the regular wage. Most companies do not offer bonuses and retirement benefits.

WORKING AND LIVING CONDITIONS

The workers in labor-intensive companies do not wear uniforms and shoes. Although some differences exist between companies, laborers in technology-intensive companies are required to wear uniforms and shoes. Most companies, even technol-

Table 13-1
Business Achievements of Each Company

		A	B	C
Wage system	Basic wage	Monthly salary for clerks; performance-based wage for laborers	Fixed wage by serial step[1]	Basic wage plus efficiency-based wage (different basic wage)[3]
	Overtime allowance	150% of basic wage for clerks; 150% of efficiency-based wage for laborers; 200% of basic wage for Sundays and national holidays	150% of basic wage from 18:00–22:00; 200% of basic wage from 22:00–06:00	150% of basic wage
	Bonus	No	No	1 month's wage
	Retirement pension	No	100%, 50%, 0%[2]	1 month's wage
	Other allowances	Full-duty pay, food allowance, medical allowance	Food allowance (about 40 yuan); medical allowance (50 yuan)	Full-duty pay
	Average wage (1 month)	Clerks: about 600 yuan; Laborers: about 400 yuan	600 yuan (2–3%); 350 yuan (60–70%); 200 yuan (remainder)	Laborers: 250–400 yuan; Managers: 450 yuan
Living environment	Company cafeteria	Located on first floor of dormitory, very small; 1 television	Located on roof of company building, very clean	Located on first floor of factory
	Meals	Breakfast provided by company	40% of meal costs subsidized by company	Employees pay for meals
	Dormitory	16–18 laborers live together with bunk beds in 50m³ space; showers and bathrooms shared; dormitory expenses paid by company	12–16 laborers live in 60m³ space, cleaner and wider than most; hot water in shower rooms	30 laborers (volunteers only) live in 100m³ space (shower room, living room, kitchen); dormitory expenses paid by company
	In-company clubs	No	Photography; music; library; recreation room	No
	In-company activities	No	Picnics on holidays	Picnics on holidays
	Opinion box	No	Yes	No
	Welfare benefits	No	English and Korean classes	No
Business achievements	Productivity	33% of Korean company; low productivity balanced by low wage; overall production cost is 50% of Korean	30% of Korean company	50% of Korean company; low productivity balanced by low wage; overall production cost is 50–80% of Korean
	Break-even point	—	1 year	3 years
	Business problems	High rate of turnover; quality improvement	Low productivity because of bad image in China; 30% discount for products although same as those made in Korea	High freight transportation between Xiamen and Hong Kong; high rate of turnover

Table 13-1 (continued)

		D	E	F
Wage system	Basic wage	Basic wage plus title-related wage[4]	Performance-based wage for sewing machine operators; fixed wage for others (from 250 yuan)	70% basic wage plus 30% efficiency-based wage (based on performance)
	Overtime allowance	150% of basic wage	150% of final performance wage for sewing machine operators; 150% of basic wage for others	Laborers: less than 1 yuan per hr. Managers: 1.5 yuan per hr.
	Bonus	—	—	No
	Retirement pension	—	—	No
	Other allowances	—	—	—
	Average wage (1 month)	—	Sewing machine operators: 380–650 yuan; Others: 300–400 yuan	Laborers: H.K.$900–1000; Clerks: H.K.$600–800
Living environment	Company cafeteria	Located on first floor of dormitory; television; public washing machine	Located on first floor of dormitory	Located on first floor of dormitory; 1 television
	Meals	—	20% of meal costs subsidized by company	Paid by company
	Dormitory	16 laborers live in 40m³ space	16 people live in 40m³ space; dormitory expenses paid by employees	8 people live in 20m³ space; dormitory expenses paid by company
	In-company clubs	No	Ping-pong table	Ping-pong table
	In-company activities	No	No	1 song contest per year
	Opinion box	No	No	No
	Welfare benefits	No	No	child birth leave (7 months without pay)
Business achievements	Productivity	50% of Korean company	50% of Korean company	40% of Korean company
	Break-even point	—	1 year	—
	Business problems	Labor relations; quality control; high rate of turnover	Too much time spent for transportation; quality control; high rate of turnover	Low productivity; management problems

Table 13-1 (continued)

		G	H	I
Wage system	Basic wage	Fixed wage	Fixed wage[6]	Basic wage plus title-based wage plus efficiency-based wage[7]
	Overtime allowance	Laborers: H.K.$2 per hour; Foremen: H.K.$3 per hour	150% of basic wage	150% of basic wage
	Bonus	H.K.$20 per year	1 month's wage if employed at least 1 year	—
	Retirement pension	No	No	—
	Other allowances	Technology allowance[5]	Full-duty pay	Full-duty pay; price-related allowance
	Average wage (1 month)	Laborers: 400 yuan; Foremen and higher: H.K.$1,150	—	—
Living environment	Company cafeteria	No	Located on first floor of dormitory	Yes
	Meals	33% of meal costs subsidized by company	70% of meal costs subsidized by company	33% of meal costs subsidized by company
	Dormitory	10 persons live in 30m³ space; showers and bathrooms are shared	10–14 persons live in 35m³ space; 50% of expenses paid by company for laborers; 100% of food and dormitory expenses for foremen paid by company	8 persons live in 28m³ space; 4 yuan of dormitory expenses paid by company
	In-company clubs	No	No	Music; soccer; volleyball; library
	In-company activities	No	No	Song contest
	Opinion box	No	No	Yes
	Welfare benefits	Medical expenses paid by employees; doctor's salary paid by company	50% of medical expenses paid by company	No
Business achievements	Productivity	30% of Korean company	50% of Korean company	—
	Break-even point	1.5 years	1.5 years	First year
	Business problems	Low productivity; high rate of turnover	High rate of turnover; quality control	High rate of turnover; high rate of defective products

Table 13-1 (continued)

		J	K	L
Wage system	Basic wage	Fixed wage	Fixed wage[8]	20% basic wage plus 80% efficiency-based wage (based on sales)[9]
	Overtime allowance	150% of basic wage from 18:00–22:00; 185% of basic wage from 22:00–06:00	Laborers: 1.5 yuan per hr. Foremen: 2.5 yuan per hr. Heads: 2–3 yuan per hr.	0.5 yuan per hr. plus efficiency-based
	Bonus	1 month's wage	1 month's wage	1 month's wage
	Retirement pension	No	No	—
	Other allowances	—	—	—
	Average wage (1 month)	450–525 yuan	Laborers: 300–380 yuan; Higher than foremen: 550 yuan	H.K.$900
Living environment	Company cafeteria	Located between dormitory and factory	Located on first floor of dormitory	Located on first floor of dormitory
	Meals	Lunch provided by company	33% of meal costs subsidized by company	Breakfast provided by company
	Dormitory	Volunteers live free in dormitory; power and water costs paid by employees; showers and bathrooms are shared	10 persons live in 30m³ space; showers and bathrooms are shared	10–14 persons live in 35m³ space; 50% of expenses paid by company
	In-company clubs	No	No	Ping-pong table
	In-company activities	No	Dance party	Dance party; song contest
	Opinion box	No	No	No
	Welfare benefits	No	4-month child birth leave; work injuries paid by company	2-month child birth leave (basic wage paid; medical expenses paid by company
Business achievements	Productivity	—	—	50% of Japanese company
	Break-even point	5 years	1.5 years	—
	Business problems	Quality control; employee education	Quality control; low productivity	Quality control

Table 13-1 (continued)

		M	N	O
Wage system	Basic wage	Basic wage plus efficiency-based wage[10]	Fixed wage[12]	Fixed wage
	Overtime allowance	150%	H.K.$6 per hr.	2 yuan per hr.
	Bonus	1 month's wage	1 month's wage	1 month's wage
	Retirement pension	No	No	No
	Other allowances	Full-duty pay[11]	Technology allowance[13]	Full-duty pay of 20 yuan; performance-based allowances[14]
	Average wage (1 month)	Laborers: 350 yuan	—	300 yuan
Living environment	Company cafeteria	No	Located on first floor of dormitory	Located on first floor of dormitory
	Meals	Employees pay for lunch	Employees pay for meals	30% of meal costs subsidized by company
	Dormitory	No	7–8 persons live in 20m^3 space; shower (cold water only) shared by all	14 persons live in 50m^3 space; 1 shower and bathroom for every 20 people; 90% live in dormitory; 15 yuan of expenses paid by employees
	In-company clubs	Ping-pong table; library	Ping-pong; music; hiking	No
	In-company activities	Picnic; dance party; song festival	Song contest	No
	Opinion box	No	Yes	No
	Welfare benefits	Welfare fund of 120 yuan per person per year	No	No
Business achievements	Productivity	30% of Korean company	50% of Japanese company	—
	Break-even point	10 months	First year	3 months
	Business problems	High rate of turnover; low productivity; strong administrative power	High rate of turnover; quality control	High rate of turnover; friction with government agencies

Table 13-1 (continued)

		P	Q	R
Wage system	Basic wage	Performance-based wage	10% basic wage plus 30% title-related wage plus 60% encouragement wage	Performance-based wage[15]
	Overtime allowance	—	—	—
	Bonus	—	—	—
	Retirement pension	—	No	—
	Other allowances	Full-duty pay of 30 yuan per month	100 yuan per month paid by company for full-duty pay and inflation	Full-duty pay of 120 yuan per month
	Average wage (1 month)	400 yuan	400 yuan	400–600 yuan
Living environment	Company cafeteria	Located on first floor of dormitory	Located on first floor of dormitory	Located on first floor of dormitory
	Meals	60 yuan of meal costs subsidized by company	Employees pay for meals	40% of meal costs subsidized by company
	Dormitory	7 people live in 30m^3 space; 1 bathroom for every 35 people; 100% live in dormitory; 15 yuan of expenses paid by employees	8 persons live in 1 room; fixed laborers provided with housing after marriage	6 persons live in 20m^3 space; 100% live in dormitory; expenses paid by company
	In-company clubs	No	Hiking; music; reading	No
	In-company activities	Movie festival	No	No
	Opinion box	No	No	No
	Welfare benefits	8% of medical expenses paid by company	Medical expenses paid by company; day-care center (up to 3 years of age) provided	12 yuan per month paid by company
Business achievements	Productivity	—	Deficit until 1987	—
	Break-even point	2 years		—
	Business problems	High rate of turnover; quality control; market opening	High rate of defective products; market opening; difficult management of fixed laborers	Family registration law

Source: Interviews with the managers of each company, January 4–May 15, 1991. To protect privacy, companies are listed A–R.

Notes:

1. There are 100 salary steps; 20th salary step given during internship; 35–40th steps given when offical contract is made.

2. 100% of basic wage paid for 3-month prior notice of resignation; 50% for 2-month notice; 0% for sudden resignation.

Table 13-1 (continued)

3. There are 10 salary steps beginning with 220 yuan; difference between steps is 20 yuan.

4. Basic wage: 95.4 yuan. Title-related wage—Training period: 0 yuan; Wind II period (6 months): 90 yuan; Wind III period (6 months): 120 yuan; Wind IV period (5 months): 160 yuan; Q.A. period (2 months): 200 yuan; Leader: 300 yuan.

5. For example, 100 sewing machine operators each receive H.K.$50 per month.

6. Each job has different wage level per day—cutting: 5.5–10.5 yuan; sewing: 6–11.5 yuan; finishing: 5.5–10.5 yuan.

7. Basic wage: 120 yuan, 158 yuan after 3 months. Title-related wage: 1–20 steps paid in H.K.$. Efficiency-based wage: 60 yuan per month after base is established.

8. Sewing: up to maximum 145 yuan; Others: up to maximum of 135 yuan.

9. Begins with 50 yuan and increases to 55 yuan after 1 year.

10. Differs according to monthly performance level, but averages one third of basic wage; difference among laborers is maximum of three times basic wage.

11. 15% of basic wage; 7% for 1 nonattendance; 0% for 2 nonattendances.

12. Employed less than 1 year: 273 yuan; 1–1.5 years: 318 yuan; over 1.5 years: 364 yuan.

13. 350 employees are paid a maximum of 5 times the basic wage in H.K.$.

14. 5% of employees receive excellent performance wage (H.K.$100–500).

15. Graded for each stage of production—1 point: 0.03 yuan; 10,000 points: 300 yuan. When performance exceeds the perfect score, 1 point is calculated at 0.04 yuan.

ogy-intensive companies, because they are assembly factories, are messy compared to those in Japan and Korea.

At Company A, the cafeteria is located on the first floor of the dormitory. However, it is extremely small, dirty, and hot during the summer—not even a fan is installed inside the cafeteria—so most workers eat outside. Regarding this matter the president of Company A said, "Chinese people have a habit of eating outside the cafeteria. Therefore, it is not necessary to worry about the cafeteria when operating a factory in China." However, my research found otherwise. For example, Company B has its cafeteria on the seventh floor of the factory building. I found the cafeteria clean and its food excellent. No laborer ate outside the cafeteria at this company. Therefore, it seems that laborers of Company A eat outside the cafeteria not because the Chinese have a habit of eating outdoors but because the cafeteria is not fit or comfortable for dining inside.

The menu at Company K's cafeteria, whose food is considered good, includes a choice of dumpling, bread, porridge, or fried noodles for breakfast; five items of rice, fried vegetables, fried pork, fried beef, and fried fish for lunch; and dinner is the same as lunch. However, laborers still complain because dishes on the menu never live up to the fancy names they are given. Companies subsidize food generally by one-third to one-quarter of the expenses to the laborers. However, despite the subsidy, laborers still pay one-third to one-fifth of their monthly wage for food. This is a heavy burden on those who came to the special economic zones to earn and save money. As a result, some prepare food themselves instead of eating in the company cafeteria.

Most laborers live in dormitories. A dormitory has steel bunk beds along both sides of the walls and little space. Only two persons can pass through the middle aisle. Companies supply beds and blankets only; no lockers are provided. Eight people commonly share a dark cramped room, which is lit by only one light bulb. There are many reasons why living conditions are so poor. Company O, for example, pays 10,000 yuan to the Baoanxian government of Shenzhen every month for the management of its laborers' living quarters. However, the dormitory facilities are outrageously poor when one considers the amount of money being spent on them. Company O suspects that embezzlement has been going on, causing friction between the company and the municipal government. The problem has not yet been solved. Frictions over dormitory operation expenses are especially serious for commissioned processing companies and mergered companies.

Most companies do not have recreation facilities, although some have ping-pong tables. Sometimes, a song contest or a dance party is offered. Some companies have TVs, but usually these are in the cafeterias, and laborers can watch them only during meal times. Managers explain that this is to keep laborers from wasting work time.

LABOR PRODUCTIVITY

Labor productivity is generally 30–50% of that of the home countries of foreign-capital companies. In the case of Company B, its productivity in China is only one-fifth of its productivity in Korea. However, Chinese laborers do not accept that Korean workers are five times as productive as them or that the quality of products made by the Koreans is better. Low productivity in China results from (1) a small number of skilled laborers due to high turnover rate, (2) the prevalence of egalitarianism (or communistic values), (3) low levels of education, and (4) a lack of business management skills. Despite low productivity in China, these companies realize high profits because of the low wages.

Labor productivity and wages are closely connected. Hong Kong and Chinese labor-intensive companies pay wages based on ability and productivity (Companies A, P, and R). It is an effective system. Laborers can be seen working even during meal times in companies using the ability-oriented system. On the other hand, Companies B, G, and H, which are also labor-intensive, adopt the seniority system. However, even here, the unhealthy practices of egalitarianism cannot be completely avoided. They set goals that can be achieved during the eight hours of the working day and pay differently according to performance.

For example, Company G pays the entire wage when at least 80% of the goal is achieved, and it pays a bonus for exceeding 100%. However, when performance is below 80% of the goal, the whole amount is not given. The basic wage makes up only one fifth of total wages in mergered type company L and only one-tenth of total wages in the Chinese company Q. This resembles the ability-oriented system. This system is not limited to foreign-capital companies. Chinese companies in the special economic zones also adopt the ability-oriented system or a similar system in order to solve the chronic problem of egalitarianism.

BUSINESS ACHIEVEMENTS

In the past many companies that established business in the special economic zones reported business deficits, but it is now otherwise. Although companies in the zones have various problems, they generally yield profits. It usually takes just one year to reach the break-even point, a result of low wages, low cost, and inferior working and living conditions offered to workers.

BUSINESS PROBLEMS

When doing business in the special economic zones, management faces difficulties that are unique to China. An example is the previously discussed family register system. Abuse of administrative power is another big problem. For example, Company K was forced to buy rat poison that cost 90 yuan from the local government. In addition, it was asked to install an unnecessary emergency alarm in the factory at a cost of 3,000. If the company had not installed the alarm, it would have faced bureaucratic difficulties from the local government. These abuses of administrative power were especially concentrated in foreign-capital companies and many companies I visited suffered them. In another case, Company I was asked to buy as many 90-yuan government bonds as the total number of laborers in the company: 3,500 bonds. When the company refused, it received a notice from the local government stating that temporary residence cards for the company's laborers would not be issued unless the company bought the bonds. In addition to these demands by the local government, company

employees were required to participate in environment clean-ups and road maintenance activities. Sometimes the company was even asked to donate money. Companies
doing business in China have to accept this reality.

OVERALL EFFECTS OF FOREIGN-CAPITAL COMPANIES

Currently, the typical worker in the special economic zones is a female temporary
laborer around twenty years old from the rural areas of Guangdong Province, working
without job security in small-scale assembly factories. The work itself is usually simple,
and does not require special education facilities or training programs. Welfare facilities
are rare, labor regulations are violated, the labor union does not function, and
employers fire laborers at will. Holidays are few and working hours are long. Living
quarters are very small, fit only to sleep in, not to live in. One shower room and one
bathroom are assigned to twenty to thirty persons, and in winter, people wash their
bodies with warm wet towels because hot water is not provided. Most production
facilities and raw materials used in the foreign companies are imported from other
countries. Many products made for export only illegally find their way into the
domestic markets.

Under these circumstances, companies in the special economic zones usually
achieve good business results. Laborers, however, do not always benefit. In the zones,
the labor turnover rate is once every two to three years. Workers are forced to return
to their hometowns by the family register system, one of China's many population
control policies, which permits nonresident workers to stay in the zones for only a
limited time. Upon returning to their homes, most return to farming because they
either were not able to acquire enough skills to take on other factory jobs or else they
find their new skills irrelevant. Some open stores with money saved from working in
the special zones. Against this structure, I feel that the outcomes China expected from
the special economic zones when they were first established, such as the transfer of
advanced technology and advanced business management skills, are difficult to realize.

PART IV

Significance of Special Economic Zones to the Chinese Economy

14

Economic Relations with Hong Kong, Macao, and Taiwan

Special economic zones present many unforeseen problems although they have produced remarkable economic development. To discuss the significance of China's special economic zones to the entire Chinese economy it is necessary to analyze the following areas: the role of the zones as export processing areas, their role as representatives of China; the return of Hong Kong and Macao to China in 1997 and 1999, respectively; unification with Taiwan, and economic relations between the zones and internal areas. This is examined in Chapter 15.

ECONOMIC SIGNIFICANCE OF HONG KONG, MACAO, AND TAIWAN TO THE SPECIAL ECONOMIC ZONES

Economic relations between the zones and Hong Kong, Macao, and Taiwan have become closer since the zones were established in 1980. The current status of each zone is explained in the areas of investment, trade, and cross-border exchange.

Shenzhen Special Economic Zone

Of the five zones, economic relations between Hong Kong–Macao–Taiwan and Shenzhen Special Economic Zone are most active.

Investment

Most foreign-capital companies in Shenzhen Special Economic Zone are from Hong Kong, Macao, and Taiwan. From 1987 to 1989, those countries accounted for 63% ($782.55 million) of total investment ($1.24 billion). They invested in 99% of over 5,000 Sanlaiyibao corporations in Shenzhen, covering a wide range of business areas, including industry, commerce, basic construction, tourism, and agriculture.[1]

Trade

In 1989, Shenzhen's exports and imports were $2.17 billion and $1.58 billion, respectively. Seventy-eight percent of total exports and 67.5% of total imports were traded to Hong Kong, Macao and Taiwan.[2] Most products made in Shenzhen are exported to Southeast Asia, Australia, Europe, and North America via Hong Kong–Macao–Taiwan, and this explains the growth of trade between those countries and Shenzhen Special Economic Zone.

Cross-Border Exchange

Transport development between Hong Kong–Macao–Taiwan and Shenzhen has increased tourist traffic (see Table 14-1). The case of Hong Kong and Shenzhen is particularly remarkable. In order to better accommodate and efficiently process the increasing overland cross-border traffic, the Wenjindudao customs department was expanded with a new office in Shatoujiao. A train runs directly between Guangzhou and Giulong three times a day carrying over ten million Hong Kong and Macao residents and other foreign tourists annually. The Huanggang seaway in Fujiantuan in Shenzhen, which connects Luomazhou to Hong Kong, was opened in December 1989 and carries 3000 passengers per day. Since the establishment of the Shenzhen Economic Zone ten years ago, 13.1 million foreign tourists, mostly from the Chinese Diaspora, have visited. Of these, about 95% are from Hong Kong–Macao–Taiwan. With the increase in visitors to Shenzhen, demand for hotels, restaurants, shopping malls and recreational facilities has been rising also. Foreign tourists are an important source of currency in Shenzhen, generating 2.18 billion yuan (foreign currency convertible note). In 1989, the total inflow of foreign currency was $830.11 million, and 15.5 percent ($128.8 million) of it was from foreign tourists.[3]

Zhuhai Special Economic Zone

Investment

Total foreign capital directly invested in Zhuhai from 1980 to 1989 was $461.8 million. Of that, Hong Kong and Macao contributed $255.1 million and $186.1 million, respectively, the sum of which forms 96% of the total. This shows that Zhuhai depends on Hong Kong and Macao for its foreign capital more than Shenzhen does. The major investment areas are industry and tourism.

Table 14-1
Travel Times between Hong Kong and Shenzhen

		Via land		Via sea
		Direct train	Direct bus	High-speed ship
Shenzhen	Lahu	40 minutes	90 minutes	—
	Shakou	—	—	50 minutes

Trade

Zhuhai's total trade in 1989 amounted to $636.25 million, 32.8 times that of 1980. Exports formed $421.05 million, 88.4% of it going to Hong Kong and Macao.[4]

Cross-Border Exchange

Zhuhai and Macao are one hour apart overland. Thanks to this convenient thruway, more than 2.2 million foreign tourists, including overseas Chinese, visited Zhuhai from 1980 to 1989. Eighty-six percent (1.9 million) of them were from Hong Kong, Macao, and Taiwan. Foreign tourists contributed 1.238 billion yuan (foreign currency convertible note) in foreign currency. This amounts to 62.9% of Zhuhai's foreign currency inflow, twenty-two times that of 1980.[5]

Shantou Special Economic Zone

Investment

Most foreign direct investment in Shantou is by Hong Kong, Macao, and Taiwan. In 1987, there were ninety-one cases of foreign direct investment, and eighty (87.9%) of them were by Hong Kong and Macao. In 1988, that figure represented seventy-one of the total seventy-eight cases (91%). In terms of actual investment, those two countries accounted for 86.9% of investments, amounting to $50.64 million. If Taiwan's investment of $2.81 million is added to this, 91.7% of the total was invested by Hong Kong, Macao, and Taiwan. The major investment area was industry.

Trade

In 1989, Shantou's total trade amounted to $299.38 million, sixty-six times the 1984 figure. Exports to Hong Kong and Macao represented $264.77 million, forming 88.8% of total trade.[6] Ninety-five percent of total 1987 imports ($125.32 million) originated from Hong Kong.[7]

Cross-Border Exchange

Planes, buses, and ships operate daily between Shantou and Hong Kong, taking forty minutes, twelve hours, and thirteen hours, respectively.[8] From 1984 to 1989, the total number of foreign visitors was 64,159, most from Hong Kong, Macao, and Taiwan. Foreign currency earnings from those visitors from 1985 to 1989 amounted to 136.84 million yuan (foreign currency convertible note).

Xiamen Special Economic Zone

Since Xiamen became a special economic zone in 1980, its economic relations with Hong Kong, Macao, and Taiwan have deepened, especially with Taiwan.

Investment

Most foreign direct investment in Xiamen was by Hong Kong, Macao, and Taiwan. From 1980 to 1989, their share of foreign direct investment was 82.3% (557 cases).

This accounted for 83% ($1.02 billion) of total investment. Major investment areas included industry, real estate, and services.

Trade

Hong Kong and Macao are the largest markets for Xiamen's exports and imports, which amounted to $970 million in 1989. This was 3.14 times the 1985 figure. Total exports were $324.5 million, 42.3% of this to Hong Kong and Macao. The major exported items were consumer goods, such as TVs, tape recorders, telephones, beverages, and cooking oil.[9]

Cross-Border Exchange

In 1989, 138,508 foreign tourists visited Xiamen: 32,476 of them foreigners or nonethnic Chinese, 2,375 Chinese, 73,118 Taiwanese, and 30,541 were from Hong Kong and Macao. The Taiwanese represented over 50% of the total, and if the number of ethnic Chinese from Hong Kong and Macao is added to this, the total comes to 103,659 or 75% of the total. Foreign currency earnings from these tourists amount to 113.52 million yuan (foreign currency convertible note), making 25.8% of total foreign currency earned by banks in Xiamen.[10]

Hainan Province Special Economic Zone

Investment

As of 1989, based on negotiated cases, Hong Kong, Macao, and Taiwan accounted for 84.6% of foreign investment in Hainan Province. Their share in terms of investment value was 74%. The major areas were industry, real estate, and services.

Trade

From 1986 to 1989, 75.5% of total exports went to Hong Kong, Macao, and Taiwan, while 78% of total imports (1987 to 1989) originated from Hong Kong.

Cross-Border Exchange

Travel times between Hong Kong and Hainan Province are shown in Table 14-2. In 1989, 110,473 foreign tourists visited Hainan Province. Hong Kong, Macao, and Taiwan visitors made up 80% of them. They spent 44.3 million yuan (foreign currency convertible note).

To summarize, the economic importance of Hong Kong, Macao and Taiwan to the special economic zones is investment, trade, and cross-border exchange. First, as

Table 14-2
Travel Times between Hong Kong and Hainan Province

		Direct bus	Passenger ship	Plane
Hainan	Haikou	24 hours	22 hours	50 minutes
	Sanya	—	40 hours	—

analyzed in Part II, the flow of foreign capital to the special economic zones is not so large. Foreign capital provided only an auxiliary mode for economic progress, but the economic development of those special zones would not have been possible without it. Whether foreign capital was the core factor in the development of the special economic zones is difficult to prove, nevertheless, it was essential. Since all five special economic zones depend on capital from Hong Kong, Macao, and Taiwan, the entry of those countries' companies to the special economic zones was crucial. Second, the largest markets of each special economic zone are Hong Kong, Macao, and Taiwan. Trade in the zones could not have been so successful without these markets. Finally, the large influx of tourists from Hong Kong, Macao, and Taiwan has been essential to the economic advancement of the special economic zones, providing a considerable amount of foreign currency.

ECONOMIC SIGNIFICANCE OF THE SPECIAL ECONOMIC ZONES TO HONG KONG, MACAO, AND TAIWAN

The following examines the advantages of doing business with China's special economic zones for Hong Kong, Macao, and Taiwan.

Production Cost Advantage

Many companies from Hong Kong, Macao, and Taiwan set up operations in the special economic zones, and the most important factor influencing their decision to enter was the abundant supply of low-cost labor. Wages in Shenzhen Special Economic Zone, the highest among the five zones, are only one-tenth of Hong Kong's (see Table 14-3). This wage disparity gets even wider over time. There are two reasons for this: (1) labor shortages in Hong Kong, Macao, and Taiwan and (2) changes in the exchange rate. Unemployment in Hong Kong was 4.5% in 1983, but declined to the current (full employment) rate of 1.6% (1990).[11] This decline caused a shortage of labor, a drastic increase in wages, and many changes in the employment structure of laborers.

As shown in Table 14-4, the number of laborers employed in the manufacturing sector decreased, while numbers in finance and services sectors increased. This change can be explained by higher wages and easier work in the latter sectors. Therefore, corporations (especially manufacturing companies) enter the special economic zones, where labor is sufficient and wages are low, to avoid labor shortages and higher wages in their home countries.

The 35% upward revaluation of the Taiwanese dollar against the U.S. dollar over the past ten years, shown in Table 14-5, combined with the 18% decline in the Chinese yuan, brought Taiwanese corporations into China.[12] The revaluation of the new Taiwanese dollar lowered the competitiveness of Taiwanese products in international markets and dealt a strong blow to Taiwan's exports, making it favorable for small- and medium-sized manufacturing corporations focusing on exports to establish business in China where production unit cost is low. Hong Kong and Taiwan companies entered the zones to take advantage of this, as did companies from Korea and Singapore.

Table 14-3
Comparison of Wage Levels among Areas (unit: yuan, %)

	Hong Kong	Taiwan	Shenzhen	Zhuhai	Shantou	Xiamen	Hainan Province
1980	—	3,901	1,133	733	—	718	—
1981	—	5,268 (35.0)	1,196 (5.6)	978 (33.4)	—	—	—
1982	21,170	5,938 (12.7)	1,408 (17.7)	1,031 (5.4)	—	797	—
1983	23,499 (11.0)	6,330 (6.6)	1,610 (13.7)	1,219 (18.2)	—	870 (9.2)	—
1984	25,468 (8.4)	8,938 (41.2)	2,266 (41.5)	1,463 (13.3)	1,143	1,023 (17.6)	—
1985	26,611 (4.5)	11,106 (24.2)	2,524 (11.4)	1,727 (18.0)	1,446 (26.5)	1,337 (30.7)	1,020
1986	28,098 (5.6)	14,943 (34.5)	2,568 (1.7)	1,832 (6.1)	1,594 (10.2)	1,556 (16.4)	—
1987	30,795 (9.6)	18,917 (26.6)	2,798 (9.0)	2,093 (14.2)	1,894 (18.8)	1,734 (11.4)	1,233
1988	33,132 (7.6)	—	3,543 (26.6)	2,764 (32.1)	2,489 (34.6)	2,336 (34.7)	1,399
1989	37,440 (13.0)	—	3,919 (10.6)	3,266 (18.1)	3,263 (31.0)	2,771 (18.6)	1,640

Sources: Hong Kong Economic Report, ed., 1990, p. 20; Economic Affairs Division of Hong Kong City Government, 1990, p. 48; Council for Economic Planning and Development of Republic of China, 1988, p. 18; State Statistical Bureau of China, 1990, p. 864; Shenzhen Special Economic Zone Yearbook, ed., 1985–1990; interviews with the staffs of the Statistical Bureau of Shenzhen and Zhuhai Statistics Bureau, January 4–May 15, 1991; Shantou Special Economic Zone Yearbook, ed., 1990, p. 344; Xiamen Special Economic Zone Yearbook, ed. 1990; Statistical Bureau of Hainan, various years.

Notes: ( ) is rate of progress from previous year. Averages of Hong Kong and Taiwan are for manufacturing sector only. China's special economic zones show average for all industrial sectors.

Table 14-4
Change in Structure of Employment in Hong Kong (unit: person, %)

	1984 Dec.	1985 Dec.	1986 Dec.	1987 March	1987 June	1987 Sept.	1987 Dec.	1988 March	1988 June	1988 Sept.	1989 March	1989 Dec.	1990 March
Manufacturing	898,900 (5.1)	847,600 (-5.7)	865,600 (2.1)	864,900 (2.8)	895,600 (1.1)	875,300 (0.6)	867,900 (0.3)	849,100 (-1.8)	869,900 (-3.0)	844,600 (-3.5)	810,582 (-5.0)	787,641 (-2.8)	764,700 (-3.0)
Banks, insurance, real estate	169,500 (4.8)	180,900 (6.7)	194,300 (7.4)	197,200 (6.2)	204,700 (8.1)	209,900 (9.8)	212,200 (9.3)	213,900 (8.4)	225,700 (10.3)	230,500 (9.9)	247,502 (7.4)	255,401 (3.2)	263,300 (3.0)
Trade, wholesale and retail	395,600 (8.1)	427,000 (7.9)	438,100 (2.6)	437,900 (3.3)	464,000 (7.5)	463,800 (7.4)	473,600 (8.1)	486,900 (11.2)	517,600 (11.5)	512,200 (10.0)	514,800 (0.5)	572,000 (11.1)	572,000 (0.0)
Hotels	178,200 (7.3)	173,400 (-2.7)	182,000 (5.0)	182,100 (6.2)	184,600 (3.0)	181,900 (0.5)	184,200 (1.2)	186,400 (2.4)	192,800 (4.4)	186,300 (2.4)	187,302 (0.5)	205,428 (9.7)	201,400 (-2.0)
Construction	68,200 (-2.8)	66,300 (-3.3)	70,800 (6.8)	71,800 (8.7)	71,900 (10.8)	71,300 (3.4)	72,500 (2.4)	74,100 (3.3)	70,300 (-0.8)	73,100 (2.5)	72,716 (-0.6)	69,006 (-5.1)	74,200 (7.0)
Government employees	173,500 (2.2)	174,900 (2.2)	178,100 (1.8)	179,100 (2.4)	180,400 (2.7)	181,800 (3.1)	182,200 (2.9)	182,800 (2.1)	183,700 (1.8)	184,900 (1.7)	186,516 (0.8)	188,400 (1.0)	188,400 (0.0)

Source: Economic Affairs Division of Hong Kong City Government, 1987–1990.

Note: ( ) is rate of progress from previous year.

Table 14-5
Exchange Rate between New Taiwanese Dollar and U.S. Dollar

Time classification	Buying	Selling
1978, 12	35.95	36.05
1979, 12	35.98	36.08
1980, 12	35.96	36.06
1981, 12	37.79	37.89
1982, 12	39.86	36.96
1983, 12	40.22	40.32
1984, 12	39.42	39.52
1985, 12	39.80	39.90
1986, 12	35.45	35.55
1987, 12	28.50	28.60
1988, 12	27.70	27.80

Source: Council for Economic Planning and Development of Republic of China, 1989, p. 199.

The entry of foreign-capital companies into the special economic zones was caused by various incentives including tax exemptions, cheap rent, and low power and water expenses. The labor-intensive textile companies of Asia's newly industrialized nations got a setback when they were excluded from the special customs exemption by the United States starting in 1989, prompting corporations to look for a new production base, such as the special economic zones in China. Noneconomic incentives are shared culture, language, and family between Guangdong and Fujian Provinces, where zones are located, and Hong Kong, Macao, and Taiwan.

Advantage as an Export-Import Market

The special economic zones are important markets for exports and imports from Hong Kong, Macao, and Taiwan. With the progress of China's open-market policy, Hong Kong imports a considerable quantity of products from all areas of China, especially from the special economic zones, where those products are re-exported to other countries. Similarly, Hong Kong imports goods from other countries and re-exports them to all areas of China, especially the special economic zones, that is, Hong Kong plays the role of trade transit area. Trade relations among the special economic zones, Hong Kong, Macao, and third countries are shown in Figure 14-1.

Imports to Hong Kong and Macao from the special economic zones amounted to $28.68 million in 1989.[13] Hong Kong and Macao exported $12.48 million worth of goods to the special economic zones.[14] The role of the special economic zone as a

Figure 14-1

Trade Relations among Special Economic Zones, Hong Kong, and Third Countries

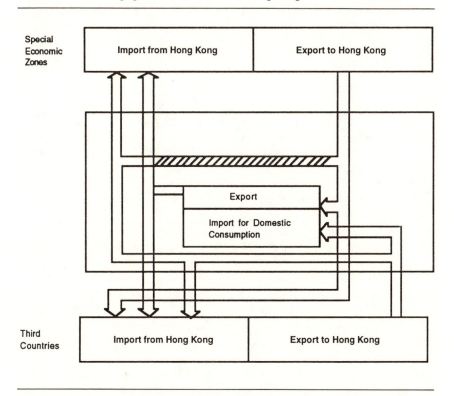

Note: The cross-hatching represents the route through which products are imported from the special economic zones to Hong Kong and re-exported to the special economic zones via Hong Kong.

market for exports and imports does not affect only Hong Kong and Macao. It also affects Taiwan and even Korea. China re-exports to or re-imports from Taiwan and Korea through Hong Kong and Macao. From 1979, when China began to enact its open economic policy to foreign countries, its indirect trade with Taiwan was H.K.\$27.17 billion as of 1989, and H.K.\$16.12 billion with Korea (1988). China has continuously had trade deficits in the indirect trade with Hong Kong since 1980, and the gap is becoming larger. This shows that Taiwan has particularly enjoyed great economic profits through indirect trade with China.

Cheap foodstuffs dominate this trade. Hong Kong's agricultural sector has performed poorly in the industrial structure, providing only 20% of the city-state's food supply. Therefore, it depends highly on imports for most foodstuffs. About 40% of its food imports come from China. However, it is difficult to assess how much of the food was imported through the special economic zones. Judging from the dependency of exports and imports of the special economic zones on Hong Kong, it is assumed that the special economic zones have played a very important role as suppliers of cheap foodstuffs to Hong Kong. Chinese foodstuffs that are cheap, fresh (due to geographical proximity), and agreeable to the Chinese taste have played a very important role in containing the increase of living expenses in Hong Kong where food expenses form over 50% of total living expenses.

Other Advantages

Water and electricity are essential to Hong Kong industry and both are supplied from Shenzhen. Hong Kong has been depending on Shenzhen for electricity since 1992. In February 1985, China and Hong Kong established the Guangdong United Limited Corporation of Nuclear Power in the form of a merger in Shenzhen. The Guangdong Nuclear Power Plant was constructed in 1992 by this corporation in the coastal area of Dayawan, forty-five kilometes away in a straight line from Shenzhen city, fifty-three kilometers in a straight line from Hong Kong city. This power plant has an annual power capacity of 10 billion kw, and will continue to supply 45% of its produced power to Hong Kong until the year 2012.

With the industrial development in Hong Kong, the consumption of water including water for industrial use increased continuously to the point where demand exceeded supply. As a result, the Hong Kong government constructed a reservoir and built a pipe line linking Shenzhen Reservoir and Hong Kong in 1960. Since then, Hong Kong has been supplied with 13 million tons of water each year.[15] At the outset of the 1980s, demand for water continued to increase, reaching 430 million tons in 1987 (see Table 14-6). The water supply from Shenzhen forms 57% of Hong Kong's total water consumption. Hong Kong's dependency is expected to increase in the future.

As Hong Kong, Macao, and Taiwan have played an important role in the progress of the special economic zones, the zones have also played an important role in the economic advancement of Hong Kong, Macao, and Taiwan. This has been especially true in the case of Hong Kong. It is not an overstatement to say that the economic progress of Hong Kong would not have been achieved without the special economic zones. Taiwan also has enjoyed considerable profits through direct investment in and trade with the zones.

During the past ten years, the special economic zones and Hong Kong, Macao, and Taiwan have practically become one large trading area. When the return of Hong Kong and Macao, and the future closer relationship with Taiwan are considered, the future of economic exchanges between Hong Kong, Macao, Taiwan, and China through the special economic zones looks positive. I believe this development will be the most consequential benefit of the special economic zones.

Table 14-6
Water Consumption in Hong Kong (unit: 1,000 tons)

	Consumed amounts	Supplied from China	Rate of dependency on China (%)
1976	405,403	91,304	22.54
1977	386,945	131,377	33.95
1978	412,372	144,496	35.04
1979	467,011	148,277	31.75
1980	508,004	171,627	33.78
1981	501,412	210,912	41.57
1982	519,461	239,352	46.08
1983	592,030	250,748	42.35
1984	627,109	285,472	45.52
1985	636,977	319,378	50.14
1986	703,015	360,191	51.24
1987	750,115	431,664	57.55

Source: Census and Statistics Department of Hong Kong Government, 1976–1987.

15

Economic Relations with Chinese Cities and Provinces

INVESTMENT

Many internal corporations have entered the special economic zones using the following three methods of entry:

1. Joint venture between a company in the special economic zones and an internal company. This method can be further classified into the following two types.

    (a) Mutual Investment between an internal corporation and a special zone corporation that is based in the special economic zone: About 3,900 corporations of this type have been established in Shenzhen Special Economic Zone since its inception.

    (b) Mutual investment between an internal corporation and a special zone corporation in a company that is based in the internal areas: As of 1990, such corporations in the Shenzhen Special Economic Zone have eighty-six factories and branches in twenty-eight provinces, cities, and independent districts across China.

2. An independent investment by a single internal corporation or a mutual investment between several internal corporations.

3. A triangular mutual investment among a special zone corporation, internal corporation, and a foreign corporation. This type of investment is based on the understanding that these three parties will utilize resources and technology of the internal corporation; geographical and political superiority of the economic special zone; and the supply of foreign capital, market openings, and design development of the foreign corporation. As of 1990, there were 1,200 corporations of this type in Shenzhen.

Besides these investment types, many other companies form public corporations with the types mentioned above in the special economic zones. In the early stages of development, many corporations entered with investment methods one and two, but in recent years investment arrangements between public corporations and investment method three have become more frequent.

Stages of Entry

The entry process of internal corporations into the special economic zones during the past ten years can be divided into the following stages:

First Stage (1980–1982)

Internal corporations entered the special economic zones. As each area became a special economic zone, the rapid increase of population created a large demand for basic needs such as food, housing, and clothing. Accordingly, the internal corporations that entered the zones focused on farming, restaurants, hotels, tourism, and other services.

Second Stage (1983–1985)

During this stage, internal corporations invested extensively in the special economic zones. The background reasons were (1) improved investment conditions in the zones and (2) advocacy by high-ranking officials in the central government, starting with Deng Xiaoping. In May 1983, the Shenzhen municipal government announced the formulation of Regulations on Preferential Measures for Internal Corporations Investing in Shenzhen Special Economic Zone. These regulations provided clear-cut guidelines concerning land rentals, laborers' family registers, taxes, selling of products, raw materials, and supply of facilities to internal corporations running businesses in the zones. As a result of these regulations, internal corporations and foreign-capital corporations in the special economic zones began to receive equal treatment.

During this period, many corporations from Guangdong Province and other provinces and cities across China established businesses in the zones. Corporate business type changed from small businesses to relatively larger industries. In addition, the investment method changed from joint venture between corporations in the same province or city to that between corporations in different locations. Moreover, the joint-venture corporations changed from producing similar items to producing various kinds of items. During this period, about 2,000 internal corporations from all areas of China were set up in Shenzhen.[16] This entry of internal corporations into the special economic zone played a very important role in attracting foreign capital.

Third Stage (1986–Present)

During this stage, the internal corporations that had entered the special economic zones during the second stage underwent changes in industry structure leading to adjustments in the business sectors of existing internal corporations, and channeling newly entering corporations into advanced technology- or export-oriented industries. This strategy was drafted in 1986 during the Convention for the Special Economic Zones. The convention prescribed the pursuit of high production, a high level of technology, and high profits. It also concluded that the industrial base of the special economic zones should be export-oriented industries. Based on this new development in policy for the special economic zones, local governments encouraged newly entering internal corporations to produce major raw materials in the internal areas of China, to process the materials in the special economic zones, and then to export semifinished or finished goods. In addition, internal corporations in the zones were also encouraged to acquire advanced technology and business management skills.

In July 1987, under the slogan "The entire nation supporting the special zone, the special zone working for the entire nation," the Shenzhen government created the Regulations on Internal Corporations' Business Management for the Progress of the Shenzhen Special Economic Zone. These regulations supplemented the 1983 Regulations on Preferential Measures for Internal Corporations Investing in the Special Economic Zones. The following is a summary of the 1987 regulations.[17]

1. Raw materials and accessories imported by internal corporations for the production of export goods are exempt from tariffs and the consolidated industry and commerce tax. Internal corporations producing tobacco, liquor, and a few other items are also exempted from 50% of the consolidated industry and commerce tax if products are sold within the special economic zones. With a few exceptions on government regulated goods, other products—if sold within the zones—are also completely exempt from this tax.

2. A corporate income tax of 15% is imposed on the profits of internal corporations. However, corporations that entered the special economic zones after January 1, 1986, and have been in business for over ten years, are exempted from such tax for the first year after yielding a profit and liable to pay only half the tax for the second year. Corporations emphasizing advanced technology exports are exempted from the tax entirely for two years after yielding profit and liable for half the tax for the third year.

3. Internal corporations are charged the same level of utility charges as state-run corporations in the zones for operational expenses such as water, electricity, transportation, and communication.

4. Internal corporations' investments of fixed capital in the zones follow the basic construction plan of the special zones, not of the internal areas, which works to the internal corporations' advantage.

5. Any internal corporation that invests independently in the special zones technically cannot borrow from a bank in the special economic zone. However, it is allowed to take out loans for its operating fund at the same interest as other special zone or state-run corporations.

6. Internal corporations do not have to follow the laws concerning foreign currency management for foreign currency earned through exports. They only have to follow a few regulations required by the local government. Therefore, internal corporations can more or less freely manage their foreign currency.

7. When an internal corporation exports over 70% of its products or its yearly export volume exceeds U.S.$500,000, its products are entitled to customs clearance. Such preferential treatment encouraged many internal corporations to establish business in the special economic zones during the past ten years, and these incentive policies contributed greatly to the progress of the zones.

The special economic zones depend greatly on the internal areas not only in terms of the direct investments made by internal corporations, but also in terms of the supply of funds. As of 1988, the total amount of loans given out by Shenzhen's various financial agencies was 17.37 billion yuan. Of this, 89% came from the internal areas.[18] What advantages did the internal corporations gain by coming to the special economic zones? Although complete statistics are yet to be published, the profits earned by internal corporations in the Shenzhen Special Economic Zone have been estimated to exceed 2 billion yuan over the past ten years using available data. In Zhuhai, the profits in 1988 were 200 million yuan, and internal corporations in Shantou paid 3.5 million yuan in taxes to the local government in 1986.[19] As for acquiring advanced technology and managerial skills, from 1986 to 1989, over 100 out of 500 cases of advanced technology that had been introduced to the Shenzhen Special Economic Zone were transferred to the internal areas.[20]

TRADE

As discussed, the special economic zones have been a conduit between foreign countries, including Hong Kong, and the internal areas of China (see Figure 15-1).

Figure 15-1
Trade Relations among Internal Areas, Special Economic Zones, and Foreign Countries

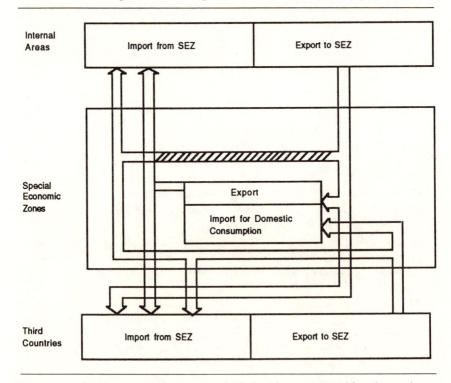

Note: The cross-hatching represents the route through which products are imported from the special economic zones to Hong Kong and re-exported to the special economic zones via Hong Kong.

Because the special economic zones were established from scratch, a considerable amount of human and physical resources was needed for their construction. However, because of a high demand for goods and services and a short supply to fill the needs in the new cities at the outset, serious shortages arose, especially in farming and construction materials. The local governments made up for this shortfall with supplies from the internal areas. Shenzhen procured 70% of construction materials used during the past ten years and 60% of consumer goods as of 1989 from the internal areas.[21] In terms of trade, 32.7% ($710 million) of the materials exported through Shenzhen Special Economic Zone in 1989 was produced in internal areas. Although fluctuations exist, from 1987 to 1989, an average of over 40% of goods were made in the internal areas and exported through Shenzhen Special Economic Zone (see Table 15-1)

The zones purchased a considerable amount of materials from the internal areas during the past ten years. This has been an important factor contributing to the progress of the zones. According to statistics, 40% of exports from the special economic zones were the transit trade type.

LABOR

The acute shortage of labor, especially skilled labor, in the special economic zones was eventually remedied. In Shenzhen Special Economic Zone, over 60,000 skilled laborers came from the internal areas of China. Each special economic zone underwent a drastic increase of population over the past ten years, Shenzhen especially, with an average annual increase of 30.4%. In 1980, when Shenzhen Special Economic Zone was first established, its population was only 94,000, but this increased elevenfold to 1,026,000 in 1989. Most new residents had immigrated from internal areas.

With this dramatic increase in population, the ratio between the permanent population and the temporary population is becoming larger. This is because the temporary population is growing at a rate about 3.5 times faster than the annual increase rate of the permanent population, which is 17.6%. (The household register of Shenzhen Special Economic Zone is selectively given to technicians, managers and college graduates among the people from the internal areas.)

Table 15-1
Exported Goods in Shenzhen Special Economic Zone by Industrial Area
(unit: U.S.$10,000, %)

	1987		1988		1989	
	Total	Percentage	Total	Percentage	Total	Percentage
Special economic zone	82,085	58.0	97,788	52.9	132,279	63.1
Areas outside the special zone	59,269	42.0	87,161	47.1	71,098	32.7

Source: Interview with the staff of the Statistical Bureau of Shenzhen, January 4–May 15, 1991.

The economic relations between the special economic zones and internal areas in the areas of investment, trade, and labor can be regarded as one of codependence, that is, economic cooperation is an essential factor for the development of the special economic zones, while internal corporations have enjoyed high profits by entering the zones.

16

Chinese Multipolar Economic Block and the Special Economic Zones

In previous studies, the status of the special economic zones in the Chinese economy is discussed by analyzing the role of the zones within a national framework. Such an analysis, however, has many problems because China is a country of multiple economic areas: China may be just one country, but from the economic perspective, it is more appropriate to see it as akin to an international economic system rather than a national economy. China is a giant country in terms of both land size and population. Unlike typical national economies, with equal distribution of economic power and a free flow of production factors (capital, goods, and labor), China's economic structure is composed of several strata of development, with sharp differences between each stratum.

For example, when the per capita incomes between provinces are compared, there is about a ninefold difference between the highest, Shanghai City, and the lowest, Guizhou Province. When compared with Hong Kong or the special economic zones, the difference is even larger. Hong Kong's per capita income is about 100 times that of Guizhou Province and between these two areas exist many economic zones with various differences. In addition, many restrictions are imposed on the movement of production factors between economic zones.[22]

With these facts in mind, it is more appropriate to discuss the nature of the Chinese economy by looking at China as an economic union composed of many different economic entities rather than as a single, uniform economic entity.

MULTIPLE STRUCTURE OF THE CHINESE ECONOMY

The zonal classification of China's economic structure has been changed several times.[23] This book follows the classification method of the Seventh Five-Year Plan, which divides the economy into the developed East Zone, the transit Central Zone, and the undeveloped West Zone.[24] The East Zone consists of twelve provinces

(Liaoning, Hebei, Tianjin, Beijing, Shandong, Jiangsu, Shanghai, Zhejiang, Fujian, Guangdong, Hainan, and Guangsi); the West Zone consists of nine provinces (Shanxi, Gansu, Ningxia, Sichuan, Yunnan, Guizhou, Qinghai, Xinjiang, and Xizang); and the Central Zone consists of nine provinces (Heilongjiang, Jilin, Nei Mongol, Shansi, Henan, Anhui, Hunan, Hubei, and Jiangsi).

Major social and economic indexes of these three zones in 1989 are shown in Table 16-1. There are considerable differences among the three zones in terms of geography, natural resources, and economic and technological levels. Land and minerals are concentrated in the Central and West Zones, while industries, high population, and large cities are centered in the East Zone.

The size of the East Zone is relatively small, but it has a high population density. Agriculture and industry are relatively well developed. In 1989, the East Zone occupied 13.4% of land mass, 32.7% of agricultural land, 41.3% of the population, and 43.3% of agriculture. Its shares of social production, industrial production, and national income were all over 50%. The West Zone, on the other hand, has a large land size and a low population density, but it relatively lags behind in agriculture and industry. In 1989, its shares of the nation were 56.9% of land, 24.0% of agricultural land, 23.1% of population, 20.2% of agriculture, 15.8% of national income, and less than 15% of social and industrial production.

The population and production densities in the East Zone, Central Zone, and West Zone are 332 persons/m^2 and 71.14 yuan/m^2, 130 persons/m^2 and 17.41 yuan/m^2, and 44 persons/m^2 and 4.48 yuan/m^2, respectively. In 1989, the ratio of population density among the three zones (East:Central:West) was 1:0.40:0.13, the ratio of production density 1:0.24:0.66, and the ratio of agricultural land per person 1:1.55:1.73. From the perspective of economic development, the ratio of production for agriculture and industry combined per person in the zones is 1:0.58:0.45 (East:Central:West), while that of only industrial production per person is 1:0.50:0.36. However, the ratio of consumption per person, 1:0.85:0.71, does not vary too much between the zones, a result of the central government's income redistribution policy.

The three zones show differences in economic efficiency. For example, the increase in social production relative to fixed capital investment with 100 yuan as a base was 151 yuan in the East Zone, 117 yuan in the Central Zone, and 85 yuan in the West Zone, a ratio of 1:0.77:0.56. The increase in national income earned through 10,000 yuan investments in basic construction from 1952 to 1985 was 1,060 yuan in the East, 710 yuan in Central, and 560 yuan in the West, a ratio of 1:0.67:0.53. As for corporate profits, in 1985, the profits self-supporting accounting companies earned from 100 yuan were 30.4 yuan in the East, 18.5 yuan in Central and 16.8 yuan in the West, a ratio of 1:0.61:0.55.

Overall, economic development is fastest in the East Zone and slowest in the West Zone. Accordingly, the three zones can be described as the developed East Zone, the transit Central Zone, and the undeveloped West Zone.

THREE ECONOMIC ZONES AND THE SPECIAL ECONOMIC ZONES

What role do the special economic zones have in China's multiple economic structure? Unfortunately, it is not possible to obtain sufficient data for this specific question. Nevertheless, I have attempted a partial analysis of the special economic zones vis-à-vis China's tripartite economic structure.

Investment

Because data could not be obtained on the origins of internal corporations, numbers of provincial and municipal representative offices entering the special economic zone were used instead. As shown in Table 16-2, 55.2% of representative offices in Shenzhen come from the East Zone, 12.1% from the West Zone, and 32.7% from the Central Zone. From this perspective, it can be said that Shenzhen Special Economic Zone has strong economic relations with the East Zone. Furthermore, entry from Guangdong Province is the largest in the East Zone. When other special economic zones besides Shenzhen are included, this tendency is even stronger.

Trade

No specific data reveals the origin of materials supplied to the special economic zones. However, judging by the percentage of provincial and municipal representative offices that enter the special economic zones, it seems that the East Zone, particularly Guangdong Province, is the largest supplier.

Labor

There are no statistics available on the city or province of origin for the huge numbers of laborers who come into the special economic zones from the internal areas. However, based on the estimate of corporate research shown in Part III, it can also be said with confidence that most laborers are from the East Zone centering around Guangdong Province.[25] For an example, among the 296 laborers of Company K, only four have family registers in Shenzhen. The rest of the laborers are from provinces and cities of the internal areas, of which 208 are from Guangdong Province. Of the remaining 84, 20 are from the East Zone; 54 from the Central Zone; and 10 from the West Zone. In percentages among the total laborers, 78.4% are from the East Zone, 18.3% from the Central Zone, and 3.3% from the West Zone.

Percentages for the home origin of laborers working in Shenzhen and Zhuhai Special Economic Zones as of 1988 are shown in Table 16-3. Of the total number of laborers, 83.1% in Shenzhen and 96.4% in Zhuhai are from Guangdong Province alone. When other provinces and cities of the East Zone are included, 87% of the total laborers in Shenzhen and 96.4% in Zhuhai are from this zone.

Table 16-1
Major Economic Indexes in China's Economic Zones, 1985

		Zones			Percentage of nation (%)			Ratio of indexes of three zones (East = 1)	
Indexes	Unit	East Zone	Central Zone	West Zone	East Zone	Central Zone	West Zone	Central Zone	West Zone
Total									
Land size	10,000m²	129.37	281.95	541.37	13.4	29.7	56.9	—	—
Agricultural land size	10,000mu	48,034	63,556	35,264	32.7	43.3	24.0	—	—
Population	10,000 people	42,995	37,125	23,987	41.3	35.6	23.1	—	—
Social production*	100 million yuan	9,203.95	4,906.48	2,424.95	55.6	29.7	14.7	—	—
Agricultural and industrial production	100 million yuan	6,927	3,520	1,721	56.9	28.9	14.2	—	—
Industrial production	100 million yuan	5,664	2,457	1,134	61.2	26.5	12.3	—	—
Agricultural production	100 million yuan	1,263	1,063	587	43.3	36.5	20.2	—	—
National income**	100 million yuan	3,804	2,200	1,094	53.4	30.8	15.8	—	—
Density									
Density of population	person/m²	332	130	44	—	—	—	0.40	0.13
Density of production	10,000 yuan/m²	71.14	17.41	4.48	—	—	—	0.24	0.06
Level of development									
Agricultural land per capita	yuan	1.1	1.7	1.9	—	—	—	1.55	1.73
National income per capita	yuan	896	595	462	—	—	—	0.67	0.53
Agricultural and industrial production per capita	yuan	1,611	948	718	—	—	—	0.58	0.45
Industrial production per capita	yuan	1,317	661.8	472.7	—	—	—	0.50	0.36

Table 16-1 (continued)

	Indexes	Unit	Zones			Percentage of nation (%)			Ratio of indexes of three zones (East = 1)	
			East Zone	Central Zone	West Zone	East Zone	Central Zone	West Zone	Central Zone	West Zone
Efficiency	Consumption level per capita	yuan	459	391	326	—	—	—	0.85	0.71
	Net income per farmer	yuan	463	389	322	—	—	—	0.84	0.70
	Increased amount in social production from investment of 100 yuan of fixed capital in 1975–1985	yuan	151	117	85	—	—	—	0.77	0.56
	Increased amount of national income from investment of 10,000 yuan of basic construction in 1952–1985	yuan	1,060	710	560	—	—	—	0.67	0.53
	Interest from 100 yuan of capital by self-supporting industrial company	yuan	30.4	18.5	16.8	—	—	—	0.61	0.55

Source: State Statistical Bureau of China, 1986.

Notes: *Invariable price in 1980. **Variable price.

Table 16-2
Provincial/Municipal Representative Offices in Shenzhen Special Economic Zone

East Zone	Number	West Zone	Number	Central Zone	Number
Beijing	2				
Tianjin	3	Sichuan	5	Shansi	3
Hebei	4	Guizhou	3	Nei Mongol	1
Liaoning	7	Yunnan	3	Jilin	5
Shanghai	2	Xizang	1	Heilongjiang	6
Jiangsu	17	Shanxi	3	Anhui	10
Zhejiang	18	Gansu	2	Jiangsi	6
Fujian	5	Qinghai	1	Henan	7
Shandong	9	Xinjiang	1	Hubei	8
Guangdong	23	Ningxia	1	Hunan	8
Hainan Province	1				
Total	91	Total	20	Total	54

Source: Interview with the staff of the Statistical Bureau of Shenzhen, January 4–May 15, 1991.

SUMMARY

Local economies are in reality nothing more than the administrative offices of the provinces—independent districts and cities are under the direct control of the central government. The provincial government, which serves as the principle administrative body of the local economy, functions simultaneously as an administrative, social, and economic organization. Of these three, administrative and social organizations are primary, and the economy takes a subordinate position, its objectives determined by the former.

The social objectives of the local government are (1) satisfying consumer needs of the local area, (2) securing full employment of the urban population within the area, (3) ensuring the safety of local society, (4) securing equal distribution of basic welfare to urban and rural residents, and (5) promoting the development of local society. Because such social objectives are given high priority, the local government operates its economy in the following ways. First, the local government conducts business management without causing any bankruptcy mainly in order to satisfy the needs of the local society for employment. Second, by making the companies having good financial conditions and companies having poor financial conditions equal, the gap between them is eliminated. Third, sometimes, actual object distribution is conducted, for example, the distribution of housing or other insufficient goods. Fourth, allowances of food staples, subsidiary food, or vegetables are given in kind, and distribution is

Table 16-3

Breakdown of Laborers' Hometown in Each Special Economic Zone (unit: %)

	Hometown	Shenzhen	Zhuhai
East Zone	Guangdong	83.16	
	Beijing	1.06	
	Hebei	0.40	
	Fujian	0.27	
	Gangsi	0.53	
	Shanghai	0.27	96.36
	Jiangsu	0.40	
	Liaoning	0.27	
	Shandong	0.13	
	Zhejiang	0.13	
	Total	86.62	96.36
Central Zone	Henan	3.18	
	Jilin	0.13	
	Hubei	0.93	3.64
	Hunan	1.19	
	Jiangsi	0.13	
	Total	5.56	3.64
West Zone	Sichuan	3.71	
	Shanxi	2.92	
	Guizhu	0.93	
	Qinghai	0.13	
	Xinjiang	0.13	
	Total	7.82	

Source: Gu Nianliang, ed., 1989, p. 238.

based on egalitarianism. Finally, the method of "Small and all, Big and all" (having all whether large or small) is followed to promote the development of local economy. However, such an industrial system of one unit (Small and all, Big and all) overlaps with the national investment, decreases economic efficiency, and wastes resources.

After examining the relations between the special economic zones and the various economic areas in terms of investment, trade, and labor force, one can see the close relationship between the special economic zones and the internal areas, particularly in the East Zone. This is significant in the economic development pattern of China, where regional differences are large. The special economic zones have tightened mutual relations among Hong Kong, Macao, and Taiwan, the internal areas, especially the East Zone, and the special zones themselves. Through this, remarkable economic development was achieved in the entire region. One can say therefore that the economic zones played a vital role in forming this region's economic network, which has been named the Southern Chinese Economic Block. The southern coastal areas of Fujian, Guangdong, southern areas of Guangsi, Taiwan, Hainan Province and all islands along the southern coast belong to this block. Certain areas of the economic special zones, economic open areas and economic technology development areas, which are located near the sea and Hong Kong and Taiwan, also belong to this economic block. It is in the Southern Chinese Economic Block that the open economic policies to foreign countries are most highly developed. This external expansion, or internationalization, of the Chinese economy has direct consequences not only to China, but to the entire East Asian economy, which also includes the ASEAN network.

As the special economic zones and Hong Kong, Macao, and Taiwan become united, Guangdong Province and the East Zone accomplish their economic progress, though some believe that their economic gap with other zones is growing larger. Regarding this matter, A. Takahashi, describes characteristics of the China's open policy to foreign countries: "With 1978 as a starting point, China began to step into unbalanced development. Companies, laborers, and farmers in some areas acknowledge that they are enjoying a higher standard of living by earning a bigger income earlier than others. By expanding these effects to apply to the whole nation, one can foresee the development of entire state economy."[26] He also indicates the limitations of special economic zone policy and coastal areas development strategies:

The experiences of Japan and southeast Asian countries show that external development is impossible without a balance in internal development. In particular, the strategy of concentrating resources in some regions and making that a symbolic core can provoke disharmony among the people by expanding disparity among regions, classes, and sectors. Therefore, although there may not be big problems in the short term, the development of state economy may be eventually impeded in the long term.[27]

The establishment of the Southern Chinese Economic Block around the local economic network of the special zones is a sign that the Chinese economic structure is slowly changing from a group of state-controlled administrative units to an economic network shaped by market conditions. In the past, the Chinese economic structure was not formed based on economic theory. The political, social, and economic branches were placed under a single body, with priority on government and social welfare, while the economy took a subordinate role. China's original economic structure comprises the central state, local governments, corporations, and Renmin Gongshe. The central government has control over the business activities of medium- and large-scale state-run corporations, economic planning committees, and various cabinet level committees of industrial and agricultural ministries. It receives and conveys instructions to local and state-run corporations through various central management agencies, such as the Chinese People's Bank, according to the vertical management-based central economic plan. As for the corporations and Renmin Gongshe, they cannot be considered economic organizations, but a form of communal production and community welfare system that functions as a complex web of government, economy, and society.[28]

Summary and Conclusion

Prior to China's economic reform and the establishment of the special economic zones, the overall economic development and the accumulated mechanism of low consumption and high investment had been in a state of paralysis owing to out-dated technology, policies focused on heavy industry, and inefficient corporate management. In the rural sector, productivity was bottlenecked due to excessive labor and a decline in farmers' morale. This led to low prices in agricultural products, low wages, low consumption, and high inventory, paralyzing the economy. Under these circumstances, China was forced to seek new sources of investment and technology. In addition, it faced the huge task of integration with Hong Kong, Macao, and Taiwan, whose levels of income and economic development were far ahead of China's. Pressed by these circumstances, China had no choice but to reform its economic system and open its economy to foreign technology and capital. The first step in its reform policy was the establishment of the special economic zones.

The purpose and features of the special economic zones are the evidence of China's open-economy policy. By establishing the special economic zones the central government provided the following economic assistance. It allowed the use of foreign capital and the adjustment of economic activities according to the market mechanism. It gave priority to business-related administrative processing, such as obtaining permits, to those corporations entering the zones. Most importantly, it gave autonomy to the management council of each special economic zone concerning economic affairs. In return, the central government expected the special economic zones to achieve the following objectives: (1) to foster closer relations with Hong Kong, Macao, and Taiwan and (2) to serve as testing grounds for the nation's domestic economic system. It also hoped that the zones would bring about an improvement in domestic economic indicators, such as employment, foreign currency earnings, and technology transfer.

The special economic zones can be seen as facilitating these objectives. They can be defined as districts, confined to areas that meet certain requirements, that promote the country's overall economic development; that operate in a free management system different from the rest of the country; that allow many types of corporations to conduct business activity, including wholly-foreign capital investment; and that contain a wide range of businesses, including industry, agriculture, livestock, fishery, commerce, real estate, tourism, finance, and insurance. In this regard, the special economic zones go beyond their former status as free ports or export processing areas and can truly be called overall economic development areas.

Many arguments have been put forth regarding the character of the special economic zones. The author believes that defining the special economic zones as "controlled capitalism" existing in a socialist state is the most appropriate. This is because the collective ownership and state-controlled economic management which characterize socialism are rare in the special economic zones, and even these restrictions are gradually decreasing.

Fifteen years since their inception, the zones have developed rapidly, expanding employment, increasing income,, raising living standards, attracting foreign capital, encouraging Chinese internal corporations, and increasing foreign currency earnings. Agriculture, the traditional industry of China, is slowly disappearing because of rapid industrialization and urbanization. On the other hand, the services sector has developed due to improvements in distribution networks and the growth of small businesses.

The development of Shenzhen Special Economic Zone has been particularly outstanding. In 1989, Shenzhen's income increased 52 times from 1979, and 2,295 joint-venture and wholly-foreign companies (one-seventh of all joint-venture and wholly-foreign companies across China) set up businesses there. From 1979 to 1989, foreign currency earnings increased 4.1 times to $830 million, and from 1978 to 1989, the average yearly wage increased 5.8 times to 3,943 yuan. This dramatic growth has transformed Shenzhen, which used to be a small fishing town, into a major industrial city with the highest income in China.

The central government has recently put its efforts into the development of Pudong (located in Shanghai), creating competition with the Guangdong Province–centered special economic zone for corporate investments. Government agencies connected to the Department of State and Shanghai City introduced nine new regulations on the development of Pudong. These regulations are expected to lead to fierce competition between Pudong and the other special economic zones for foreign-capital companies, because Pudong's incentives for the foreign-capital companies are as good as those offered by Shenzhen, and Shanghai has the highest level of industrial strength and labor quality in China. Based on limited national support, Guangdong Special Economic Zone faces the challenge of establishing a new development strategy.

A close examination of the causes of growth in the special zones' reveals that, contrary to China's original expectations, economic development was not accomplished by foreign capital alone. Indeed, other factors were stronger determinants of growth. These included investments by the central and local governments, loans from financial agencies, the advantages accruing from being a transit trade area, and the zones' geographic proximity to Hong Kong and Macao.

The introduction of foreign capital did not really bring about the dramatic changes that China expected. Foreign-capital companies did not contribute greatly to the expansion of employment because, unlike Chinese companies, they tended to be capital intensive rather than labor intensive. Since wages paid by foreign-capital companies were not much higher than those paid by Chinese companies, the effect of gaining foreign currency through wages was also negligible. In addition, since the production processes of foreign-capital companies that entered the zones usually involved only simple assembly, most companies did not offer training or educational programs or facilities, and the introduction of advanced technology and skills has not taken place as hoped. Finally, most production equipment and raw materials used by foreign corporations in the zones are imported rather than purchased from the Chinese market. Therefore, the entry of foreign capital has not vitalized the Chinese economy as much as it could have.

Foreign-capital companies, on the other hand, enjoyed high profits by selling their raw materials and products in the Chinese domestic market. Such economic activity took place both legally and illegally, and smuggling and illegal resales are still major social problems. Illegal trade, a serious byproduct of economic development, is not, however, the responsibility of foreign companies alone. China's "look-the-other-way" policy sometimes allows foreign-capital companies in the special economic zones to freely conduct illegitimate business activities.

An analysis of the corporate structure in the special economic zones reveals that the typical laborer is a young female around twenty years old from the rural areas of Guangdong Province. She usually works as a temporary laborer, a very insecure position, under inferior working conditions. Since China's family register system restricts laborers to work for only two to three years on average, most workers return to their homes in the countryside after this period is over. There, they have few opportunities to employ what skills they acquired in the zones. This is a negative aspect of the special economic zones.

Many other problems exist in the zones. They have not taken adequate advantage of their comparative superiority in low production costs (which includes low wages). The labor market is fully the purchaser's market. Wages are low and the labor union has very little power. As a result, laborers are expendable commodities, hired and fired at will. Another serious problem in the zones is the formation of slums and shanty towns, a consequence of drastic increases of temporary farmers, individual stores, and temporary laborers; loose supervision of the public welfare agencies; and high laborer turnover rate. This has yet to become a crucial social issue, but will become a major problem in the near future if it remains ignored. Such structural problems are, of course, difficult to solve, but if they are not addressed, it will be difficult to realize the transfer of advanced technology and management skills as well as the interindustry-related effects that China expects to achieve.

The major cause of these problems is poor and immature management. Although structural problems such as the family register issue can be cited as examples of poor management, the real problem lies in the attitude of local government officials. For example, local officials have been guilty of not taking the time to grasp the significance of, or to enforce, employment contracts between companies and their employees, and of being lax in their inspection of raw materials and export goods entering the zones. Such problems, which stem from both negligence and inexperience, have turned the special economic zones into havens for smuggling and facilitated the abuse of temporary laborers.

CONCLUSION

When all these factors are combined, it can be concluded that the special economic zones were not very successful in their role as export processing areas. However, as discussed before, the significance of the zones goes beyond export processing. One must not forget to take into consideration the significance of the zones in the triangular relationship between the zones, China's internal areas, and Hong Kong/Macao/Taiwan. Through joint efforts, the special economic zones and Hong Kong/Macao/Taiwan are gradually becoming integrated, at least on an economic level. In light of the fast approaching unification of Hong Kong and Macao with the Chinese mainland in 1997 and 1999, respectively, as well as with Taiwan in the near future, this integration is a valuable achievement indeed. In fact, this can be said to be the most important result of the special economic zones.

Although the effects of the special economic zones have yet to be felt throughout the nation, the remarkable economic growth of the East Zone is a direct result of the zones within it. From this, one can infer that the influence of the special economic zones will spread. This process has already begun. Through close cooperation with the East, as well as with Hong Kong, Macao, and Taiwan, the zones are trying to achieve external economic expansion of the entire Southern Chinese Economic Block. The economic success of this block has incited similar movements along the coastal areas with the purpose of forming regional economic networks. This has led to the creation of Both Coastal Economic Block, Greater Shanghai Economic Block, Bohai Economic Block, and the Northeast Economic Block. The formation of an independent economic network is also planned in the internal areas. In the long run, such efforts are expected to contribute to the strengthening and expansion of the entire ASEAN and East Asian economy.

The formation of the Southern Chinese Economic Block has brought about a monumental change in China's economic structure, especially in terms of the vitalization of regional economies. This is because, in contrast to the former system in which the provincial administrative districts served simultaneously as economic units, economic divisions are now determined by the market mechanism. In this light, it can be said that the special economic zones have pioneered the changing economic structure of China. This structural change, which transformed the Chinese economy from a national to an international economic framework, is a landmark in the history of the Chinese economy.

Notes

PROLOGUE

1. *Beijing Zhoubao* (Beijing Weekly Newspaper), January 2, 1979.

PART 1

1. He Zhusheng, 1984, pp. 77–78.
2. Ibid., pp. 77–78.
3. Nakagane, 1985, p. 178.
4. Inagaki, 1986, p. 29.
5. Ibid.
6. Deng Xiaoping, 1987, p. 48. At this time, Deng Xiaoping also mentioned the possibility of applying the open policy to foreign countries for some port cities besides the zones. "Besides the existing economic special zones, port cities such as Dalian and Chingdao must be open, too. They are not called special economic zones, but the same policies being conducted in special zones can be enacted in these cities."
7. China's open economic policy for foreign countries can be divided into two periods according to its position in the Chinese economic development strategy. The first period (1978–87) lasted from the Third General Meeting of the 11th Central Committee of the Communist Party to the announcement of the economic development strategy for the coastal area. During this period, trade with foreign countries and funds, materials, and technology from foreign countries were not major independent factors in the Chinese economy, but were understood only as a means of supplementing Chinese economic development. The second period began with the introduction of the economic development strategy for the coastal area in 1988 and runs to the present. The most significant characteristic of China's open economic policy for foreign countries during this period is that the policy itself became an independent component of the reproduction mode. In other words, China wanted to accomplish its economic development by depending on foreign markets, materials, and funds.
8. Yabuki, 1986, p. 90.

9. This also relates to the question of whether the special economic zones are defined as an essential factor in Chinese economic growth or as an extraneous, supplementary factor. In addition, in terms of selection of industry, this relates to the question of whether the government should first emphasize attraction of labor-intensive industry which would be transformed into technology/knowledge-intensive industry, or whether it should emphasize attraction of technology-intensive industry for attraction of foreign capital and coalition of domestic market (*Renmin Ribao* [People's Daily], August 12, 1985).

10. *Renmin Ribao* (People's Daily), January 7, 1986.

11. Gu Liji, 1984.

12. U.S. Department of Commerce, Bureau of International Commerce, 1970, p. 14.

13. Other interpretations of the special zones include the place where new democratic economical factors exist, allowing various economic factors such as state economy, cooperative economy and private capitalism economy to co-exist; the zone where two types of economy, socialism and capitalism, co-exist; and the zone with the double character of socialism and capitalism.

14. Liu Zhigang, 1989, p. 143.

15. Ibid., pp. 153–54.

16. Tang Huozhao, 1990, p. 35.

17. Zheng Tianlun, Chen Zhuohua, eds., 1990, pp. 241–45.

18. Tang Huozhao, 1986, pp. 124–32.

19. Liu Zhigang, ed., 1989, p. 36.

20. The biggest problem faced after the transformation from a fixed price to a free price system was high inflation. According to an interview with the Statistical Bureau staff in Shenzhen city, the price index recorded a drastic increase after the inauguration of price reform. The rise was especially serious during the establishment of the special zones from 1979 to 1981 and in 1984, when food and oil were no longer subsidized by the government.

21. Despite the formation of competitive business in the producer goods market, state-run corporations still occupy most of the market share. The occupancy rates for state-run producer goods companies in 1986 and 1987 were still extremely high, although they had decreased slightly from previous rates. The rates for oil, coal, and gas, for example, are all above 50%. In this situation, it is difficult to remove the bad custom of bureaucratic management from the producer goods market.

22. Liu Zhigang, ed., 1989, p. 75.

23. (1) Foreign capital, 18.5%; (2) loans from domestic financial agencies, 23.6%; (3) investment by the central government, 2.9%; (4) investment by committees of the central government/provinces/cities, 12.1%; (5) self-fund of companies in Shenzhen City, 20.7%; (6) internal companies, 4.1%; (7) Shenzhen city budget, 13.9%; and (8) others, 4.2%. Liang Wensen, 1989, p. 7.

24. Liu Zhigang, ed., 1989, p. 84.

25. Ibid., p. 85.

26. Ibid., p. 87.

27. Stocks issued by the Shenzhen Development Bank in 1987 amounted to 8 million yuan and were sold out immediately after they were issued. Stockholders consist of 111 corporations and 7,298 individuals. Of the total amount of issued stocks, state-owned companies possess 51.3%, collective ownership companies 17.1%, and individuals 31.6%. *Shenzhen Tequbao* (Shenzhen Special Zone Daily), February 4, 1988.

28. Liu Zhigang, ed., 1989. p. 88.

29. Shenzhenshi zihua bangongshi (The Planning Office of the City Council in Shenzhen), 1989, p. 295.

30. *Xinxi Ribao* (News Daily), September 1, 1989.

31. *Kaiyiebao* (Newsletter of Opening), August 2, 1988.

32. *Shenzhen Tequbao* (Shenzhen Special Zone Daily), February 14, 1989.

33. Ibid., April 12, 1989.

34. Liu Zhigang, ed., 1989, p. 161.

35. Yu Guangyuan, 1983.

36. Liang Wensen, 1982.

37. Fu Dabang, 1983, pp. 585–86.

38. Xu Dixin, 1984.

39. Ibid.

40. For information on the socialistic remodeling of private companies during 1949–1955 after the establishment of New China, refer to Xue Muqiao, Su Xing, and Lin Zili, eds., 1960.

41. The phenomenon of incomplete use of labor arose with the establishment of the New China. China had many unemployed people at that time who could not be ignored after the communist government was set up, because a key tenet of communist ideology is that unemployment does not exist in a socialist state. In order to eliminate the social problem of unemployment, it absorbed surplus labor in both urban and rural sectors in the form of overemployed labor.

42. The point where the overemployed labor in urban and rural sectors disappears is as follows: (1) In the rural sector, until invested capital for each period (Ka^i) reaches the amount of invested capital at the point where the overemployed labor disappears in the rural sector (Ka^t); average labor productivity per person at the point of Ka^t (Aa) is larger than average labor productivity per person according to actual inputted labor in the rural sector (Ba^i). When overemployed labor disappears, $Ka^i = Ka^t$, $Aa = Ba^i$. (2) In the urban sector, until the invested capital for each period in the urban sector ($K_b i$) and the amount of invested capital at the point where the overemployed labor disappears in the urban sector ($K_b t$) become equal, average labor productivity per person according to the actually inputted labor in the urban sector (A_b) is larger than average labor productivity per person according to the actually inputted labor in the urban sector ($B_b i$). When $K_b i = K_b t$ is made, $A_b = B_b i = B_b t$ (average labor productivity per person when L_b and $K_b t$ are inputted) is accomplished. When comparing the urban and rural sectors, the point where the overemployed labor disappears ($A_b = B_b i = B_b t$) arrives earlier in the urban sector than the rural sector. This is because capital productivity in the industrial sector is higher than in the rural sector.

43. *Beijing Zhoubao* (Beijing Weekly Newspaper), June 28, 1988.

44. The scissors differential is also called the x-shape price differential. This term explains the divergence between the prices of agricultural products and manufacturing products, which happens in an X shape. This phenomenon is particularly noticeable in a capitalist economy. Because the pace of development in agriculture is slower than that of manufacturing, prices of agricultural products are kept down, while prices of manufactured products keep rising in a scheme by the capitalists who control manufacturing.

45. *Qi shi niandai* (1970s), 1979, No. 3.

46. *Renmin Ribao* (People's Daily), October 6, 1978.

47. *Cheng Ming*, no. 5 (1979)

48. The consumption fund is the remainder after deducting the accumulation (payment of agriculture tax/overall commercial taxes, payment of profits, other obligations to the state plus redemption of production cost/management expenses and spendings for nonproduction sectors such as the accumulated fund for expanded reproduction and welfare) from the total gain of each economic core unit, such as corporation management committee, production battalion, or production division. The percentage of the consumption fund in the total amount of gain is

generally around 65–70%, although some differences exist according to the production and technology level of the production division.

This consumption fund is distributed in accordance with the socialist distribution principle called distribution by labor, which is a combination of the wage and supply systems (therefore, called partial wage–partial supply). In general, the wage system makes up 70% of the fund, while the supply system makes up the remaining 30%. The wage is divided into the basic wage and the subsidy, and the basic wage is determined by each management organization according to the public evaluation method. The subsidy is again divided into three parts (corporation, battalion, and platoon) and paid with the basic wage after a small evaluation on the tenth day and a large evaluation at the end of the first month for individual, group and each part according to the completion of the plan.

49. Yamamoto, 1980, pp. 50–52.

50. Wakabayashi, 1992, p. 70.

51. Oshima, 1987, p. 298.

52. During the first five-year planning period, there were twelve instruction-type indexes which were applied to (1) total production, (2) production amount of major products, (3) trial production of new products, (4) major technology, (5) decrease rate of the basic cost, (6) amount of decrease of the basic cost, (7) total number of employees/laborers, (8) the number of laborers at the end of year, (9) total amount of wage, (10) average wage, (11) labor productivity, and (12) profits. During the period of the Great Leap, there were four instruction-type indexes: (1) production amount of major products, (2) total number of employees/laborers, (3) total amount of wage, and (4) profits. The remaining eight indexes were left to the discretion of the company. Recently, among the eight instruction-type indexes such as (1) production amount, (2) quality, (3) profits, (4) product items, (5) raw materials, (6) consumption amount of labor, (7) labor productivity, and (8) expenses, only four are still instruction-type indexes and the remaining indexes are left to the judgment of the company.

53. *Far Eastern Economic Review*, August 29, 1985.

54. Sato, 1986, pp. 12–39.

55. Uehara, 1987, pp. 3–22.

56. Okabe, 1986, pp. 159–93.

57. *Hong Kong Standard*, May 26, 1988.

58. *Far Eastern Economic Review*, June 23, 1980.

PART II

1. Yang Chanzhu, 1990, p. 97; Shantou Special Economic Zone Yearbook, ed., 1986–89.

2. Shenzhen Special Economic Zone Yearbook, ed., 1989, p. 50.

3. Calculated from data found in Statistical Bureau of Hainan, 1989.

4. *Renmin Ribao* (People's Daily), August 27, 1990.

5. Shenzhen Special Economic Zone Yearbook, ed., 1990, p. 645; Xiamen Special Economic Zone Yearbook, ed., 1990, p. 332.

6. Shenzhen Special Economic Zone Yearbook, ed., 1989, p. 528.

7. The industrial and commercial tax is a liquid tax levied on the sales of products and services. This tax is levied on the income of units engaged in industry, commerce (farm produce, wholesale, retail, and import), transportation, and services; the income of individuals; and profits earned from selling goods. Since this tax amounts to three-quarters of the total tax, it is an important way to control the income level of companies. Tax rates are different for different products and businesses, which are determined according to the level of prices or profits. For

example, gas and water have a rate of 3%; radios and TVs, 13%; cosmetics, 51%; and luxury cigarettes, 69%. The tax is levied on the production cost for industrial items, on the wholesale price for farm produce and imported goods, and not levied on the income from retail sales. For more information, refer to Kojima, 1989, pp. 108–9.

8. Xiamen Special Economic Zone Yearbook, ed., 1990, pp. 156, 168; Statistical Bureau of Hainan, 1990, p. 623.

9. *Renmin Ribao* (People's Daily), August 27, 1990. The total amount of social production in Zhuhai had shown a growth rate of 25.6% every year for ten years (1989: 6,754.83 million yuan). GNP in 1989 and GNP per resident were 2.57 billion yuan and 3,594 yuan, respectively. These figures were recalculated from the figures obtained through interviews with officials in the Zhuhai Statistics Bureau by the System of National Accounts (SNA) method. For more information on the SNA method, see Kojima, 1989, pp. 145–50.

10. Shantou Special Economic Zone Yearbook, ed., 1984–1989; Xiamen Special Economic Zone Yearbook, ed., 1990; Statistical Bureau of Hainan, 1987–89.

11. The first introduction of direct foreign capital to China occurred during the first Five-Year Plan. During this period, four China–Soviet Union merged companies were established. They included an oil corporation (with a contract period of thirty years), a colored scarce metal corporation (contract period of thirty years), a private airline corporation (contract period of ten years), all in Xinqiang; and a shipping corporation (contract period of twenty-five years) in Talian. According to their stated contracts, China was responsible for land, buildings, and construction materials, while the Soviet Union was responsible for machine facilities, equipment, aircraft, and aircraft-related materials. Both China and the Soviet Union were jointly responsible for business management. Products were equally distributed to China and the Soviet Union, and both partners shared equal profits or losses (Dangdai zhongguo conghshu bianji weiyuanhui bian [Series on Contemporary China], ed., 1989, pp. 317–19).

12. Xiamen Special Economic Zone Yearbook, ed., 1990, p. 43.

13. *Beijing Zhubao* (Beijing Weekly Newspaper), August 8, 1976.

14. Shenzhen Special Economic Zone Yearbook, ed., 1985, p. 95.

15. This figure was attained by dividing the total investment from 1979 to 1989 by the number of companies.

16. From an interview with the staff of the Statistical Bureau of Shenzhen, January 4–May 15, 1991.

17. From an interview with the staff of the Zhuhai Statistics Bureau, January 4–May 15, 1991.

18. Lin Wuru, 1990, p. 351.

19. Calculated from data found in Shenzhen Special Economic Zone Yearbook, ed., various years.

20. From an interview with the staff of the Zhuhai Statistics Bureau, January 4–May 15, 1991.

21 Calculated from data found in Shantou Special Economic Zone Yearbook, ed., various years.

22. Xiamen Special Economic Zone Yearbook, ed., 1990, p. 171.

23. Calculated from data found in Statistical Bureau of Hainan, various years.

24. From an interview with the staff of the Statistics Bureau of Shenzhen, January 4–May 15, 1991.

25. From an interview with the staff of the Zhuhai Statistics Bureau, January 4–May 15, 1991.

26. Xiamen Special Economic Zone Yearbook, ed., 1990, p. 339.

27. The total amount of labor wages in the special economic zone was calculated as 1.96 billion yuan because other companies (such as state-owned and collective ownership companies) in addition to foreign-capital companies have to pay 25% of the basic wage for a social welfare fund for laborers.

28. Calculated from data found in Xiamen Special Economic Zone Yearbook, ed., 1990.

29. Calculated from data found in Statistical Bureau of Hainan, various years.

30. Calculated from data found in Shenzhen Special Economic Zone Yearbook, ed., various years, and Xiamen Special Economic Zone Yearbook, ed., 1990.

31. Shenzhen Special Economic Zone Yearbook, ed., 1990, p. 654.

32. From an interview with the staff of the Zhuhai Statistics Bureau, January 4–May 15, 1991.

33. Lin Wuru, 1990, p. 351.

34. Shantou Special Economic Zone Yearbook, ed., 1990, p. 318.

35. Xiamen Special Economic Zone Yearbook, ed., 1990, p. 154.

36. Statistical Bureau of Hainan, 1989.

37. Calculated from data found in Statistical Bureau of Hainan, various years.

38. Because of limited data regarding the percentage of foreign-capital companies for exported industrial/mineral products, this was estimated based on the percentage of foreign-capital companies for the total amount of industrial production.

39. Until 1987, 2,658 internal companies were located in Shenzhen, which was one-third of the total number of companies in the city. These companies came from 28 provinces, central government-controlled cities, and independent districts across the country. Their total investments amounted to 2 billion yuan. According to sector, there were 81 companies in farming, forestry, livestock, and fishery; 674 in industry; 104 in construction; 10 in transportation and communications; 1,408 in commerce and services; 318 in real estate; 9 in sanitation and sports; 3 in finance; and 45 in sports, scientific technology, and advertising. In 1987, however, the amount of production by internal companies formed 70% of the total amount of industrial production in the city. In addition, of the total volume of exports in the city ($1.44 billion in 1987), internal companies formed 43.7% ($618 million).

40. From an interview with the staff of the Statistical Bureau of Shenzhen, January 4–May 15, 1991. According to their area of origin, 8.2% of internal companies are from Sichuan Province, 7.7% from Shanghai, 6.8% from Guangdong Province, 6.1% from Hunan Province, 5.8% from Beijing, and 6% from Zhejiang Province.

41. Calculated from data found in Shantou Special Economic Zone Yearbook, ed., 1990, p. 315.

42. Xiamen Special Economic Zone Yearbook, ed., 1990, p. 46.

43. Xiamen Special Economic Zone Yearbook, ed., 1990, p. 334.

44. Statistical Bureau of Hainan, 1990, p. 616.

45. There are no precise statistics available that indicate the extent of resale in Shenzhen. Therefore, the extent of resale was estimated according to which type of corporation, central or local, trade-related companies belonged to. Of course, not all imports and exports carried out by trade corporations belonging to the central government and Guangdong Province are the result of resale trade. Imports and exports of trade corporations belonging to the municipal government are not necessarily free from resale either. However, when seen as a whole, central government and Guangdong Province trade corporations tend to resell businesses more than trade corporations of municipal governments. This holds true for the other special economic zones as well.

46. Xiamen Special Economic Zone Yearbook, ed., 1990, p. 107.

PART III

1. Of the gross domestic production in Shenzhen Special Economic Zone in 1989, 62.9% was in industry, and over 50% of the total labor was engaged in the industrial sector. Shenzhen Special Economic Zone Yearbook, ed., 1989, p. 528.

2. I visited eighteen corporations in the zone (including companies from China, Hong Kong, Japan, Korea, Taiwan, and the United States) and conducted interviews between January 4 and May 15, 1991. All quotes from company managers are taken from these interviews. Since the managers wanted information that may identify the company and themselves kept confidential, the companies are designated as companies A to R.

3. Penalties, such as those inflicted on workers who receive overseas educational programs and quit before five years elapse, have been illegal in Japan for the past ten years. However, such penalties still take place in the special economic zones according to Japanese managers and Chinese laborers.

4. The official exchange rate of H.K.$100 is 66 yuan in the bank, but the rate is 77 yuan in the black market (as of 1990).

PART IV

1. Zheng Tianlun, Chen Zhuohua, eds., 1990, p. 187.

2. Shenzhen Special Economic Zone Yearbook, ed., 1990, p. 213.

3. From an interview with the staff of the Statistical Bureau of Shenzhen, January 4–May 15, 1991.

4. From an interview with the staff of the Zhuhai Statistics Bureau, January 4–May 15, 1991.

5. Ibid.

6. Fang Lingsheng, 1990, pp. 40–41.

7. Lin Wuru, 1990, p. 372.

8. Shantou Special Economic Zone Yearbook, ed., 1991, pp. 179-89.

9. Xiamen Special Economic Zone Yearbook, ed., 1991, p. 107.

10. Ibid., p. 332.

11. Economic Affairs Division of Hong Kong City Government, 1991, p. 50.

12. State Statistical Bureau of China, 1990, p. 692.

13. Shenzhen Special Economic Zone Yearbook, ed., 1990, p. 213; Shantou Special Economic Zone Yearbook, ed., 1991, p. 338; Xiamen Special Economic Zone Yearbook, ed., 1991, p. 107; and State Statistical Bureau of China, 1990, p. 644.

14. Shenzhen Special Economic Zone Yearbook, ed., 1990, p. 213; Lin Wuru, 1990, p. 372; and State Statistical Bureau of China, 1990, p. 644 (Zhuhai and Xiamen are not included in this figure.)

15. Yukari, 1990, p. 260

16. Liu Zhigang, 1988, p. 231.

17. Ibid., p. 245.

18. Zheng Tianlun, Chen Zhuohua, eds. 1990, p. 175.

19. Lin Wuru, 1990, p. 353.

20. Zheng Tianlun, Chen Zhuohua, eds., 1990, p. 177.

21. Ibid. p. 175.

22. The multilayer economic structure in China's economy is not a phenomenon that is appearing for the first time. This structure was formed in the course of history, and has its origins

in the establishment of the People's Republic of China. For more information on this subject, refer to M. Takahashi, "China World Economy," 1991.

23. In its early stage, the nation was divided into two zones: the coastal and internal areas. In 1958, at the time of the Great Leap, the entire nation was divided into seven zones, then, in 1961 redivided into six zones (Northeast, South, Northwest, East, Southwest and Central). During the Third Five-Year Plan the theory of the Three-Line Construction was introduced. Of the three lines, the first line refers to the provinces along the coastal zone, the third line refers to the southern zone of Yunnan, Sichuan, and Gansu Provinces, and the second line refers to the middle zone. During the Third and Fourth Five-Year Plans, development of production focused on the third line. During the Fifth and Sixth Five-Year Plans, the focus of development was put on the coastal zone.

24. There are various opinions in China regarding how the zones should be divided. Some of the major ones are: (1) dividing the entire nation into six economic blocks centering around major cities; (2) dividing the nation into two zones, one along the big rivers in a vertical line and the other along the coast in a crosscutting line, linking all cities located near the dividing lines; (3) dividing the nation into the big three economic zones: the most popular idea among academic circles. The reason for the disparity of opinions on the division of economic zones is that advocates tend to claim that their zone deserves the highest priority for development. However, they do not explain why the zones should be divided in that particular way, what kind of relationships will be formed between the zones when the nation is divided as such, or how the economic circulation mechanism of the local economic areas within the same economic zone is expected to work. The reason for dividing economic zones in China, in my opinion, should not be to determine the priority order of which zone should be developed first, but to study the special features of each zone in order to provide appropriate development strategies for each.

25. The labor income of Shenzhen Special Economic Zone exceeds 4 billion yuan.

26. A. Takahashi, 1992, p. 378.

27. Ibid.

28. The company must provide not only welfare for its employees, but also school education, hospitals, houses and children's employment. For the Chinese unit society, see Ro Feng, 1989.

Bibliography

CHINESE

Cao Fanyi. *Shijie jingji tequ yu fazhan zhanlue* (World Special Economic Zone and Development Strategies). Guangzhou: University of Zhongshan, 1990.

Cao Hongwen. "Laodongli liudong yu tequ fazhan" (Labor Shift and Special Economic Zone's Development). *Tequ jingji* 4 (1989).

Cao Quhong. *Tequ shiqui jingji xiediao fazhan yanjiu* (Research on the Special Economic Zones' Social Economic Cooperation Development). Guangzhou: Guangdong People's Press, 1990.

Chen Wenhong. *Zhongguo jingji wenti* (China's Economic Problems). Hong Kong: Guangjiaojing Chubanshe, 1989.

———. *Zhongguo waihui wenti* (China's Foreign Exchange Problems). Hong Kong: Guangjiaojing Chubanshe, 1989.

Chen Yuguang. "Laodong renkou de jiuye" (The Employment of Labor). In *Dangdai zhongguo renkou* (Contemporary China's Population), edited by Dangdai zhongguo conghshu bianji weiyuanhui bian (Series on Contemporary China). Beijing: China Social Science Press, 1988.

Chen Yun. "Dui jingji congzuo de ji dian yijian" (Several Opinions on Economic Affairs). *Zhonggong yanjiu* 7 (1984).

Da Dan. "Shenzhen tequ fazhan zhong de bianqian" (The Changes of Shenzhen Special Economic Zone's Development). *Tequ jingji* 3 (1989).

Dangdai zhongguo conghshu bianji weiyuanhui bian (Series on Contemporary China), ed., *Zhonghua renmin gonghuaguo jingji guanli dajishi* (The History of Chinese Economic Management). Beijing: Chinese Economic Press, 1986.

Deng Xiaoping. *Jianshe you zhongguo tesede shihuizhuyi* (The Construction of Chinese-Style Socialism). Hong Kong: Sanlian Press, 1987.

Fang Lingsheng, ed. *Zhongguo jingji tequ 10 nian congshu: shantou fen juan* (Series on Ten-Years of Chinese Special Economic Zone: Shantou). Hong Kong: China's

Special Economic Zones Data and Research Unit, Center for Contemporary Asian Studies, The Chinese University of Hong Kong, 1990.

Fang Sheng. *Shenzhen tequ jingji kaocha* (An Inspection of Shenzhen Special Economic Zone). Shenzhen: Economic Research Center of Shenzhen University, 1984.

———. "Zhongguo dalu ye Taiwan, Xianggang de jingji hezuo yu lianhe" (Economic Cooperation and Linkage of Mainland China, Taiwan, and Hong Kong). *Tequ jingji* 1 (1991).

Fang Xiaqiu. *Zhongguo jingji gaige tequ kaifa* (China's Economic Reform and Special Economic Zone's Development). Beijing: Economic Science Press, 1988.

Fu Dabang. "Jingji tequ de jingji xingzhi" (Economic Characteristics of the Special Economic Zone). In *Zhongguo jingji tequ nianjian* (China's Special Economic Zones Yearbook), edited by Zhongguo jingji tequ nianjian bianjibu (China's Special Economic Zones Yearbook). Hong Kong: Zhongguo jingji tequ nianjian chubanshe, 1983.

Gu Liji. "Cong quanju zhi changyuan de quandian kanquan ban tequ de zong zhi" (The Significance of the Special Economic Zone with Longterm Prospects). *Gangao jingji* 3 and 4 (1984).

Gu Nianliang, ed. *Zhongguo jingji tequ de diquxing yingxiang* (Characteristics of China's Economic Zones as Special Economic Zones). Harbin: Heirongjiang People's Press, 1989.

He Bozhuan. *Shanao shang de zhongguo* (China on a Mountain Ledge). Guizhou: Guizhou People's Press, 1988.

He Zhusheng. "Jingji tequ de youlai, choujian he fazhan" (Construction and Development of Special Economic Zones). In *Zhongguo jingji tequ* (China's Special Economic Zones), edited by Zhao Yuanhao. Guangzhou: Kexue puji chubanshe guangzhou fenshe, 1984.

Hu Dunai, and Xue Tianbiao, eds. *Xianggang yu neidi maoyi* (The Trade of Hong Kong and Mainland China). Beijing: Zhongguo duiwai jingji maoyi chubanshe (China's Foreign Economic Trade Press), 1984.

Hu Mengzhou. "Jingji tequ de laodongli guanli" (Labor Management of Special Economic Zone). In *Dangdai zhongguo de laodongliguanli* (Contemporary China's Labor Management), edited by Dangdai zhongguo congshu bianji weiyuanhui bian (Series on Contemporary China). Beijing: Chinese Social Science Press, 1990.

Huang Zhaohong. "Liyong waiyi" (Use of Foreign Capital). In *Dangdai zhongguo de duiwai jingji hezuo* (Contemporary China's Foreign Economic Cooperation), edited by Dangdai zhongguo congshu bianji weiyuanhui bian (Series on Contemporary China). Beijing: China Social Science Press, 1989.

Liang Wensen. "Shenzhen jingji tequ jingji moushi chutan" (First Search of the Economic Model in Shenzhen Special Economic Zone). *Jingji daobao* 6 (1982).

———. "Shenzhen 2000nian fazhan zhanlue" (The Development Strategy of Shenzhen 2000). *Tequ jingii* 4 (1990).

Liao Guangsheng, ed. *Mianan jingji fazhan yu yatai quyu hudong* (Interrelationship between Bi-Coastal Economic Block and Asian Countries). Hong Kong: Center for Contemporary Asian Studies, The Chinese University of Hong Kong, 1991.

Lin Wuru, ed. *Zhongguo jingji tequ jianzhi* (A Simple History of China's Special Economic Zones). Guangzhou: Guangdong People's Press, 1990.

Liu Guoguang, ed. *Zhongguo shehui zhuyi jingji de gaige, kaifang he fazhan* (China's Socialist Economic Reform, Open and Development). Beijing: Economic Management Press, 1987.

Liu Zhigang, ed. *Shenzhen shichang tixi toushi* (Prospective of Market System in Shenzhen). Shenzhen: Haitian Chubanshe, 1989.

——. "Shenzhen 10 nian jingji shehui fazhan hujgu yu qianzhand" (Review and Prospective of Shenzhen's Ten Years of Socio-Economic Development). *Tequ jingji* 4 (1990).

Ma Hong, ed. *Xiandai zhongguo jingji cidian* (Modern Chinese Economic Dictionary). Beijing: China Social Science Press, 1982.

Ro Feng, "Unit: A Special Form of Social Organization," *Chinese Social Science* 1 (1989).

Shenzhenshi zhengzhi bangongshi (The Office of Policies of Shenzhen). *Ten Years of the Shenzhen Special Economic Zone*. Shenzhen: Haitian Press, 1990.

Shenzhenshi zihua bangongshi (The Planning Office of the City Council in Shenzhen). *Shenzhen jingji shihui caoyian* (Shenzhen Social and Economic Survey). Shenzhen: Shenzhen zihua bangongshi, 1989.

Su Yucai, ed. *Zhongguo jingji tequ 10 nian congshu-hainan fen juan* (Series on Ten Years of Chinese Special Economic Zone: Hainan). Hong Kong: China's Special Economic Zones Data and Research Unit, Center for Contemporary Asian Studies, The Chinese University of Hong Kong, 1990.

Tang Huozhao. *Shenzhen jingji mianmian guan* (Every Aspect of the Shenzhen Economy). Shenzhen: Haitian Chubanshe, 1986.

——. *Shenzhen 10 Years: 1980–1990*. Kunlun: Kunlun Press, 1990.

Wang Luolin, and Xu Chuxuan. *Xiamen jingji tequ de xian zhuang yu zhanwang* (Present and Future Prospects of Xiamen Special Economic Zone). Hong Kong: Center for Contemporary Asian Studies, The Chinese University of Hong Kong, 1986.

Wang Renxiang. *Yanhai kaifang chengshi yu jingji tequ shouce* (Handbook of Coastal Open Cities and Special Economic Zones). Beijing: China Outlook Press, 1988.

Xue Muqiao, Su Xing, and Lin Zili, eds. *Zhongguo guominzingzide shiheizhuyide gaizhu* (Chinese People's Economic, Socialistic Remodeling). Beijing: Beijing waijiao chubanshe, 1960.

Yang Chanzhu, ed. *Zhongguo jingji tequ 10 nian congshu-zhuhai fen juan* (Series on Ten Years of Chinese Special Economic Zone: Zhuhai). Hong Kong: China's Special Economic Zones Data and Research Unit, Center for Contemporary Asian Studies, The Chinese University of Hong Kong, 1990.

Yu Guangyuan. *Tantan dui shenzhen jingji tequ de jige wenti de yiyi* (The Significance of the Argument About Several Problems in Shenzhen Special Economic Zone). Beijing: Jingji yanjiu, 1983.

Zhang Fengging. "Xiamen jingji tequ de dui taishang touzi wenti" (Taiwan's Investment Problems in Xiamen Special Economic Zone). *Tequ yu gangao jingji* 3 (1989).

Zhang Minru, and Zhao Shili. "Shenzhen shi de renkou qian yi yu liudong" (Population Movement and Flow of Shenzhen City). *Shenzhen daxue xuebao* 1 (1990).

Zheng Tianlun, and Chen Zhuohua, eds. *Zhongguo jingji tequ 10 nain congshu-shenzhen fen juan* (Series on Ten Years of Chinese Special Economic Zone: Shenzhen). Hong Kong: China's Special Economic Zones Data and Research Unit, Center for Contemporary Asian Studies, The Chinese University of Hong Kong, 1990.

ENGLISH

Andors, Phylis. "Women and Work in Shenzhen." *Bulletin of Concerned Asian Scholars* 20, no. 3 (1988).

Bachman, David. "Differing Visions of China's Post-Mao Economy: The Ideas of Chen Yun, Deng Xiaoping, and Zhao Ziyang." *Asian Survey* 24, no. 3 (1986).

Burns, John P. "Immigration From China and The Future of Hong Kong." *Asian Survey* 27, no. 6 (1987).

Chai, Joseph C. H., and Chi-Keung Leung, eds. *China's Economic Reforms*. Hong Kong: Center of Asian Studies, University of Hong Kong, 1987.

Chan, Thomas M. H. "A Critical Review of China's Special Economic Zone Policy: Based Primarily on the Experience of the Shenzhen Special Economic Zone." In *Perspectives on China's Modernization: Studies on China's Open Policy and Special Economic Zone*, edited by K. Y. Wong, C. C. Lau, and Eva B. C. Li. Hong Kong: Center for Contemporary Asian Studies, The Chinese University of Hong Kong, 1988.

Chang, David Wen-Wei. *China Under Deng Xiaoping*. Hong Kong: The Macmillan Press, 1988.

Fangyi Huang. "China's Introduction of Foreign Technology and External Trade: Analysis and Options." *Asian Survey* 27, no. 5 (1987).

Hang Seng Bank. *On Estimating the Stock of Hong Kong Dollar in China*. Hong Kong: Hang Seng Bank, 1990.

Hsia, Ronald. *The Entreport Trade of Hong Kong with Special Reference to Taiwan and the Chinese Mainland*. Taiwan: Chung Hua Institution for Economic Research, 1984.

Ho, C. Y., and L. C. Chau, eds. *The Economic System of Hong Kong*. Hong Kong: Asian Research Service, 1988.

Jao, Y. C., and C. K. Leung. *China's Special Economic Zone*. Hong Kong: Oxford University Press, 1986.

Ledic, Michele. "Hong Kong and China Economic Interdependence." *The Pacific Review* 2, no. 2 (1989).

Liu, William. "Post-Mao Economic Strategy on Hong Kong-Macao Reversion." *East Asian Studies* 23, no. 4 (1987).

Lo, Shiu-Hing. "Decolonization and Political Development in Hong Kong: Citizen Participation." *Asian Survey* 28, no. 6 (1988).

Martellaro, A. Joseph, and H. B. Sun. "The Special Economic Zones: A New Dimension in Chinese Socialism." *East Asian Studies* 23, no. 1 (1987).

Nomura Research Institute. *The Economic Prospects of Hong Kong for 1991 and Beyond*. Hong Kong: Nomura Research Institute, 1991.

Overholt, William H. "Hong Kong and the Crisis of Sovereignty." *Asian Survey* 24, no. 4 (1984).

Peebles, Gavin. *Hong Kong's Economy*. Hong Kong: Oxford University Press, 1988.

Pepper, Suzanne. "China's Special Economic Zone: The Current Rescue Bid for a Faltering Experiment." *Bulletin of Concerned Asian Scholars* 20, no. 3 (1988).

Scobell, Andrew. "Hong Kong's Influence on China." *Asian Survey* 28, no. 6 (1988).

Sit, Victor F. S. "China's Export-Oriented Open Areas: The Export Processing Zone Concept." *Asian Survey* 28, no. 6 (1988).

Song, Yun-Wing. "China's Entry Into World Markets: The Role of Hong Kong in China's Export Drive." *Australian Journal of Chinese Affairs*, no. 15 (1986).

U.S. Department of Commerce Bureau of International Commerce. *Free Trade Zones and Related Facilities Abroad*. Washington, D.C.: U.S. Government Printing Office, 1970.

Vogel, Ezra F. *One Step Ahead in China*. Cambridge: Harvard Univesity Press, 1989.

———. *Canton Under Communism*. Cambridge: Harvard University Press, 1969.

White, Lynn T. III. *Shanghai: Uneven Taxes in Reform China*. Hong Kong: Center of Asian Studies, University of Hong Kong, 1989.

Wong, Richard Y. C., and Joseph Y. S. Cheng, eds. *The Other Hong Kong Report.* Hong Kong: The Chinese University Press, 1990.

Wong, Kwan-Yiu, and K. Y. David Chu, eds. *Modernization in China: The Case of the Shenzhen Special Economic Zone.* Hong Kong: Oxford University Press, 1985.

Wong Pui Yee, ed. *China's Special Economic Zones: Towards Industrialization and Internationalization.* Hong Kong: China's Special Economic Zones Data and Research Unit, Center for Contemporary Asian Studies, The Chinese University of Hong Kong, 1988.

———. *Economic Relations Between China's Pearl River Delta, Special Economic Zones, and Hong Kong.* Hong Kong: China's Special Economic Zones Data and Research Unit, Center for Contemporary Asian Studies, The Chinese University of Hong Kong, 1988.

JAPANESE

Abo, T., ed. *Japanese Manufacturing in America: Automobiles and Electronics: The Application and the Adaptation of Japanese Management.* Tokyo: Toyo Keizai Shinbusha, 1988.

Association for the Study of National Economic Security. *A Frontline of China's Open Economy.* Tokyo: The SIMUL Press, 1989.

China Research Center. "Chinese Special Economic Zone." *Quarterly Chinese Study* 17 (1989).

Hamada, K., ed. *Socialist Countries in Asia under the Economic Open Policy.* Tokyo: The Institute of Developing Economies, 1985.

———. *Chinese Economy under Deng Xiaoping.* Tokyo: Aki Shobo, 1987.

Hashimoto, K. *The Challenge of Shenzhen Special Economic Zone.* Tokyo: Nikan Shobo, 1990.

Hujimori, A., ed. *Export Processing Zones in Asian Countries.* Tokyo: The Institute of Developing Economies, 1978.

Inagaki, K. "Total Review of Special Economic Zones.: *Sekai Shuho* 5 (1985).

———. *How to Perceive Chinese Markets.* Tokyo: PHP Research Center, 1986.

———. *Investment Environments in China.* Tokyo: SouSou Sha, 1988.

———. "External Economic Relations and Policy Changes." In *A Turn of Chinese Economics,* edited by K. Yamanouchi. Tokyo: Iwanami Shoten, 1989.

Ishikawa, S. "Mid and Long Term Economic Prospects for China: A Preliminary Study." In *Mid and Long Term Economic Prospects for China,* edited by Japan and China Economic Associate Co. Tokyo: Japan and China Economic Associate Press, 1984.

———. "China's Economic Development: A Study Using Economic Development Theories." In *A Turn of Chinese Economics,* edited by K. Yamanouchi. Tokyo: Iwanami Shoten, 1989.

Kataoka, S. *A Challenge to the World Economy: Theoretical Backgrounds of China's Economic Open Policy.* Tokyo: Tokyo Press, 1986.

Kojima, R. *Chinese Economics and Technology.* Tokyo: Keisou Shobo, 1975.

———, ed. *Chinese Economic Reform.* Tokyo: Keisou Shobo, 1988.

———, ed. *A Commentary of Chinese Economic Statistics and Laws.* Tokyo: The Institute of Developing Economies, 1989.

———, ed. *The Industrialization of Hong Kong: The Nucleus of Asia.* Tokyo: The Institute of Developing Economies, 1989.

Liang Wensen. "The Economic Development and Experiences in Shenzhen Special Economic Zone." *Quarterly Chinese Study* 17 (1989).

Mizuno, Z., and S. Yahata. *Work Division and Technical Transfer Between Japanese Companies and Native Enterprises: A Case of Automobile Industry in Thailand.* Tokyo: The Institute of Developing Economies, 1988.

Nakagane, K. "The Current Situation and Prospects of Special Economic Zones: By Shenzhen's Experiences." In *A Study on the Prospects of the Asia-Pacific Region,* edited by NIRA (National Institute for Research Advancement). Tokyo: NIRA Press, 1985.

———. "China's Industrialization and Its Mechanism." In *A Turn of Chinese Economics,* edited by K. Yamanouchi. Tokyo: Iwanami Shoten, 1989.

———. *The Political Economy of Agro-industrial Relationships in Contemporary China.* Tokyo: University of Tokyo Press, 1992.

Okabe, T. "On 'Chinese-Style Socialism.' " In *Reexamination of Chinese Socialism,* edited by T. Okabe, T. Sato, and K. Mohri. Tokyo: The Japan Institute of International Affairs, 1986.

Oshima, H. T. *Economic Growth in Monsoon Asia.* Tokyo: Keishoshobo, 1989.

Ren Wenxia. *China's Economic Reform and Business Management.* Nagoya: University of Nagoya Press, 1990.

Sato, T. "A Prolegomenon to Comparative Study of the Chinese and the Soviet Economic Systems." In *Reexamination of Chinese Socialism,* edited by T. Okabe, T. Sato, and K. Mohri. Tokyo: The Japan Institute of International Affairs, 1986.

Sawada, Y. "Hong Kong: A Nucleus of Asia." In *The Industrialization of Hong Kong: A Nucleus of Asia,* edited by R. Kojima. Tokyo: The Institute of Developing Economies, 1990.

Tajima, T. "Structure of Investment and Industry in Chinese Economy." In *Multi-Level Structure of Chinese Economy,* edited by K. Ishihara. Tokyo: The Institute of Developing Economies, 1991.

Takagi, Y. *Economic Analysis of Developing Countries: Dual System, Economic Assistance, and Accumulated Debts.* Tokyo: Toyo Keizai Shibun Sha, 1988.

Takahashi, A. "Progress and Problem of Strategies in Special Economic Zones." In *Economic Reforms in China: Reflections and Prospects,* edited by Y. Sekiguchi, S. Zhu, and M. Uekusa. Tokyo: University of Tokyo Press, 1992.

Takahashi, M. "China World Economy." In *The China Which We Are Anxious to Learn About,* edited by K. Nomura and M. Takahashi. Tokyo: Koubuntou, 1991.

———. "The Civil Economic Reform and Its Problems." In *A Turn of Chinese Economies,* edited by K. Yamanouchi. Tokyo: Iwanami Shoten, 1989.

Taniguchi, K., ed. *Development of Taiwanese and Korean Overseas Investment.* Tokyo: The Institute of Developing Economies, 1990.

Tomioka, M., and H. Kajimura, eds. *A Study about the Economy of Developing Countries.* Tokyo: Sekai Shoin, 1981.

Uehara, K. *China's Economic Reform and Open Policy.* Tokyo: Aoki Shoten, 1987.

Wakabayashi, K. *Chinese Population Problem.* Tokyo: University of Tokyo Press, 1989.

———. *Population Management of China.* Tokyo: Akishobo, 1992.

Wong Pui Yee. "Current Status of Shenzhen Special Economic Zone and Expected Economic Relationship between Hong Kong and Shenzhen Special Economic Zone." *Quarterly Chinese Study* 17 (1989).

Xu Dixin. "About the Characteristics of China's Special Economic Zone." *Beijing Zhoubao* (Japanese edition), January 24, 1984.

Xue Muquao, ed. *The Socialistic Reconstruction of China's National Economy.* Beijing: Foreign Language Press, 1960.

Yabuki, S. *China Syndrome: Socialism Much the Same with Capitalism.* Tokyo: SouSou Sha, 1986.

———. "The Development of the Open Door Policy: From Special Economic Zones to Development Strategies for Coastal Regions." In *Chugoku no Sekai-Ninshiki to Kaihatsu-Senryaku-Shiza no Tenkan to Kaihatsu no Kadai* (China's Perception of Contemporary International Relations and Its Development Strategy), edited by K. Kobayashi. Tokyo: The Institute of Developing Economies, 1990.

Yamamoto, T. "The Quest for Chinese Industrializaion (Development Strategies)," In *History of Chinsese Industrialization*. Tokyo: Law and Cultural Press, 1982.

Yamamoto, Y. *Peking 35 Years*. Tokyo: Iwanami Shinsho, 1980.

Yukari, S. *Asian Core—Hong Kong*. Tokyo: The Institute of Developing Economies, 1990.

Zhang Fengfu. *Macroeconomic Analysis in China*. Tokyo: Yuhikaku, 1989.

KOREAN

Cha Dongse. *Analysis of Effects of Foreign Capital*. Seoul: Korea Institute for Industrial Economy and Trade, 1986.

STATISTICS

Census and Statistics Department of Hong Kong Government. *Hong Kong Monthly Digest of Statistics*. Hong Kong: Census and Statistics Department of Hong Kong Government, various years.

Council for Economic Planning and Development of Republic of China. *Taiwan Statistical Data Book*. Taiwan: Council for Economic Planning and Development of Republic of China, various years.

Economic Affairs Division of Hong Kong City Government. *Economic Status*. Hong Kong: Economic Affairs Division of Hong Kong City Government, various years.

Hainan Special Economic Zone Yearbook (Hainan tequ jingji nianjian bianji weiyuanhui), ed. *Hainan tequ jingji nianjian* (Economic Yearbook of Hainan Special Zone). Beijing: Xinhua chubanshe, various years.

Hong Kong Economic Report (Xianggang jingji daobaoshe), ed. *Xianggang jingji nianjian* (Hong Kong Economic Yearbook). Hong Kong: Xianggang jingji daobaoshe, various years.

Huang Hanqiang, ed. *Aomen jingji nianjian 1984–1986* (Economic Yearbook of Macao 1984–1986). Macao: Huaqiaobao, 1986.

Lin Hechun, ed. *Zhongguo jingji tequ yu yanhai jingji jishu kaifaqu nianjian 1980–1990* (The Yearbook of China's Special Economic Zones and Coastal Economic Technical Open Area: 1980–1990). Beijing: Gaige chubanshe, 1991.

Ministry of Foreign Economic Relations and Trade (MOFERT) of China. *Zhongguo duiwai jingji maoyi nianjian* (Almanac of China's Foreign Economic Relations and Trade). Beijing: Zhongguo shihui chubanshe, various years.

Research Center of Hong Kong and Macao (Gangao yanjiusuo). *Xianggang jingji tongji ziliaobian* (Statistical Data on the Hong Kong Economy). Beijing: Zhongguo tongji chubanshe (Chinese Statistics Publishing House), 1990.

Rong Quiyu, ed. *Zhuhai jingji nianjian 1979–1986* (Zhuhai Economic Yearbook 1979–1986). Guangzhou: Guangdong renmin chubanshe, 1986.

Shantou Special Economic Zone Yearbook (Shantou jingji tequ nianjian bianji weiyuanhui), ed. *Shantou jingji tequ nianjian* (Shantou Special Economic Zone Yearbook). Guangzhou: Guangdong renmin chubanshe, various years.

Shenzhen Special Economic Zone Yearbook (Shenzhen jingji tequ nianjian bianji weiyuan-hui), ed. *Shenzhen jingji tequ nianjian* (Shenzhen Special Economic Zone Yearbook). Guangzhou: Guangdong renmin chubanshe, various years.

State Statistical Bureau of China (Guojia tongjiju). *Yanhai jingji kaifangqu jingji yanjiu he tongji ziliao* (Economic Research and Statistic Material of Coastal Open Area). Beijing: Zhongguo tongji chubanshe (Chinese Statistics Publishing House), 1989.

———. *Zhongguo tongji nianjian* (Statistical Yearbook of China). Beijing: Zhongguo tongji chubanshe (Chinese Statistics Publishing House), various years.

State Statistical Bureau of China and the Population Census Office of the State Council (Guojia tongjiju renkou tongjisi). *Zhongguo renkou tongji nianjian* (Statistical Year-book of Chinese Population). Beijing: Zhongguo zhanwang chubanshe, various years.

State Statistical Bureau of China and the Social Statistics Office of the State Council (Guojia tongjiju shehui tongjisi). *Zhongguo laodong gongzi tongji ziliao 1949–1985* (Statistical Material of Chinese Labor Wage 1949–1985). Beijing: Zhongguo tongji chubanshe (Chinese Statistics Publishing House), 1987.

Statistical Bureau of Guangdong Province (Guangdongsheng tongjiju). *Guangdongsheng tongji nianjian* (Statistical Yearbook of Guangdong). Beijing: Zhongguo tongji chubanshe (Chinese Statistics Publishing House), various years.

Statistical Bureau of Guangzhou (Guangzhoushi tongjiju). *Guangzhoushi sishinian 1949–1988* (Forty years, 1949–1988, of Guangzhou City in China). Beijing: Zhongguo tongji chubanshe (Chinese Statistics Publishing House), 1990.

———. *Guangzhou tongji nianjian* (Statistical Yearbook of Guangzhou). Beijing: Zhongguo tongji chubanshe (Chinese Statistics Publishing House), various years.

Statistical Bureau of Hainan (Hainansheng tongjiju). *Hainan tongji nianjian* (Hainan Statistic Yearbook). Beijing: zhongguo tongji chubanshe (Chinese Statistics Publishing House), various years.

Statistical Bureau of Shenzhen (Shenzhenshi tongjiju). *Shenzhen gaige kaifang de shinian* (Ten Years of Reform and Open Policy in Shenzhen). Shenzhen: Shenzhenshi tongjiju, 1989.

Xiamen Special Economic Zone Yearbook (Xiamen jingji tequ nianjian bianji weiyuanhui Xiamen), ed. *Xiamen jingji tequ nianjian* (Xiamen Special Economic Zone Year-book). Beijing: Zhongguo tongji chubanshe (Chinese Statistics Publishing House), various years.

The Yearbook of Zhuhai (Zhuhai nianjian bianji weiyuanhui), ed. *Zhuhai nianjian* (The Zhuhai Yearbook). Guangzhou: Guangdong renmin chubanshe, various years.

Zhuhai Statistics Bureau (Zhuhaishi tongjiju). *Zhuhaishi shehui jingji shinian cengzhang sudu* (The Development of Zhuhai Social Economy for Ten Years). Zhuhai: Zhuhaishi tongjiju, 1990.

NEWSPAPERS AND MAGAZINES

Beijing Zhoubao (Beijing Weekly Newspaper), August 8, 1976, January 2, 1979, January 28, 1988.

Cheng Ming, no. 5 (1979).

Far Eastern Economic Review, June 23, 1980, August 29, 1985.

Hong Kong Standard, May 26, 1988.

Kaiyiebao (Newsletter of Opening), August 2, 1988.

Qi shi niandai (1970s), no. 3 (1979).

Renmin Ribao (People's Daily), October 6, 1978, August 12, 1985, January 7, 1986, August 27, 1990.

Shenzhen Tequbao (Shenzhen Special Zone Daily), February 4, 1988, February 14, 1989, April 12, 1989.

Xinxi Ribao (News Daily), September 1, 1989.

Index